MW01169877

CRITICAL THINKING
AND **ANALYTICAL MIND**

The Art of Making Decisions and
Solving Problems. Think Clearly,
Avoid Cognitive Biases and Fallacies
in Systems. Improve Listening Skills.

Be a Logical Thinker

MARCUS P. DAWSON

TABLE OF CONTENTS

Part 1. Critical Thinking

Part 2. Analytical Mind

PART 1

CRITICAL THINKING

INTRODUCTION

Do you know that your brain works like a computer? In fact, your brain, which is actually a 3-pound mass, is a natural supercomputer that acts as your body's command center. It is critical to the functioning of all parts of your body, just as it is involved in everything you do in your life. It is the part of your composition that determines how your thoughts flow, how you direct your actions and also how your social disposition is. It is actually the same brain that regulates what kind of person you become, controlling your thoughts, your politeness, your degree of rudeness, how you handle dangerous situations and even how you behave with strangers, colleagues, family and friends.

It is correct to say that your brain is in charge of your emotional well-being. It also influences how you relate to people of the opposite sex. Essentially, what you have to understand is that your brain is involved in virtually everything you are involved with throughout your life. That's why you need to nurture it, feed it, exercise it, and understand how it works if you want to succeed in polishing your creative thinking skills. Needless to say, only when you are able to manage critical thinking are you in a position to solve problems and handle difficult situations in a way that makes things better for you and those you are trying to help.

Your brain is actually more complex than a computer. For example, the brain has 100 billion nerve cells, and all nerve endings have connections to many other cells. You may find this hard to believe, but that same brain that you may think is not very large has many more connections within it than the number of stars in the universe. Despite the physical connections, just know that you become the best you can be in your workplace, in relationships, in recreation, and in all other areas when you put effort into optimizing your brain function.

When it comes to exercise, the brain needs as much exercise as the physical body, so some people choose to lift weights regularly, do yoga, eat healthy foods, and do other things to improve the health of the brain. Often, the way the brain works can tell you how your soul is doing, because it is that brain that houses the computer that runs your life. It doesn't matter what your age is. The fact is that your brain needs to be exercised, and when you exercise it regularly, the positive effect is manifested in your life. In short, when you want your brain to continue to be able to solve problems, even the most difficult ones, you have to take care of it, both in what you feed it and in how regularly you exercise it.

This book is about critical thinking that includes intelligent strategies and logical thinking. It also discusses the best decision-making skills you need to acquire. Everything discussed in the book requires very high level reasoning, which means that your brain must, by necessity, be in excellent shape. It is for this reason that this book explains what you need to do to exercise your brain, and what you can do to become a logical thinker. You will also learn from this book the best techniques to sharpen your decision making skills.

CHAPTER 1
BENEFITS OF BEING A CRITICAL THINKER

Critical thinking involves a good deal of thought, energy and time (although it involves less and less the more you do it). So why do you do it? After all, many people make life-changing decisions based on incomplete information, judging things according to unexamined assumptions, or simply doing what everyone says they should do without ever asking why.

Setting aside value judgments about how someone should live their life, the following are some practical benefits of incorporating critical thinking into your life:

You'll Achieve the Best for You

Although certain academic disciplines and professions are popularly associated with critical thinking, it transcends any subject or function. Critical thinking represents a deeper examination of things, understanding of problems, situations, questions, and even people on a much more substantive level. It can be applied in various areas of one's life, allowing one to analyze and evaluate an important decision or a lengthy project according to the facts and to move forward with confidence.

You'll Anticipate (Most of) the Unexpected

"Measure twice; cut once" is an old proverb that reminds us that even a little extra time at the beginning of a project can help avoid mistakes later on, while hasty actions can have unforeseen negative consequences. Critical thinking, taking the time to analyze the facts, evaluate the information, and develop a plan according to those considerations may not anticipate all the problems, but it will help you see what can happen and be prepared for the unexpected.

You'll Stay One Step Ahead

George C. Parker was the man who infamously tried to sell the Brooklyn Bridge to unsuspecting and naive people. Parker eventually went to jail for fraud, but in the meantime, many people lost their hard-earned money - and perhaps their dignity. While not all con artists are on this level, unfortunately, we live in a world full of people and organizations trying to manipulate us into giving away our money, our support, and whatever else they want to get their hands on. If you thought something was too good to be true, critical thinking allows you to examine things to find out if it is true.

You'll Sharpen Your Mind

Just like you can work out at the gym to get in shape, critical thinking is the best way to keep your brain in shape. Critical thinking challenges you to look at things in depth, not to accept easy answers or superficial explanations, and to think a lot about the world around you.

You'll Improve Your Performance

Professional development courses, executive training and other programs aimed at improving productivity teach some form of critical thinking. They may use different terms or apply them to different situations, but they all rely on self-awareness, clear thinking, and rational analysis as tools for "getting ahead" in the workplace. Regardless of your job, critical thinking can make your job easier and increase productivity, which is good for both you and your boss!

You'll Understand More

Although critical thinking can take a long time and often requires concentration, the more you do it, the more naturally it will come to you and the more you will find yourself applying it out of habit. Daily tasks begin to look like opportunities for imaginative problem solving. Conversation becomes deeper and more interesting, for one does not only listen to what people have to say, but considers how they may have reached a certain conclusion or developed a particular perspective. Looking at the world critically does not mean finding fault with everything around you. It means looking at familiar attitudes and experiences in a new light.

Importance of Being a Critical Thinker

The ability to analyze your thoughts and present them with evidence instead of accepting your ideas without sufficient evidence is called critical thinking. There are many benefits to critical thinking, as well as the importance of critical thinking. Critical thinking skills are used in classrooms to solve problems as well as in real world situations. It is a valuable skill that should be mastered by students and employees alike.

There are a variety of skills that can be learned through critical thinking skills that can be applied anywhere, requiring reflection, planning, as well as analysis. A mastery skill is the skill you need in every aspect of your life. Critical thinking skills are needed in every area of life. Regardless of where you work, be it in education, research, the legal profession, administration, etc., you need critical thinking skills. The ability to reason objectively and provide solutions systematically is a great advantage in whatever industry you are in. There are many areas in which critical thinking skills are applied and play an important role. These include:

Economy

In the new knowledge economy, critical thinking is very important. Information and technology are what drive the global economy. One must be in a position to deal with change effectively and quickly. Increasing the demand for people who are not only obsessed with one aspect of the intellect is done. The capacity for critical thinking, as well as the analysis of information and the incorporation of different sources of knowledge to solve problems, is an added advantage. Good critical thinking promotes this type of skill, making it extremely vital today.

Language and Presentation Skills

Critical thinking improves your presentation skills and language. Systematic and clear thinking improves the way you express your thoughts. Through understanding the ways to evaluate the logic behind any text, your comprehension improves significantly.

Promotes Creativity

Finding an ingenious solution to a problem is often more than just an idea. New ideas must be relevant to the task at hand; therefore, critical thinking is very crucial to evaluate new ideas, decide on the best ones and adjust them when necessary.

Self-Reflection

Self-reflection is very important for living a meaningful life. Critical thinking assists a person in self-reflection by providing the tools necessary for self-evaluation.

Foundation of Science and a Democratic Society

To be able to experiment and confirm theories, scientists require critical thinking skills, since these are the fundamentals that make up the modern, technological and progressive civilization in which we find ourselves - which essentially depends on the capacity and willingness of the general population to critically perceive reality and offer their judgment with the general good in mind.

Academic Performance

For a student, learning critical thinking skills is very important because it improves performance. Studies have made it clear that students who can critique and analyze information also suggest the intersection with the various social phenomena we experience daily through the application of these in their daily lives, as they understand the content at a deeper level.

Rather than relying on teachers and classrooms for instruction, students who have critical thinking skills are independent, self-directed learners. They are also able to assess how they learn, examine areas where they are strong and weak, and direct the path they wish to take in school.

CHAPTER 2
ARE YOU A GOOD CRITICAL THINKER?

Critical thinking is a valued trait by many employers, and they are likely to test your critical thinking skills during the interview process. However, if this trait was not tested, your work will show how good a thinker you are. A weak critical thinker will begin to make costly mistakes. These mistakes will be repeated, demonstrating a lack of learning, and a weak thinker will be unable to determine where action is needed. These people will make assumptions, and most of their assumptions will be wrong. This list continues to grow as better ways of evaluating a critical thinker are developed.

Main Features of a Critical Thinker

Most people have to meet someone in their life who constantly puts critical thinking skills into practice. This is probably the person who knows certain issues very well, forms his or her own opinion about things, is always looking for solutions to problems, and usually knows the best way to solve these problems.

However, have you ever thought about what makes them different as critical thinkers? Are there any characteristics that they seem to show in everyday situations that distinguish them as someone who uses critical thinking skills on a daily basis?

To illustrate the different characteristics of certain people, think of two people faced with a situation. These people would be considered the critical thinker and the passive thinker.

Both people work in a store and are faced with a situation where a customer wants to return an item. Returns in this store are complicated, and they are not sure how to do it on their own. The differences in their thinking patterns determine how each person will respond to this situation.

The passive thinker is not someone who is creative. Although they have been trained for the return process, the returns are difficult, and they have difficulty remembering all the steps.

They do not take the time to assess the situation and seek out the resources available to them to help them make the return. Instead of examining the situation thoroughly, they do not make an effort to find a solution to the problem.

The passive thinker assumes the mentality that he does not know what to do, and conceives that a task is impossible. He may feel defeated, or may even convince himself that it does not matter. They tell the client, "I'm sorry, I don't know how to do this. Come another time," and leave the situation as it is.

However, the critical thinker takes a different approach. Curious and resourceful, the critical thinker immediately takes it upon himself to find a solution. With an open-minded perspective and the ability to manage uncertainty, he or she walks through all the steps of critical thinking while trying to find an answer.

They go through all their options: clicking on the computer system to find out, reviewing the instruction manuals provided by the store, calling customer service and the store manager. Finally, after exhausting all their options and analyzing the situation as thoroughly as possible, they find an answer to the problem.

Certain characteristics distinguish a critical thinker from a passive thinker. It involves everything from how they see the world, their approach to a problem, and the steps they take to find answers.

The passive thinker gives up easily, has a narrow perspective, and does not take the initiative to discover answers that are not very clear to them.

However, these are some different characteristics that distinguish critical thinkers from others.

Curiosity

One could say that this is the first step in becoming a critical thinker. People who are good critical thinkers have to be curious about the situations in which they find themselves and about righteous living. They ask who, where, when, what, why, and how that allows for complete and comprehensive answers and even innovation.

To take the retail situation, for example, the difference in the way the critical thinker and the passive thinker approached the situation began with curiosity. The passive thinker did not bother to ask questions about the situation. On the other hand, the critical thinker asked how can I do this? They wanted to acquire a new skill and were curious about how to accomplish what had been so difficult for them in the past.

A Wide Perspective

This is another essential characteristic for being a critical thinker. If someone is narrow-minded and not open to new possibilities, then they will not find themselves able to accept new ideas, new strategies, and be able to accept new possibilities. A broad perspective allows the critical thinker to get out of his box and discover what lies ahead.

In the retail example, the critical thinker might use the resources available to him, such as the guidance provided by the store and the customer service line, because he is open to the possibilities of how to make this return and help the customer. In contrast, the mind of a passive thinker did not come up with the idea of using any resources. With the narrow-minded thinking of "I don't know what to do so I can't do this", it is a negative premise, a closed perspective, and did not leave them with the open-mindedness necessary to solve the problem at hand.

Broad Knowledge

What you will have noticed about the critical thinkers in your life is that they have a vast knowledge of a variety of subjects. Critical thinkers often read books, consume news of current events, and go out to experience things firsthand, like going to a museum.

Learning is such an essential step in strengthening your critical thinking skills because the more you know about a variety of topics, the more often you will think critically about any situation or issue that comes your way. If someone is very knowledgeable about history, they will notice patterns in current events that reflect past events and infer what happened at an earlier time. Or if someone is very knowledgeable in politics, he or she has more of an advantage when it comes to the ability to think critically about political events such as presidential debates.

Being Properly Informed About the Subject

When it comes to critical thinking, while much knowledge is important, it is even more important to have accurate knowledge. A person can learn as much as they want, but if they are not well informed about a subject, then their knowledge is useless.

Go back to being a history buff. A person can be extremely interested in history and have consumed several books on various historical periods. But if his knowledge of a subject is completely uninformed, for example, ancient Rome, then his argument that today's America is reflecting the fall of Rome becomes inaccurate.

Examining the Reasoning and Possible Biases and the Assumptions Behind Them

Critical thinkers can not only formulate precise and sound reasoning behind an argument, but they also possess the ability to recognize any kind of bias between that reasoning, whether their own or someone else's. If given a political argument, they can recognize the bias that comes with party membership and separate it from the situation to create a solid argument. Or if a new teacher comes to their school and they are wonderful, the critical thinker can set aside their own prejudices and explain objectively why this teacher is so great.

The Possession of Reasoning Based on Sound Consistent Logic

If the logic behind the reasoning of an argument is inconsistent, then, ultimately, the whole argument falls apart. If the premises of an argument are: "Water is wet, rain is water", but conclude with: "Rain is not wet", there is no logic behind that argument. The critical thinker not only possesses this reasoning, but does so without emotions or social pressure behind it. Their own emotions or the pressure they experience from their peers only serve to make their argument biased, which they try to avoid in the first place.

Ability to Handle Uncertainty

This is very important in situations where critical thinking is necessary. Sometimes there is a problem that needs to be solved, and the answers are not obvious. The critical thinker does not crumble and give up when uncertainty arises. Like the retail worker, the critical thinker possesses the ability to remain calm in uncertain situations. He or she can determine the steps for the task at hand while remaining sensible.

CHAPTER 3
A PRACTICE KNOWN AS METACOGNITION

Metacognition is the realization and understanding of how a person thinks and learns. Research has shown that there are specific strategies that can be used to improve an individual's ability to learn and retain information. People who use metacognition know which learning strategies are right for them and how to plan their learning process.

This activity helps the brain create a new neural pathway to bring memory into awareness, which improves retention.

Both the instructor and the student can begin this self-assessment at any time by asking the following questions:

What went well? This question can be helpful in identifying students who have overestimated their abilities, as well as students with low self-esteem. The term "illusion of ability" is often used to describe students who think they know more and/or perform better than they are. After listening to the student's self-assessment, the instructor can provide specific information by comparing the student's actual performance to desired performance levels. Conversely, for the student with low self-esteem, the instructor can reinforce all the things the student does correctly and improve his or her self-confidence.

Then ask these questions: What went wrong? What is missing (knowledge/skills)? These questions encourage students to think about what went wrong and why. Is it due to a lack of knowledge, skills that need further development, lack of attention, or a combination of factors?

Finally, ask the student: What will you do differently next time? Encourage the student to work independently or in collaboration with his or her coach to improve.

Metacognition: Thinking About Thinking

These thought processes are embedded in our brain. We use them constantly and automatically. But we do not always use them effectively. Effective students know how to intentionally access these different ways of thinking and apply them to different types of tasks.

This process involves metacognition: "thought for thought". Cognitive strategies help students analyze the task or problem, identify the type of thinking required, and activate the correct cognitive processes for the task at hand. A student with strong metacognitive skills understands several perspectives on thinking and can apply them intentionally and successfully.

Make Thinking Obvious With Mind Maps

Thinking maps make cognitive processes perceptible and clear to students. Each map is directly compared to a specific cognitive process.

The use of the maps represents the visual processing centers of the brain and helps students to identify and analyze patterns in the data. As students become capable of using the maps, they also become capable in the cognitive process to which they adapt.

Students also learn to relate maps and views to core academic vocabulary. For example, they will discover that words like "source", "effect", or "outcomes" are related to circumstances, and thinking about logical outcomes and require a multiple flow map, while words like "request", "group", and "association" are related to classification. In addition, they require a tree map. After some time, the use of the maps is programmed to initiate and imagine essential psychological cycles. By the time they hear explicit key words or types of questions in a task, they know precisely what guide to use to initiate the right perspective for the task. Therefore, the Maps act as keys to open the cognitive processes. Using the Maps to illustrate their reasoning helps students become more productive, adaptive, and powerful thinkers and learners.

The Phases of Critical Thinking

"Learning to think better by improving thinking skills" can be defined as critical thinking. Critical thinkers use the process of thinking to analyze (examine and ponder) and synthesize (reconstruct) what they have learned or are currently learning. Unfortunately, much of everyone's reasoning seems to be partial, inaccurate, vague, misinformed, and biased. Critical thinking is necessary to improve its quality and value as it becomes very restrictive.

The development of critical thinking is a gradual process. It requires: overcoming the stagnation of learning, as well as monitoring the system itself, modifying personal patterns of thinking, which appear to be long-term tasks and a significant time of progress.

Critical Thinking

Attributes Critical thinkers incorporate certain characteristics and these characteristics help to identify people as "deep thinkers", distinguishing them from more traditional "ordinary thinkers". Critical thinkers tend to be self-disciplined, self-directed, self-controlled, and self-correcting. They ask important or critical questions and problems and then articulate them clearly and precisely. Critical thinkers collect, gather, analyze, and evaluate relevant information. They arrive at the right assumptions, conclusions, and ideas while measuring and testing specific expectations and parameters. They also keep an open mind to alternative systems of thinking, constantly recognizing and evaluating their assumptions and thoughts. Over time, critical thinkers communicate effectively with others to seek and find answers to questions and problems.

There are usually six phases of evolutionary thinking that lead to the "mastery" of the art of critical thinking. Through extensive practice and application of the process, people can expect to begin to change their thinking habits and eventually change them. Each phase of progress is described below.

Phase One: The Reflective Thinker - People are generally unaware that there are significant problems with their present thought patterns.

Phase Two: The Challenging Thinker-People are aware that existing problems in their thinking process are evident or apparent.

Phase Three: Beginning Thinker - Beginning individuals seek to facilitate changes in their thinking, but without focusing on routine, reliable training.

Phase Four: Practicing Thinker - Individuals recognize the importance of regular practice in developing their thoughts and strengthening them.

Phase Five: Advanced Individual Thinkers continue to develop according to the amount of practice provided to the system.

Phase Six: Thinker Accomplished - Individuals become professional and structured when critical, rational, evaluative logic becomes second nature.

Individuals will only move to these stages if they accept the fact that there are serious problems with their current thinking processes and strategies and can accept the difficulty of their reasoning and get regular practice started to refine and reinforce the elements and skills of critical thinking.

CHAPTER 4
THE KEY TO SUCCESSFUL CRITICAL THINKING

Improving critical thinking skills is a lifelong study worth pursuing. Critical thinking is at the heart of the accumulation of knowledge and experience. After you have begun the practice of critical thinking, the question will be how to continue to improve critical thinking skills. What wisdom can be shared with students that will help them maintain their skills just as well after their school years?

Teaching critical thinking skills does not require much in the way of planning or equipment, but only open and curious minds and some strategies like the ones we will discuss below. These are everyday approaches designed to help you on the journey of improving and perfecting critical thinking skills so that they become an unconscious daily practice in a life of learning.

Review the strategies below carefully, internalize them, and begin incorporating them into your daily practices. Slowly, critical thinking will begin to become second nature to you.

1. Do Not Waste Time

There are times when we have lost time and sadly realize that we cannot get it back. The time lost, unfortunately, can never be recovered. It is important to try to minimize the amount of time lost in trivial things. For example, instead of sitting in front of a TV after work flipping through the channels, you can spend that time reviewing how and when you practiced thinking throughout the day. Ask yourself these questions:

- What time did you think the worst?
- When did you think the best?
- What did you think?
- If you had to repeat the day, what would you do differently?
- Were you able to find out anything?

You can ask that question and even ask more, spending as much time as you can analyzing your answers to the questions. The more you practice this, the more you will improve your thinking patterns and habits.

2. Learn New Things Every Day

Make learning a lifelong habit. Learn something new every day. What have you always wanted to learn? Do it. Keep learning until you find the answers you're looking for, no matter what question you want answers for. Ignore what others may say, but focus on gaining knowledge every day. It is very important to satisfy an intellectual need and develop habits of curiosity to learn more.

It is never too late to learn new things, nor is it too late to start doing them. Look at history, people who started new projects at an age when many would think it was impossible. If you have ambitions to learn more, don't be discouraged; go for it. Learning has no limits - you are free to be curious in any field and learn. Improving critical thinking skills is not for your age. It is not about conquering the world - it is just learning a new skill that will help you in all aspects of your life. Believe in your potential and learn every day.

3. Have a Questioning Mind

Since the beginning of time, the human mind has been curious about everything under the sun and even beyond. In modern times, we encourage and teach our children to question, be curious and explore possibilities. Questions are the essence of learning.

The ability to ask meaningful questions that result in useful and constructive answers is the core of critical thinking and a lifetime of learning. Taking a guiding question approach to learning ensures that both students and providers not only accept the information presented to them, but question it and seek different points of view because they take nothing for granted. For example, think of something you have heard and ask yourself some of the following questions:

· Who said it?

Is it someone you know?

Is the person in a position of power or authority?

Whoever told you this, does it matter?

- What was said?

Did they provide opinions or facts?

Did they provide all the necessary information?

Did they leave out anything?

Questions like these will let you make an informed decision because you will have applied the critical thinking process.

4. Practice Listening Actively

There is a common expression that "many people are waiting for their chance to speak". What do you mean by actively listening when someone is talking? Secondly, how are you able to actively listen to improve your critical thinking skills? Studies have shown that people are inefficient listeners most of the time, that after listening to a 10-minute presentation, the average listener has understood and retained only 50 percent 48 hours after the presentation, and continues to decline with the other participants.

Listening is not easy - it's hard work. Active listening requires even more work. Active listening means making a conscious and determined effort to hear every word that is said and, most importantly, to understand the message that is being conveyed. It is also about full understanding of the speaker's intention - therefore, having empathy for the speaker and the information being conveyed. So, how do you improve active listening?

Like any other communication skill, active listening can be learned, taught and even practiced. The following tips will help you learn, improve, and practice active listening:

a. Talk less - it is not possible to talk and listen at the same time. Hold on to answers and interruptions and be open by giving the speaker your attention and everything they need, understanding what they are saying.

b. Adopt a listening mode - silence your environment and your mind, open your mind to listening and be comfortable while listening. Be sure to maintain eye contact.

c. Make the speaker comfortable - nod your head, use your body gestures, or do anything that makes the speaker realize you are listening and interested in what you have to say. Seating is also important for both the speaker and the listener. Where does the speaker feel most comfortable? When sitting behind his or her desk or at his or her side? If a child stands at eye level and avoids protruding above his or her eyes, he or she is intimidated and may not be able to convey the information.

d. Eliminate distractions - this involves clearing the room of anything physical that might cause distractions, putting the phone on silent, turning off the TV or computer if they are on and might cause distractions. If the speaker requires privacy, be sure to give it by asking others in the room to excuse you, and when you close the door. It also gives the speaker the confidence that you will hear and understand everything they say, and your response will be equally good.

e. Empathize - try to understand the situation where the speaker is coming from. Put yourself in their position, ask the necessary questions that lead you to understand the speaker's position and feeling about the situation.

f. Don't be afraid of silence - some people need time to form a thoughtful response. Do not rush them, and do not suggest what they should say. It prevents them from communicating honestly. Let them speak at their own pace and with understanding.

g. Put aside personal prejudices - this is also a very difficult thing to do because our experiences shape who we are. Putting aside all these experiences is a skill that requires help in order to actively listen.

h. Pay attention to your tone - be attentive to understand the tone being used. Sometimes a tone can obscure the meaning of a word, and other times, it can enhance the meaning. Make sure you know what the tone is for understanding what is being communicated.

i. Listen and identify the underlying meaning - most of the time, you realize that there is a hidden meaning in some communication. Listen for understanding or comprehension and secondly for the ideas that are being communicated.

j. Pay attention to non-verbal communication as well - you can lose a lot of information if you don't like non-verbal cues. People can communicate through body language and facial expressions - therefore, the reason why eye contact is necessary.

5. Solve the Problem

If there are so many problems and so little time to solve them, try to solve at least one. The problem will occur without our direct influence by action or choice, but it will not go away by itself. The secret is to handle them one by one every day at a time and to learn the secret to avoid them in the future.

Choose one problem a day and concentrate on finding a solution without dividing your attention. You may want to clear up a misunderstanding that has lasted a long time between you and someone else, or are you getting too distracted at work? Alternatively, have you struggled with a project and want to improve it? Maybe you have something at home that needs to be fixed? Face the problem and find a solution. To help you solve the problem, here's an example:

Sample Process

This approach will give you a guide to handle the problems you decide to face on a daily basis. The step-by-step guide will include the following:

- Define and clearly state the problem as much as possible.

- Take the time to study the problem and understand it and what is expected. If you do not have control over a certain problem, put it aside and concentrate on those for which you can find a solution.

- Find out what information you need to solve the problem, actively gather all the information needed to help you solve the problem.

- With acuity, interpret and analyze the information you have collected, choose the reasonable and appropriate inferences you can.

- Find out what you can do, either in the short term or in the long term. Clarify all your options for action, and imagine the solution that seems ideal.

- Analyze your options, taking note of their pros and cons.

- Take a systematic and strategic approach to the problem and move forward with it.

The process of improving critical thinking requires practice and time. Let us hope that the five practices or strategies above will be useful to you in improving your critical thinking skills. With daily practice, you improve your skills, and critical thinking becomes part of you.

CHAPTER 5
CAUSES FOR LACK OF CRITICAL THINKING SKILLS

Critical thinking skills are important tools, especially when it comes to personal and academic beliefs. When applied, critical thinking is a strong defense against ideas and opinions that are potentially harmful or blatantly wrong. Unfortunately, not all people have this ability, although they can be very well educated. Understanding what suppresses critical thinking is a significant step in increasing a more responsive perspective.

Instruction

Instruction is a significant obstacle to critical thinking. The moment an individual is continually surrounded and develops an uneven perspective on things like personal beliefs or politics, it stifles critical thinking. Young people and students are especially helpless against this, so critical thinking must be constantly supported. As the American Association of Colleges and Universities states, instructing students to be cautious "will help them see beyond the distortion of propaganda and allow them to judiciously evaluate the persuasiveness of strong emotional appeals.

Lack of Intelligence

A University of Phoenix article entitled "Can Critical Thinking be Educated in the Classroom? states that a critical thinker "would require a degree of cognitive and intellectual capacity. The article infers that a few people are more experienced than others in being dubious and analytical. This is reasonable, because individuals who do not know will think it is much simpler to recognize certain ideas at first glance than to invest time and energy in exploring them. As the Media Awareness Network points out, "basic reasoning is how you think, not what you think" and requires "interest, an open mind, mistrust and determination. In the end, you can't think critically if you overlook your process. Critical thinking is not assuming that everything you hear or see is potentially wrong.

Arrogance

Your disposition can profoundly affect critical thinking. Regardless of whether you are very bright, you will not think critically about the remote possibility that you are not ready to go beyond your perspectives. In the remote possibility that you are not humble, so to speak, you will be looking for options to fear that they will end up being wrong.

Cognitive Dysfunction

As the Surgeon General noted, mental disability and psychological illness can cause a variety of obstacles, such as decreased thinking and perception or cognitive impairment. Thus, individuals with these problems may be mentally disabled. Because critical thinking requires a specific level of knowledge, cognitive impairment prevents individuals from understanding the intricate guidelines and processes of critical thinking.

The 5-Step Creativity Cycle

1. Preparation

The first level is the idea of preparation, the idea that you are immersed in control. If you are a musician, you absorb a lot of the music that inspires you to create this new piece. If you are a writer, read other authors in this field. If you are an artist, you are looking at the work of another artist in the area where you want to create something. Supposedly you are a scientist, and you are looking at all the historical research. And if you're a businessman or businesswoman, you look at all the previous market research and what other companies have done in the past.

Therefore, this stage is best done in a quiet environment. In fact, at this stage, you are trying to absorb as much information as possible because this information will enter your subconscious, where it is very important to the second or second level.

2. Incubation

It begins to stir in the back of your mind, in the psyche. This is an important stage because from time to time it can take days, weeks, months or even years. You consider this thought by composing for a book or some music, and you write in it and put it aside for some time and then go back to it.

3. Insight

The third stage is what some people think of as a classical piece or display from a creative person, which is called the insight stage or perspicacity stage. Insight is the idea of the "Aha" moment, the "Eureka" moment. Although it is probably the smallest of the five steps, it can be one of the most important. One quick thing to say is that they occur more often when you do some low-level physical activity. Let's take a shower, drive a car, take a walk and then bring these ideas to mind. This is the third stage, the information stage.

4. Evaluation

The fourth level is the idea of EVALUATION. It is an area that many creative people struggle with because you often have many ideas and you have limited time. Therefore, the evaluation stage is important because it requires self-criticism and reflection. Ask yourself questions like:

"Is it a new or novel idea or one that has just been modified and done before?

It's the idea of hanging out with a small group of trusted friends and saying

"I had this idea, what do you think of it?"

It's a very important place because we only have a limited amount of time to do certain things. Often, people who are called "creative" tend to be very good at this stage, the evaluation stage.

5. Elaboration

And then we have the final stage. It's called preparation. Here he said that Edison is "1% inspiration and 99% sweat. Now the craft stage is the 99% sweat stage. It's where the work is done. Many people believe that the creative process is this perception, this "Aha" moment or part of the preparation. But in reality, a creative person is not complete, and I don't think they can do something that lasts unless they can get past it and do the hard work. Processing? Testing the idea, working on the idea, those nights in the studio, working in your office, those hours in the lab if you're a scientist, those days testing and micro-testing products. It's the craft stage.

CHAPTER 6
COGNITIVE BIASES

The memories stored in our brain of a similar event that may have created a bias will lead to this change in thinking and decision making. These biases could disrupt an entire process, leading to a choice that is not in the optimal range for the mental model.

Cognitive bias will be an error in reasoning that may divert the decision maker from making any rational deduction. To a certain extent, we will find that the cognitive bias we have is going to be a completely natural phenomenon. It is simply the way the brain is going to work. It is often going to be a very complex process for the brain to work through every piece of information that comes to it from all of our senses, from touch, taste, sound, eyes, and more.

Keep in mind that there will be some types of cognitive biases that are not considered natural. These will be created from a few different things, such as misinformation and education of parents, school, traditional practices, and more. It's not natural to have these kinds of cognitive biases, and if you realize that these are things you're dealing with, then it's something you have to deal with from the beginning.

How Cognitive Biases Weaken Your Mental Models

Each of the following solutions offered by cognitive biases also has its respective disadvantages. The key to avoiding further problems, therefore, is to be aware that shortcuts are being taken rather than making deliberate but sound decisions. Consider these four issues that stem from the overuse of cognitive biases in a person's daily life.

1. You Do Not Get to See Everything

Filters are beneficial to you if and only if they block unnecessary information only. However, in most cases, people are unable to adjust their filters accordingly, leading to the loss of key information that could be useful in making a decision.

2. Your Search for Meaning Can Lead You to Illogical or Even Harmful Assumptions

Imagining how an event has happened can quickly become a source of error and misjudgment. You are essentially fabricating a story that fits only your point of view rather than the whole truth of the situation.

3. Decisions That Are Made Too Quickly Tend to Have Serious Flaws

Hasty decisions are often selfish because you didn't have the opportunity to consider each side of the story. Sometimes, they can also be counterproductive since, most of the time, they are partially or completely wrong.

4. Your Memories Can Further Strengthen the Mental Errors You Have Made

The bits of information you save tend to fit what you already have. It means that instead of expanding your mind, you are only reinforcing both the good and bad attitudes and beliefs you have about people, objects, events and more.

Given these, you can conclude that cognitive biases are like any other you may have at your disposal. When used correctly in context and in moderation, they can be quite useful and even life-saving at times. However, when abused, over-reliance on cognitive biases can create more problems and lead to more harm. The human brain is capable of remarkable feats of ingenuity and resourcefulness. It also plays an essential role in the plans and decisions that are made for everyday life, such as remembering the conversations you have had with your friends and having a productive day at work with your colleagues.

The brain is indeed susceptible to being misled. Fortunately, it is also capable of improving the important mental structures that underlie your thoughts, attitudes, and behaviors.

Ambiguity Effect

It's where you avoid situations where you don't know if the outcome will be in your favor or not.

Anchoring

It is when you rely too much on one piece of information during the decision-making process. It is usually the first piece of information you receive.

Personification

It is where animals, objects and concepts are characterized as having the same tendencies as humans. It is giving non-humans traits, emotions and intentions that are normally reserved for humans. New paragraph, attention bias.

Attention Bias or Attentional Bias

This is where your perception is affected by the thoughts that continue to occur.

Automation Bias

It is where you believe the automated information and you rely excessively on these automated systems, and will often go against what you know is the right decision.

Availability Heuristic

When the probability of something happening is overestimated because you remember it better than other things, it can influence our memories, and our emotions can change.

Availability Cascade

This is where collective beliefs become more plausible because of the repetition the public gives them. This is the saying that if something is repeated long enough, it will become true.

Backfire Effect

It is where we refuse to believe the evidence that does not support our police.

Bandwagon Effect

It's basically where you think you're doing something just because a group of people are doing the same thing.

Base Rate Fallacy

These concerns focus on specific information that only relates to a certain situation rather than looking at the general information in front of you.

Belief Bias

This is where you skew your argument because you believe so strongly in the conclusion.

Ben Franklin Effect

Someone is more likely to do someone a favor if they have already done so. This is in contrast to if they had received a favor from the same person.

Blind Spot of Bias

It is where we see ourselves in a less partial light, and then we see other people. We are more capable of seeing prejudice and someone else than ourselves.

Biased Support for Choice

It's where we remember the choices that someone makes better than the choices they made.

Grouping Illusion

This is where we see the phantom fat patterns instead of looking at the whole picture.

Confirmation Bias

This is where we only focus on information that will confirm what we already believe.

Consistency Bias

This is where we tend to test solutions directly rather than looking for alternatives.

Conjunction Fallacy

This is where we look beyond the general conditions in favor of the very specific ones as more likely than the first.

Revision of Beliefs

It is where we refuse to reform our own beliefs, even when new information is presented to us.

The Effect of Continued Influence

This is where we continually learn information that is incorrect even after it has been corrected.

The Curse of Knowledge

This is where the best informed people have difficulty seeing something from the perspective of someone with less information.

Default Affection

This is where we favor the default solution over the other options we are given.

The Empathy Gap

It is where people often do not give credit to the influence or strength of their feelings or those of another person.

Illusion of the End of the Story

It is where we allow ourselves to believe that in the future, we will change less than in the past.

Focusing the Effect

It is where we place too much importance or value on an area of an event that is happening.

The Player's Fallacy

This is where we think any future possibility will be affected by events that have occurred before.

Difficult Affection - Easy

This is where our confidence in the judgments we are making is either too conservative or not extreme enough.

Identifiable Victim Effect

It is when we respond most strongly to someone we have identified as being in danger, rather than to an entire group of people who are in danger.

The Effects of IKEA

This is where we put a disproportionate value on objects that are not fully assembled, and the value is high. We don't look at the quality at the end of the result.

Impact Bias

This is where we tend to overestimate the duration of something or the intensity of the impact.

The Law of the Instrument

This is where we rely too much on unfamiliar tools and methods, and ignore any alternative approach.

Bias of Omission

This is where we tend to fail to judge something as harmful when compared to something that is less moral and equally harmful. It usually revolves around action against action.

Bias Towards Pessimism

This is where we overestimate the chances of negative things happening to people.

Projection Bias

This is where we overestimate how much we will have in common with our future selves.

We assume that we will have the same preferences, thoughts and values, which leads us to make decisions that are either suboptimal or inferior.

Effect of Overconfidence

This is where we rely solely on our trust to answer questions.

Restriction Bias

This is where we think we can show more restraint than we really can when faced with temptation.

Perception of Selection

This is where expectations will often alter and affect the perceptions we have.

The Bias of Sexual over-Perception

It's where we become overconfident or unsafe, except in how much someone is attracted to us.

Stereotypes

This is where we expect a certain population of people who have characteristics and traits just because that's how we think they are.

Status Quo Bias

It is where we feel that everything will remain the same.

Time - Saving Bias

This is where we don't give importance to how much time can be saved or lost depending on whether we increase or decrease the speed.

Bias Units

This is where we consider the suggested amount of something to be appropriate, and we tend to overconsume. Think about this with the suggested serving size.

Women Are a Wonderful Affect

This is where we, as a society, tend to give more positive features and pay tribute to women rather than men.

Zero Risk Bias

This is where we would prefer to reduce the small risk to zero rather than make a larger risk reduction compared to a large risk. Cognitive bias is an error in the way we think it affects our decision-making ability as well as our judgment. One of the first ways it is affected is through our personal Bias, which will ultimately affect your decision based on emotion rather than fact.

Our ethical compass is always working and always pointing in the direction we would like to believe we are including. We want to draw conclusions that are objective, reasonable in scope, and detailed with the information provided. When we are distracted, shocked, anxious, or careless, these prejudices that we work so hard to eliminate slowly slide away. Normally, we are not aware of these prejudices when we decide something. Therefore, they remain in your decision models and end up with unsuccessful decisions and judgments not based on objective facts and truths. Ultimately, you are making bad decisions.

CHAPTER 7
AN IN-DEPTH LOOK ON WHAT CRITICAL THINKING IS

It would be hard to find someone who hasn't come across the term "critical thinking" in one form or another. But what exactly does it mean, and why is it a good thing? Is it a good thing, or is it just a way of adding more stress to an already overloaded mind? These and many more questions about critical thinking will be answered.

What is Critical Thinking?

Contrary to popular belief, critical thinking does not necessarily mean criticizing (although it is possible that it can be done much more effectively after engaging in critical thinking). It is simply a way of absorbing information and contributions coming from different places, analyzing them and reflecting on them before trying to form an opinion. This is basically what the term means.

It is the way in which thoughts and arguments are rationally entertained, without rushing to form an opinion and make a judgment. You need to be able to think critically regardless of how others tell you to think because that's how you come to really form your own beliefs and convictions rather than just repeat those of others. Many of the problems we face in today's world-hate, bigotry, fanaticism, xenophobia, anger and more-would simply disappear if people learned to think for themselves. A person is not born racist or homophobic; he inherits those notions from the societies he inhabits, and never stops to think about them.

Why Do You Need Critical Thinking?

Why is it then important to have this analytical approach to everything, to consider and think carefully about the claims and arguments that are heard every day, especially in the Internet age?

Forming Your Own Beliefs

Let's face it; we are all born into a certain doctrine, whether religious, social or otherwise. Critical thinking helps you to question each and every one of those doctrines and to decide for yourself if that is really something you have to follow. There is nothing wrong with following a certain religion or becoming an atheist; it is people who follow either path without thinking about it, just because they were told that this is the right path, that they too often pose some form of threat. You will not find a religious fanatic or racist practicing critical thinking; they are more or less deluded people who never take the time to think for themselves.

When you think critically about things, you will never fall into those categories. You will never harbor hatred toward another person because of his or her sex, color, creed, religion, or any other reason. You will begin to find things that connect you to people rather than separate you.

A Better Understanding of Things

Critical thinking allows you to form a better understanding of things in general. Acquiring knowledge is never really about accumulating as much information as you can; anyone with a good memory could do it. But what good is that knowledge if you don't think about it and analyze it? Acquiring knowledge is about analyzing the inputs you receive, finding correlation and/or causality, and deducing the consequences of a particular piece of information or argument. Then, this will help you put that knowledge to good use, and you can use it to solve problems and answer bigger and more important questions.

You will find that all the scientists and great thinkers of our time and times past lived by a code to critically question everything. They built and deconstructed any information, statements or hypotheses they heard, and this allowed them to have a significantly better understanding of our universe. Critical thinking also allows us to understand the logical connection between ideas and how everything is connected, which is the foundation on which science is based.

The Rationality of Forming an Argument

We live in a time when people argue about everything; some even argue to make a living. It is very easy to appear uninformed or foolish in these times, and that is why critical thinking is needed. It will enable you to understand a very important point that could change your life: it is not a matter of being right or wrong or making judgments, except in cases where it is clear and simple enough to make such judgments, which is known as a case of "black and white. Once you fully grasp the notion that you do not need to make a judgment about everything, but rather to analyze and understand each claim from every angle, you will begin to react differently and more rationally.

Then, if and when you want to form an argument, you can do so from a rational point of view that is based on being informed and reasonable and not just impulsive. You will be able to expand your statements and explain why you do not agree with solid arguments instead of using the "I am right, you are wrong" approach, which is usually useless and does not help or contribute to make any change, which leads us to a very important use of critical thinking: problem solving. As we will explore later in the book, one of the main reasons why many people have problems with problem solving is because they rarely address the issue at hand in a critical way.

Becoming a Better Person

Critical thinking will simply help you become a better person. You will develop more empathy and begin to realize that you don't have to be right all the time; maybe the other person is right sometimes. Maybe your world view is not the only valid one, and maybe there is a different reality outside the confines of the box you are in. You begin to empathize with others, and you see other viewpoints for what they really are; only viewpoints of people who don't share your beliefs, not enemies or people you should hate for being different. Critical thinking helps you to see beyond cultural norms and to see people for who they are rather than for who they tell you they are. This, and the fact that you shed all hatred for those who are simply different, helps you to be a better person and a better leader, which brings us to the next point.

Improving as a Leader

As you read this, you may ask yourself, still, how does critical thinking help me? Well, it will help you be a better leader and manager. The empathy you gain from analyzing and thinking about others' points of view means that you will be able to show those ideas the respect and recognition they deserve. It also means you will be better equipped to make decisions because you understand that every problem must be considered from every angle. When a team member tells you about a problem they are facing, you don't get defensive and start undermining their problem, but you listen and think about it, and you may find they have a valid complaint.

If one of your team members suggests an idea to you, and you think critically about it, your ego will never get in the way. If it is really a good idea, you will accept it and push your people forward, because you will simply see that it is good for business, and what is good for business is good for you. Critical thinking will also help you communicate better, as every point or statement you make will be backed by evidence and solid reasoning rather than emotion. It will help you reach your subordinates and deliver your messages in an elaborate and clear manner.

Business and Science

What do these two disciplines have in common? Both are largely based on critical thinking, and critical thinking has played and will play an important role in their evolution. When you begin to consider problems from all angles and think about your possible options and solutions, you will become a better problem solver, which is a necessity for any professional today. Critical thinking also promotes creativity because it is what is needed to find a solution to a difficult problem that you have considered from all angles. You will not settle for an ordinary answer, because you will continue to analyze your solution and find different ways to improve it.

As for science, it goes without saying that all scientific theories and experimentation are based on critical thinking. Scientists question everything, and their theories and hypotheses are not based only on their intellectual capacities but rather on how they can build their reasoning and connect ideas.

Making Sense of the World

All of the above aside, we need critical thinking to make sense of the world, especially in a world as polarized as ours today. You are constantly being told what is right and wrong, who are the bad people you should hate; it can be a very slippery slope to take everything you hear as truth without subjecting the statements to reason and critical thinking. Critical thinking is the way you will be able to determine which statements are correct and which are false and biased, possibly serving a particular plan.

You keep hearing the term "false news," but is it false news? And if so, why is it so? That's where critical thinking comes in; it's your way of knowing what makes sense and what doesn't, and most importantly, how you should act on it. Some philosophers say there are no absolute truths, but if there were, critical thinking is how you would find them.

Does Critical Thinking Go Against Personal Beliefs and Feelings?

No, it is not. Critical thinking simply means that the arguments that are formed and the approach to problem solving are not going to be based on faith, personal beliefs or gut feelings, but on a sensible and rational consideration of the facts presented and the information available. If you want to call a person an idiot instead of showing why they are wrong, at least do it while giving a reason why they are idiots (although it doesn't help your case if you start with the insults).

CHAPTER 8
CULTIVATE YOUR INTELLECTUAL CURIOSITY

Intellectual curiosity may be one of the five main indicators/predictors of effectiveness, productivity and professional achievements of leaders. Some may be surprised, but not most. Although IQ is nuanced, complex, and advanced, it remains a competence that can be learned, trained, honed, and realized. You probably haven't learned much about the value of increasing IQ since you were in school or in your first jobs. Because these skills are seen as natural, innovative, or advanced, they often lack a practical approach to new leadership. Unfortunately, young leaders lack the opportunity to integrate the power of curiosity into their early leadership mosaic that would accelerate their career growth and development. Their curiosity fosters a deeper appreciation of the environment and its inhabitants.

Intellectual curiosity is a vital part of the great leadership equation.

Great Leadership = (IQ * CQ * EQ)

Without CQ, great leadership cannot be achieved. CQ is the vital glue that connects our perception and emotions.

Invest in yourself to become an outstanding success. The larger your investment, the more suitable it is for your business trip. It's only as you expand your career. The good news is that you have dedicated time to your personal development. Either you do it and stand out, or you don't. These are ways to improve mental and emotional intelligence.

1. Expand Your Horizons

Expanding your horizons opens the world to you when the opportunity presents itself. New experiences invite the unknown into your life. The unknown gives you diverse experiences that greatly enhance your knowledge. By creating new neural pathways, the brain responds to new things. With repetition, each new pathway becomes stronger, giving us new skills and strengths. Therefore, you should always strive to be a little outside of your comfort zone. This can be done very quickly. You can choose to visit new places, go to the office, or brush your teeth with a non-dominant hand. Habits shape the brain. The harder and more accustomed you are to dealing with change. Everything that is normal in your life prevents you from developing as you would if you did some things a little differently every day. Mix things up to train you in new ways, new people, and new environments.

2. Be Imaginative

All success begins with results, incentives and imaginary stimuli. The more creative you are, the more likely you are to develop new and successful strategies for problem solving, brainstorming and networking skills. The more imaginative you are, the greater your ability to be inspired in all aspects of life when necessary. This type of creativity gives you a confidence that helps you enormously, whether it is in your daily life or when this skill is useful in your business life. People will know that when new and inventive ideas are needed, you will be the person who will move things in a new and better direction. Creativity is the main attribute you have to be a smart innovator. You have it all, and not only does a little imagination increase enthusiasm for what you can do, but it can also make the most boring work a little more fun.

3. Pleasure Reading

Developing personal growth through reading books implies the possibility of choosing different types of books that may belong to very different categories. Whether it is a detective story, a novel, your favorite poem or a sports magazine, reading stimulates your imagination and can be a fantastic experience. Your brain translates the words into images that play in your mind like a movie without your conscious effort. Reading gives you a break, puts you in another world, and creates an emotional relationship between you and the paper words. You just have to run for a while. If you can't go on vacation, reading a book is a great replacement. In addition, reading increases your vocabulary, provides examples of good grammar in your head, and helps you become not only a better reader and writer but also a more different kind of communicator.

4. Train Your Brain

Numerous techniques are easy to use to keep the mind awake. Many word riddles and other applications such as luminosity are available on your smartphone, which offers games and problem-solving strategies designed to improve the neuroplasticity of your brain. The brain's ability to create new neural connections allows you to work at a higher level: neuroplasticity. The more neuroplastic your brain becomes, the more new connections it makes and the more easily and efficiently you process information. The significant strength lies in decision making, and yet very few train their brain every day.

5. Consistently Learn

There is still something to learn. The more you learn, the more prepared you will be to make an excellent strategy. The more knowledge you gain, the more information you will have in making critical decisions. Learning is what builds your confidence. It increases your skill base and enhances your skills. It also allows you to work smarter, not just harder. Let's assume that you will always have to learn more and experience a direct and clear increase in your ability to do so.

6. Physical Activity

Physical activity not only improves your shape, but also gives you better brain function. The brain reacts better when it is full of oxygen. It improves memory, improves concentration, and prevents cognitive decline when the brain is given the oxygen it needs for training. The brain cannot receive new information or generate new cell development without exercise. The fastest and most structured way to be smart, less stressed, less depressed, and more energy efficient is to move your body.

7. Keep an Open Mind

This is crucial if you are curious. Be open to learning, unlearning and relearning. Anything you know and believe can be wrong, and you must be prepared to recognize and change your mind.

8. Don't Take Things as Granted

Maintaining an appropriate curiosity, similar to that of children when they observe something new and want to discover as much as possible, is essential and vital, especially in adults. Never take things for granted. Try to dig deeper below the surface.

9. Don't Label Something as Boring

Every time they label something boring, without examining it, they close a possible new opportunity. Knowing how to select your priorities is a vital skill, but it is also essential for keeping an open and alert mind. Even if you don't have time to explore a specific situation, you leave the door open, and then when you have time, you can choose and evaluate how to act.

10. Play a Game

The games and cards are generally known as leisure games. These activities can also contribute to your intellectual well-being. Next time you have some free time, grab a deck of cards or play a board game. It doesn't matter if you play alone or with others. As long as your mind is thinking, there are changes.

11. Play a Musical Instrument

Music has a strong impact on our minds. A musical instrument can improve mental well-being by learning to make sounds, build patterns and emotions through music. Any instrument can enhance intellectual well-being, so start today and take up a new hobby.

12. Write Down Your Thoughts or Journal Frequently

Having time to write thoughts or notes can also benefit those who struggle to express their emotions or, more generally, anyone who wants to make sense of what they are feeling inside. You can better understand yourself and your feelings and actions by exposing your mind to deeper thought.

CHAPTER 9
MENTAL MODELS

Now that you know about critical thinking and its benefits, we get to the hard part. Yes, all of the above was an introduction to critical thinking. Now, the real issue is, how do you practice this technique of thinking? Learning how to do it is not difficult, but it is not easy or simple either. It is not because learning to think critically is complicated in itself, but rather because it takes self-discipline and a clear mind to do it.

So how can you do it? Well, the good news is that there are thousands of different ways to model your thinking. But that's also the bad news.

The mental models that we are going to explore are simply ways of explaining or thinking about a certain subject in relation to how it works. It is a concept or a framework within your own mind that will help you explain things and understand the meaning behind them.

Occam's Razor

This is the first of the mental models that we are going to explore. Occam's razor is quite simple, actually; it states that when a problem or something needs to be explained, the simplest and most direct of its explanations/responses is often the right one.

It is an approach to follow when several hypotheses are presented that compete for a dilemma. In such cases, the one that requires making the least amount of assumptions to prove its correctness is the correct hypothesis. However, it is important to know that this approach must be followed with hypotheses that explain the same occurrence, so it should not be used to explain opposing points of view. In other words, your explanations have to come to the same conclusion or prediction, but that does not mean that they are all correct.

So, let's assume that you woke up one morning and found your car parked on the street but covered with dirt. You have a couple of explanations for that incident. The heavy rain the night before may have splashed the dirt from your car. Or the neighborhood kids may have conspired against you, picked up some mud in a bucket, and slid undetected into your car to throw mud at it. As you can see, the result is the same; your car is dirty. But the hypotheses are completely different. In this scenario, the obvious probable explanation is the first one, because it requires less assumptions.

If you run out of gas on the way to work, the most likely reason is that you forgot to fill your tank the day before, not the existence of a gang of gas thieves who snuck into your closed garage at dusk and emptied your tank. Again, the same result, but Occam's razor argues that the explanation with the fewest assumptions is the most likely.

Hanlon's Razor

This is another proverb or way of thinking to explain some human behavior, and it is inspired by Occam's razor. It goes like this: "Never attribute to malice what can be adequately explained by stupidity. It is possibly one of the most functional approaches to critical thinking because it could help us avoid many unnecessary conflicts.

Hanlon's Razor simply means that sometimes bad things happen, but that does not necessarily imply bad intentions. Sometimes the other person is just stupid or incompetent, or just didn't think it through. In other words, not everyone is the enemy and people don't look for you.

Your colleague at work didn't spill coffee on your favorite shirt because they hate you; they did it accidentally, without any ill will on your part. The random person who hit you from behind on the street is not going to hit every BMW owner; they just lost concentration for a second or were too tired after a long day's work.

Imagine the kind of world we would live in if people were not constantly hostile and assumed the worst. Hanlon's Razor is a simple mental model that teaches you not to always assume the worst in people's behavior. In short, give people the benefit of the doubt; you will be surprised how much less stressful and happy your life and theirs will be.

First-Principle Reasoning

First principle reasoning is one of the most important mental models that exist and is particularly suitable for scientific disciplines. First principle thinking is a way of trying to achieve absolute truth if such a thing exists.

A first principle is an idea, notion or assumption that is sustained by its merit, since it cannot be deduced from any other assumption or theory. Aristotle was the first to propose this concept, stating that it could help us to know everything we need to know simply because we know the basic truth. When the reasoning of the first principles is used, all other assumptions, models, conventions, and false thoughts that cloud judgment and impair the search for truth are ignored. There is only the first basic principle, which you will try to find by asking the right powerful questions.

So how do you practice the reasoning of the first principle? In short, question everything. Do not take any answer for granted, and shatter everything until you are left with an undeniable truth.

Think of it as a way to reverse your thinking. Reduce everything to the most basic truth, instead of building an analogy that only repeats what others think. The main reasoning will help you seek truth because you question everything you know. The use of an analogy, on the other hand, puts you in a position where you simply accept a widely accepted truth, but is it the truth? That is the question you must ask yourself.

If you do not learn to use first principle reasoning, you will always be hooked on what people tell you is right or wrong, and you will always be trapped by the assumptions of others. But when you begin to shed everything, looking for the most basic and undisputed truths, you see the world for what it is, not for what others tell you it is.

Scenario Analysis

Scenario analysis is a fairly important critical thinking approach, and one that plays a significant role in the investment world. It is an approach to predict future events by considering all possible outcomes.

This opens up new doors for us because not only are there such alternative outcomes, but also the paths leading to them. Scenario analysis is not based on past results or analysis of past trends; it is not derived from historical inputs or market indicators, which really forces you to think outside the box.

To practice scenario analysis, you have to think about the best, worst and most probable results of a scenario, but you have to act as if all of them are plausible and all of them are probable. In general terms, it is recommended to keep the scenarios to only three, and it is necessary to think of all three as "likely to occur. Once you manage to apply this principle to any discipline you want, it is very unlikely that an unforeseen event will surprise you.

CHAPTER 10
CRITICAL THINKING VS. OVERTHINKING

Imagine that you find yourself in a problem at work where you have difficulty expanding your product exposure. It is a prime example of a situation where following the steps of critical thinking will be beneficial in laying the groundwork for creating a question, gathering information, and analyzing that information.

But instead of following the critical thinking process, the more you think about the problem at hand, the more anxious you become. You think about what could happen if you don't figure out how to solve the problem quickly: people will stop buying, you won't be able to reach enough people, and your business will have to close down eventually.

Even when you find solutions to the problem, no matter how sound they are, you question those solutions until you feel they wouldn't have worked anyway, and the whole process continually falls apart. You spend a lot of time on it, but it gets harder and harder to find solutions.

It's a good example of overthinking. In a critical thinking situation, you would work on the process in a controlled and organized way. With excessive thinking, all signs of structure fade, anxiety creeps in and your productivity disappears.

There is a fundamental difference between excessive thinking and critical thinking. Exaggerated thinking is very obsessed with a subject, usually someone else's behavior, but often your own. You keep playing with what happened in your mind as if you were trying to solve it, but the problem is that you are not trying to solve it. Judge and ask questions to prove that someone is right and someone else is wrong.

If you think too much, you end up spending a lot more time than you should be thinking about a problem, but that doesn't mean it's productive thinking. Critical thinking is productive. Doing things? It solves immediate problems and is organized and free of prejudice. However, thinking too much wastes time and mental energy.

In critical thinking, a solution to the problem is actively sought, developing the steps that can be taken to reach a conclusion. There are some strategies and skills you can use to achieve the desired solution. Because critical thinking involves a lot of thought, it helps reduce stress.

Thinking too much, on the other hand, does not use strategy. It contains rumors, worries and excessive analysis. If you think too much, you will find yourself facing a problem instead of finding a viable solution. Because of this, stress increases and the more intense you feel, the more likely you are to focus on the negative aspects of the situation. A constant cycle of stress is created and critical thinking is lost.

Thinking too much is not productive. It is catastrophic. It stops you. It keeps you from moving forward. Critical thinking, however, is about understanding. It does not involve any crisis. It's a question designed to provide useful information. Questions that bring you closer to a deeper understanding.

Studies have shown that focusing on negative events can be a major predictor of major mental health problems such as depression and anxiety. Part of the reason why excessive thinking causes so much stress is because you are hearing that inner voice criticizing you and telling you that you are wrong or inadequate. This leads you to overthink situations.

The next time you think too much instead of thinking critically, there are some strategies you can try to rethink. Then you can propose a calmer and more collected mentality and start to put your critical thinking skills to work.

Confront your negative inner voice: Your negative inner voice perpetuates your excessive thinking by making you more anxious as it goes. To prevent your negative inner voice from taking over, first, take note of what that inner voice says to you when it appears. Then think about where those words come from. Does it have to do with a current situation like work or someone you love, or is it a past life event that left you feeling inadequate as an adult? After you understand where it is coming from, you can separate it from your more positive thoughts. Finally, when those negative thoughts come back, put them away. You can do this with a set of phrases that answer the voice within, such as, "I can do this" and "I am able to solve my problems.

Choose your thoughts carefully: An effective way to stop thinking too much, to think carefully, is to learn to control or focus your attention to increase calmness and self-awareness. In this way, you are more able to understand and have control over your behavior.

It changes the way you look at problems: Instead of dealing with problems with stress and ruminating on a negative subject, it changes the way you see and address the problems you encounter. Instead of seeing a challenge as a bad thing, think of it as a positive challenge that you will be stronger to overcome. Accept that you have a lot of control over your circumstances by having a positive mindset. Commit yourself to overcome these challenges to feel powerful and proactive in the face of them.

Critical Reading and Writing

Learning to read critically involves actively participating in what we read, first developing a clear understanding of the author's ideas, then challenging and evaluating the arguments and evidence provided to support those arguments, and finally forming our own views. Reading in this way requires us to develop skills that are not necessary for more passive forms of information retrieval. However, it also allows us to get more out of what we read.

Steps for Critical Reading:

- Before reading, scan the piece to get an idea of what it is and what the main argument is. This can include reading an introduction, if available, or captions.

- As you read, continue the dialogue with the author through comments, recording their thoughts, ideas and questions. Underline, highlight, or circle significant parts and points, and compose observations in the margins.

- After reading, check your comments to get an overview of the content. You may also decide to write a summary to improve your understanding.

- If you react to the text after you have acquired a clear sense of the author's argument and thought, you can dissect the author's argument and techniques. At that point, you can construct your thoughts, perhaps on your screen.

Two Ways to Read

It is useful to consider that critical reading involves two ways of reading: reading with the author or trying to fully understand the author's opinions and reading the author critically or challenging the author's opinions. The first function is necessary to make the second possible. By reading in two ways, you can develop your ideas and theories, but only after you understand the author's arguments.

Read with the author: understand the author's point of view.

1. Make sure you understand the author's views and ideas. Summarizing and paraphrasing your argument in your own words can be helpful at this stage.

2. Briefly acknowledge the author's ideas (whether or not he opposes this idea). Use the author's ideas as a focal point for taking a look at your world, developing the author's speculations with your coordinated examples.

Critical reading of the author: participation of the author in a dialogue.

1. Look through your lens now, ask questions and challenge the author. Some things to look for are: limitations, biases, misconceptions, unanswered questions, and alternative problems or interpretations of the author's examples.

2. Now you will be able to plan your ideas and theories. Which parts of the author's ideas do you agree with? Which parts would you review? What is your point of view?

CHAPTER 11
FORMULA TO DEVELOP OPEN MINDED THINKING

As long as you are not dead, you will have thoughts and be asked to make decisions. You can still become a critical thinker; it is not too late.

We have a great capacity to carry out certain tasks and activities. In fact, those who lack talent in specific areas can hone their skills through practice. The same is true for critical thinking.

You can use the following strategies to develop open thinking skills.

Think and Focus on Your Life's Goals

Everyone has a purpose, but most people make the worst decisions because they lose sight of their goals. Ask yourself this: Why do I want to keep waking up and working hard?

Knowing what your goals are will almost instantly give you all the information you need to achieve them because your mind is ready to do so. You will know that you need to take certain steps to see that you achieve the things you set out to do. At the same time, your goals will also define every decision you make. If one of your biggest goals is to buy a home before you turn 30, then that will make you decide to get a job and set up a savings account.

Think About the Consequences of Your Action

If you want to be a critical thinker, you need to always think consciously about what is most likely to happen after you make a decision. By doing this, you immediately worry about whether your actions will backfire or give you more benefit. Also, consider other points of view that allow you to see the whole picture, and in any case that you have not made a more beneficial decision, attribute it to experience. By being aware of what could have happened, you will know how to act better the next time you find yourself in that situation.

Notice When Something Is Wrong

If your intuition tells you that a specific brand of toothpaste won't make your teeth pearly white, then you have every reason to question how it advertises. When you think about it, that's how you check every doubt you have in your mind. When you practice critical thinking, you begin to see the world as it is.

Do Not Put Too Much Emphasis on Being Right

Critical thinkers may realize that they don't have to be right all the time or have all the answers. Being a critical thinker means considering all the information before making a decision. Therefore, in case you don't know something, don't be afraid to accept and change that thought. Asking questions is important and is something you should never be afraid of as a critical thinker. Don't make any judgments or decisions if you don't have enough information to do so. Critical thinking involves making the right decision, rather than being right all the time.

Know Your Biases

As human beings, we all have certain issues that awaken passion in us. It is important to keep in mind when it comes to mastering critical thinking skills. Again, having strong feelings about one subject or another is not uncommon. Rather, it is quite normal. However, making decisions about issues that cause your thinking processes to be clouded by emotion can become a problem in terms of critical thinking.

Therefore, you should be aware of what issues may cause you to be biological or prejudiced in some way. Once you know what those issues are, you can take some time to evaluate your thoughts and understand why they affect you so much. This can help in many ways, including allowing you to articulate your opinions to others, and pushing you to think about it two or three times before making a final decision regarding this issue.

Know What You Have Power Over and What You Do Not

Thinking critically is about being efficient. Not being able to recognize which elements of a situation are within your power to change can hinder the efficiency of your thinking. Trying to change things that are not in your sphere of influence can waste a lot of time and energy. Taking the time to evaluate all the elements of the issue and noting which ones you can control will help you to use your valuable time and energy productively. Any element that is not under your control is not your concern and is not worth thinking about any more than necessary.

Do Not Rush the Decision-Making Process

One of the biggest factors affecting our ability to make informed and sound decisions is time constraints. It is true that often, when making a personal or professional decision, there is a time limit before we must make a decision and act on it. Still, try to take as much time as you need to make the right decision. Rushing the critical thinking process can lead to a lot of problems.

Look at a Situation from Every Perspective

Thinking is a fairly individual activity, but often, the more people participate in the conclusion, the more successful the result is. By consulting with others, you will get many perspectives on the same situation because everyone will bring their own experience.

As a critical thinker, you must realize that the view of a situation you have will be one-sided and biased, no matter what you do. There are always other perspectives to consider, which will reveal important aspects of the situation. One way to take advantage of this is to put yourself in the shoes of someone with whom you may have a conflict or feel the need to criticize.

Avoid over-Analyzing

When decisions are made, there is excessive analysis. While analysis is a very important part of critical thinking, overanalysis can lead to paralysis in decision making. Experienced critical thinkers can analyze data without falling into the trap of trying to force their information to fit a particular outcome or need. There is no way you can get as much information as possible because there is an infinite amount of information available. However, once you know that you have obtained as much information as you can, and that you have looked at that information thoroughly, with an objective point of view, you should be able to move towards making sensible decisions.

Realize That Learning Never Ends

Another important habit for being a critical thinker is to be always on the move, looking for more information on a wide variety of topics and issues. Thinking critically will be much better if you have more information at hand. To maintain this habit, you should make a constant effort to read and expand your information, since you never know what information will be beneficial in terms of future decisions.

Always Consider the Risk

Everything we do in life is established by navigating the perspective of certain risks. Often, risks are behind the preventive measures that we take for granted in our daily lives. Critical thinkers will do more than just prepare to deal with a risk should it occur. Rather, they will take the necessary steps to prevent the situation in which people become victims of such a risk.

Never Assume or Jump to Conclusions

Critical thinkers have a habit of never drawing hasty conclusions. Sometimes, it seems that the solution to a problem is obvious, and when that is the case, you may want to go with the first conclusion that comes to mind. However, the solution is not always the best one. Before taking action, be sure to look at all the evidence presented and think carefully about what the best solution might be. Critical thinkers reach conclusions based on evidence, not the other way around. Taking the time to gather as much information as possible will help your ability to understand a complicated situation before taking action, which may not be the best.

Eat Well

It can be a shock, but the capacity for critical thinking can be affected by what we carry in our bodies as well as our minds. To make sure your brain is sharp, there are some eating habits that should be considered.

See the Opportunities and Possibilities Around You

It cannot always be said that there is only one approach to solving a problem. At the same time, one cannot always say that the problem is only a problem. When you think about it, a problem can present itself as a dilemma that makes you nervous, but it can be an opportunity, and you may not know it.

Critical thinkers are often wrong to be optimistic, but that is not true. They don't see the world as a bleak and pitiful place to be because they know there is always an easy way to solve problems. Sometimes they even welcome problems because it gives them a chance to be creative and use a desperate situation to their advantage.

Harness Wasted or Idle Time

You have the ability to lose or use time well. Unfortunately, many of us spend most of our time watching television. Often, we don't have a particular program we're following; we just surf the channels to see what's available.

The thing about time is that once it's gone, it's gone forever. You won't come back at that point. Often, you may complain that you don't have enough time, but when asked about what you've accomplished, you're at a loss for words.

Maintain a Journal

Thinking about how you employed critical thinking and the steps involved is good, but it is not enough. Go a step further and write down the process in a journal. Something in the journal brings up often hidden feelings and thoughts.

Utilize and Develop Intellectual Standards

Accuracy, breadth, clarity, depth, precision, logic, relevance and meaning are universal intellectual norms that every critical thinker should strive to develop. The obvious way to develop these standards is to practice one intellectual standard per week. In this way, you will be able to master one standard before moving on to the next.

During your practice, you should be able to focus on stating, elaborating, illustrating, and exemplifying the standard. In this way, you will be able to cover all your bases.

Keen Observation

Observation is fundamental to any analytical process, and this is what is done primarily. In fact, human beings continue to observe things and events around them, sometimes only accidentally and at other times as a deliberate move in their critical observation.

Communicating

Communication can be taken as an exchange of thoughts and information between the parties. Isn't this what you do almost continuously? Although you may have taken it for granted, you can appreciate that serious issues tend to go smoothly as long as you have thought critically about what to say before you say it.

CHAPTER 12
STRATEGIES TO IMPROVE
YOUR CRITICAL THINKING SKILLS

Keep a Journal

Keeping an intellectual journal can also help you meet your goal of improving your critical thinking skills. You can write an entry every day to keep your entries regular. Each day, write an entry that describes a situation that was or is significant to you. Keep a record of the different problems you have managed to solve as a result of critical thinking. You need to have a format that you can follow to address each problem.

Solve a Problem Each Day

Another strategy that can help you improve your critical thinking skills is to try to solve at least one problem a day. In other words, when you start each day, you can choose one problem to work on in your free time. Then, take some time to look at the problem from a logical point of view taking note of all its elements.

Redefine Your Viewpoint

Being open to considering alternative views on a situation can help develop more refined and informed opinions. It can be difficult to accept the fact that the way you see things now may need to be adjusted, but it can help in the long run.

Question the Viewpoints of Others

This strategy is not about being argumentative and openly challenging people, especially in situations where this would be inappropriate. Rather, when you hear someone speak, don't always accept the information they share as fact.

Take Out Time

You must invest quality time in perfecting your critical thinking time. It doesn't mean you have to set aside hours every day to think. It means that when you have a moment, for example, when you are stuck in traffic or walking from one place to another, take that time to be more productive with your thinking. As you do, you will begin to observe certain factors about your thinking process and how you come to conclusions.

Deal with One Problem at a Time

Critical thinking requires your mind to be clear, so don't fill it with problems by trying to solve too many problems at once. Instead, go through one problem at a time. Doing this will allow you to clearly establish the problem in your mind and understand what kind of problem it is.

Change Your Perspective

You may have a way of being and seeing that is based on your personal and social interactions. From your experiences, you define the way you understand things. For normal thinking, this is fine, but for a critical thinker, this can be very limiting. You will find that seeing the world from a perspective means that your solutions to problems tend to follow a pattern as well.

Often, this can lead to frustration and negative emotions. Critical thinking needs to be able to redefine how you see the world in order to have a more open mind. This will make it possible to find solutions in unlikely places or scenarios.

Always Question Assumptions

It is easy to reach wrong conclusions by forgetting to question the assumptions that have already been made. Some of the best innovators in the past were people who wondered whether some of our fundamental human assumptions might be wrong.

Acknowledge the Influence of Groups

The groups have an unwritten and sometimes written code of conduct. Groups expect members to do and not do various things. In fact, some groups take their beliefs very seriously, and any member who goes against those beliefs is expelled from the group.

Group thinking is a major obstacle to critical thinking. It must be guarded against. You can protect yourself from it by recognizing the influence of groups. Analyze the group you are in, and determine what actions or behavior the group and its members expect you to conform to cause each group requires some measure or level of conformity.

Take a Breath, and Have a Thought

Begin to take even a moment before answering a question, deciding a course of action or making a decision. Train yourself to think carefully, even briefly, about what you are doing and why you are doing it. The world and the people around us seem to be moving faster every day, but incorporating critical thinking into your daily life can be as revealing as it is productive.

Talk to Yourself

If you find yourself nodding or shaking your head about something said during a conversation or on the news, take a step back and consider why you made that gesture. What do you agree or disagree with? Have you always felt that way? Can you remember the time when you thought of what you agree or disagree with as a topic for consideration - rather than something you simply agree or disagree with?

Practice Asking Critical Questions

When do you think you would receive the best answer to a question? Would it be when you ask a general question, or when you ask a specific question? And when would you expect to receive a serious and useful answer? Would it be when you ask a serious question, or when you ask it casually? If you want to receive the most useful answer to a question, how you ask it matters a lot. It is essential that you adapt your questions in a way that causes the person you are addressing to give you relevant and useful answers as well. In addition, when designing questions that will help you during the time of the research, you must frame those questions in a way that leads them to sources relevant to the topic at hand. It is also possible to locate relevant material more quickly.

Get Verifiable Evidence

It is recommended that you get into the habit of learning and supporting ideas through verifiable evidence and also through logical thinking.

Ask Questions

You may get lost when you try to think critically. You can ask so many questions that you don't even know what questions you originally asked. It's like the black hole of critical thinking. It can be exhausting and discouraging. But don't stop! Go back to the basic questions and write it all down. If you write it down, the newspaper will remember it for you.

Be Aware of Your Mental Processes

Self-consciousness, self-consciousness, self-consciousness! Becoming aware of your thought process is important, especially because it moves so fast. Be aware of those cognitive biases!

Form Your Own Opinions

Even if you are wrong, they can give you a good starting point. It's kind of like the thesis statement of your work. It helps you decide what you are trying to prove, but it may be different when you finish your work because of the evidence you found.

Do Proper Analysis

It's also a great idea to get used to analyzing any problems you have before trying to make any deductions. Another thing you need to do in the same line is the proper reasoning and also the proper evaluation of situations and challenges.

Make Reasonable Interpretation

You must learn to interpret topics extensively and deeply, as you avoid the impulse to embrace information only in appearance.

Confirm Information Veracity

It is always necessary to check the integrity of any information you intend to use, even when such information has been obtained from published books or the Internet. Even if you are collecting information from things that you or others have observed, just check its accuracy and credibility. Let's say, in fact, that you need to check the integrity of all information you are considering for use at all times. This helps you to have more accurate information at hand.

Deal With Your Ego

Self-centeredness can hinder critical thinking. If you are full of your-self, you will close your eyes and ears to new ideas or corrections. You will tend to justify your actions, to blame others, to become defensive or to point out the "deficiencies" of the person trying to correct you. Some-times, we take our self-centeredness too far by associating with people who do not challenge us and avoid the people who tend to call us.

Be Innovative

Explore alternatives to find new and better solutions. You can do this by becoming innovative. Don't be afraid to try. Don't be afraid to take risks. Your mind is a strong tool that can generate innovation. You should not settle in your comfort zone and be content with what you already know. Nor should you settle for what the world and the people around you already know.

Have a Healthy Lifestyle

Now you may wonder why this article appeared in an article on im-proving your critical thinking. Yes, living a healthy lifestyle is necessary for the improvement of the mind. A healthy mind must be housed in a healthy body. You can never release your full potential if your physique is not at its best.

Be Creative

Creativity is common among great thinkers and successful people. In the real world, creativity is not the only luxury but a necessity and a sur-vival skill. A critical thinker is a creative person. We all use our creativity in different settings, but we must follow a common process. Once the process is understood, it can be intentionally applied in any necessary sit-uation. It increases your creativity and efficiency, and also strengthens your initiative.

Know When to Move on

You may have so much optimism that you always fight for your idea. But if things don't work out so well, change your strategy. You didn't change your decision to reach your destination, you just took a different route to get there. This is a characteristic that very few people have. It's called flexibility. People who have this knowledge when their preferences are getting the best of them and are able to re-strategize and change direction. Don't be obsessed with the infinite possibilities. If you've done a thorough job and things aren't going so well, move on and stay on target. Having this skill is like having a good map. Now it is up to you to drive your critical mind towards your goals.

Diversify

A critical thinker embraces diversity. One of the most powerful skills of a great thinker is the ability to embrace diversity. We are talking here about diversity of thought or art and the process of harnessing and maximizing different ways of thinking.

A critical factor to consider is always to recognize where you are strong and where you are not. If in a certain field, you know that you are not skilled, look for others that are. And make an effort to improve this. Listen to your thoughts and listen to the new directions your thinking can provide. Learn to diversify and be open to the perspectives of others.

CHAPTER 13
HOW TO BEAT HINDRANCES TO CRITICAL THINKING

Is there anything you can point to that is not threatened by obstacles? Critical thinking is definitely not one of them and therefore one must know how to overcome such obstacles. It goes without saying that you cannot pretend to solve a problem unless you have identified the specific problems surrounding it. Therefore, in the case of critical thinking, you need to know what threatens this process. What can hinder your progress in undertaking critical thinking?

Often the threats to critical thinking are six in number, and they do not have to work together. In fact, any one of them can act to sabotage your critical thinking efforts. However, the adage of being forewarned is equivalent to being prepared to work.

8 Hindrances to Critical Thinking

1. Missing Direction

Have you heard people say something about those who don't know where they are going never reaching their destination? You will never know if you are working towards your goal unless you know what your goal is. As such, you need to articulate what your goal is, and then design a plan of action to work towards that goal. Usually, once you see your well designed action plan, your mind starts working creatively, and it generates very innovative ideas that are aimed at improving the problem solving skills you already have. It also begins to think of new ways to approach the problem. However, if you have no idea what you want done at the end of the day, you have a problem from the beginning. Management is everything.

2. Fear of Failure

When we talk about the fear of failure, we have in mind the fear related to losses, being wrong, losing money, being late and so on. So you fear that you can't succeed in business, that you might lose your investment, and that you won't be on time, and so on. Do you know what part of failure is the worst of all?

Surprisingly, it is not the actual failure that is a disadvantage, considering that you have failed in different tasks and different spheres of your life, and you are still moving forward in your life. The real disadvantage is anticipating failure. As long as you internalize the idea of failure, you will not feel motivated, and therefore will hesitate to commit yourself to something productive. In short, you are not eager to begin the problem-solving process as long as you feel you are likely to fail in it.

3. Fearing Criticism

When people fear criticism, they also fear ridicule and, in the same vein, they fear rejection. They fear being laughed at. Often, in such cases, those affected fear that they will be considered fools, or made to look like fools. This is especially true for people who are eager to please and gain the approval of others, including approval from people they barely know; people they barely care about.

Unfortunately, there are a considerable number of people who do not reach their potential simply because they fear that others may think they are too ambitious. Others fail to show their talent and experience, fearing that others may view their efforts as futile. Fear of criticism and rejection leaves you in the loser's lane, and this is simply because you choose to play it safe rather than focus on your goal. Be innovative in your thinking and ultimately put your ideas into action, despite the opinions of the detractors.

4. The Strife to Remain Consistent

How can you be creative when all you care about is being consistent with what you have done and how you have done it in the past? It doesn't matter that you have been successful in the past - there is a great potential to think about something critically, considering that there are always variables that may have changed over time. The point here is that the tendency to do what you have always done, through what experts call homeostatic impulse, is a great obstacle to success.

When you succumb to the impulse to remain constant, effectively saying that you are going to stay in your comfort zone, you end up getting stuck in a zone with no creative ability and no capacity for innovation. Before long, you are likely to start rationalizing your unwillingness to change and your unwillingness to venture outside of your familiar territory. In short, if homeostasis is maintained, progress in problem solving will be hindered. It means that you are likely to find it very difficult to succeed in business and in any other enterprise in which you may be involved.

5. Passive Thinking

Do you know that your mind does not become creative if you remain passive rather than actively involved in something? In passivity, your mind has no vitality, as it is not stimulated at all. In fact, it falls short of energy, as do any of your muscles that are not physically exercised. Where normally you would have been proactive and creative, you become passive and start doing things automatically.

One of the things that can make you passive is routine. For example, you get into the routine of getting up at a certain time every morning, and doing the same tasks that you are used to, meeting the same people that you deliberately meet, eating your meals from the same place at the same usual time, and then proceeding to watch the same television programs that you are used to today in the day. Where, then, do you have room to be creative and experimental when routine prevails? You have nothing to challenge your mind, so you end up becoming a bore. You even become complacent and make no attempt to learn other ways of doing things.

Worse yet, you often come to despise anyone who suggests you try something new, and everything they say is met with a negative attitude. Soon, you begin to show signs of being threatened every time someone suggests that you can change the way you do things.

6. Seeking Justification

How much will you get if every time you are about to make a move, you stop to explain it to the world? However, this is something that many people do. You can excuse them once you remember that human beings are rational beings, but trying to justify your actions to each and every one of them is bound to make you fall behind. For your business to succeed, and for any other business to succeed quickly, you cannot wait to formulate a good reason to give the world, and then wait for the world to give you a nod. You must leave yourself room to do what you think is right without seeking the approval of the rest of the world. The security you seek in trying to rationalize your actions is an obstacle to success.

7. Enculturation

When you take everything that your culture bequeaths to you, and you don't care to question it, you are bound to stand in the way of progress. What culture, if it can look back sharply, does not have beliefs and practices that are either bottlenecks to progress or repugnant to justice? A number of cultures have prejudices and blind spots, so taking such practices at face value can be an obstacle to success. It is necessary to ignore the gaps in their culture, to set aside traditional prejudices and biases and to adopt critical thinking regardless of what the culture stipulates.

The point here is to be bold enough to challenge the general view and think like an individual who has an independent mind and can reason. If you subject ideas - as well as beliefs - to logical scrutiny, you end up purifying them and implementing them in the most appropriate form and manner according to the circumstances.

8. Unfavorable Emotional States

Who does not value calm in a difficult situation? However, you can often find yourself making decisions without weighing up how your mental state is processing the problem. Whenever you make a decision in anger, the facts are likely to be blurred by too many negative emotions, so the decision may not be the best fit for the situation. This is the case, too, if you are depressed at the time of the decision. Forget that the great philosophers of antiquity, Plato and Aristotle, held that anger supported great reasoning, and the respected theologian, Martin Luther, stated that he thought best when he was upset. The average person does not do any good by acting when he is in deep emotions like anger and depression.

CHAPTER 14
HOW TO SHIFT YOUR STATE OF MIND
TO BE CRITICAL

Like any thinking strategy, there is a process that goes hand in hand with critical thinking. However, what we want to keep in mind about the process of critical thinking is that although there are steps that accompany it, critical thinking is not necessarily a "technique". Rather, it is a state of mind.

A true critical thinker says to himself: "I don't want to believe, I want to know". Critical thinking is intentional, it is specific, and the state of mind in which the critical thinker finds himself is one that drives him to discover concrete information that he can use in a practical sense.

Critical thinking is the process of making use of your thinking while thinking about making your thinking even better than it was before. There are two crucial things in the process of critical thinking and the state of mind that goes with it.

One is that critical thinking is not just thinking, but a means to self-improvement. Critical thinking not only involves a specific way to improve your thinking, but also requires skills such as constant learning and broadening your perspective on life, which benefits you in other areas of your life.

Another thing is that the self-improvement that comes from critical thinking comes from the ability to use the standards by which thinking would be properly assessed. In other words, it is the improvement in terms of your thinking through standards that assess your thinking.

Another reason critical thinking implies such a specific state of mind is that it involves placing certain restrictions on your thinking through intellectual norms. Thus, to raise the level of thinking to a higher level, you essentially use a method of thinking that is not familiar to you, such as spontaneous thinking or visceral thinking where you follow the current of the first thing that comes to mind. It is about making your brain work harder to raise your standards and improve your thinking patterns completely.

There are a number of basic steps that make up the critical thinking process, and the more you use them, the sharper your critical thinking skills will become. These steps are:

Reconstruct the situation: This involves breaking down the situation into its most basic form. Put it into the simplest words, you can understand it. Break down the argument into its basic premises and conclusion. Determine how they fit together. Asking questions about the evidence.

Reveal hidden issues: This would include bias and manipulation. Does the person making the argument fall into any of the traps that sabotage critical thinking, such as inherited opinions or intellectual arrogance? Or do they use certain fallacies such as false dichotomy? Also, determine what is the intent behind making this argument. Are they really trying to inform, or are they trying to manipulate the situation to get ahead?

Make the best decision: This is where you draw the conclusion from the situation. At this stage, keep in mind that instead of choosing an answer because it seems right to you, you should subject all options to scrutiny and skepticism.

One of those skills is communication. There are two types of communication that people engage in. One is surface level communication or trivial communication. This communication does not require any education or real deep thinking. Think of it as small talk or gossip, things that don't use any skill to get it right. This type of communication is not that deep.

The other communication is the kind that results in a deep, deep conversation. It involves all four modes of reading, writing, speaking, and listening. Sometimes they can be used together, or sometimes separately, but they all require a higher level of thought and effort. These four things involve problem-solving and critical thinking skills throughout the process.

You can think of communication as a transaction between two logics. For example, in reading, there is the author's logic and the reader's logic. The reader reconstructs the author's logic in his or her own experience, and evaluates it for himself or herself. There is a similar process for writing, speaking, and listening.

Another important skill for critical thinking is collaborative learning. Collaborative learning becomes useful when it is based on disciplined critical thinking. How many times have you been in a group setting where you had to work on a project or solve a problem together, but people did not take it seriously, and group members showed actions that sabotaged critical thinking, such as intellectual arrogance and not listening.

Surely not much was done on the project, or the quality of the finished project was not very good.

But if you are in a situation where everyone works hard together, everyone strives to follow in the footsteps of critical thinking and develop solid, valid, reason-based conclusions and arguments; the result is very different.

Without critical thinking, collaborative learning becomes bad collaborative learning. It is just a collection of bad thoughts thrown together in a messy way that does not give any positive result, and the bad thinking is validated among the group.

Some examples of collaborative learning are prejudices, stereotypes and collective hysteria. They come from a group of people who engage in bad thinking practices, and validate them among themselves.

However, when disciplined critical thinking is present in a collaborative learning environment, a mode of collaboration is obtained that is based on education, knowledge, and insight.

Curiosity goes hand in hand with critical thinking. For curiosity to flourish, it must evolve from research and disciplined reflection. Left to itself, your curiosity will wander, leading you into useless and, at worst, dangerous situations.

Intellectual curiosity is different. Here it is still allowing your mind to wander but in a controlled way. It includes intellectual humility, intellectual fearlessness, intellectual righteousness, intellectual persistence and confidence in reason. Intellectual interest demonstrates its value as it incites information, understanding and insight. It can also help to expand, develop and perfect our minds, making us better, more compassionate and more blessed.

However, you should be more than curious about these methods. You must be happy to work, ready to endure the clutter and disappointment, ready to face the restrictions and overcome the impediments, be available to the perspectives of others, and be eager to engage the thoughts that many individuals find compelling.

A final skill that accompanies critical thinking is self-esteem. You may think that self-esteem is not very important to your thinking process, but it plays a big role.

However, there is a healthy self-esteem that is useful for critical thinking skills, and there is an unhealthy version. If a person feels good about herself for no particular reason other than that she is full of herself, that misguided sense of self-esteem clouds her judgment, and she falls into the trap of intellectual arrogance.

But if he only has a good sense of himself and feels good about the person he is, he will be more confident in his ability to reason sensibly. You will find yourself more confident in your conclusion after following all the steps of critical thinking.

It is the variety of skills among individuals that explains the need for peer review among different individuals.

Reasons Why It Is Important to Get in Touch with Your Emotions

When you begin to feel any negative emotions, ask yourself the following questions:

What line of thought has led to this emotion? For example, if you are angry, then ask yourself, what were you thinking that caused the anger you are feeling? Are there other ways to look at this situation? Every situation seems different, depending on your perspective. A negative aspect makes everything seem dull and gloomy, and on the other hand, a positive perspective makes things lively. Whenever you feel a negative emotion coming on, try to see the mood or rationalize it. Focus on the thought process that produced the negative emotion, and you will be able to find a solution to your problem.

CHAPTER 15
DEVELOPING A POSITIVE MINDSET

Complaining is part of human nature. The problem is to live complaining about everything. Then the person only thinks and vibrates negatively. And, like everything in the Universe and governed by the Law of Attraction, what he thinks, does and speaks will be attracted and can be realized in life. He who emits a negative thought will generate more negative energy, attract more negativity, and materialize and live in negative situations. So we have to think positively.

Our mind has to believe, feel and think positive thoughts. The Positive Mind is nothing more than using the Law of Attraction to attract into our lives what we desire: love, prosperity, travel, health, joy, luck, and so many dreams and goals.

And most interesting of all, the energy we extract from the Universe to generate positivity or negativity in our lives is the same. The Universal or Vital Energy is an inexhaustible source that only generates Pure Energy for those who wish to attract to their life through the power in their mind.

What makes energy good or bad in a person's life is the thought of it. In other words, energy is always attracted. How this energy will manifest itself in your life will depend on its vibration.

Positive thinking is the first step on a long journey to make you happier and achieve your positivity. There are no miracles. There is a need for changes in habits and thoughts to begin a new life.

Start by changing your negative or stagnant mental programming, and you will begin to think positively. You will notice that you will begin to attract new opportunities and more positive people to your life.

Then we can understand that a positive mentality is a set of actions that lead to the realization of a desire through positive thinking. However, for the realization of the selected desires, the mental procedure must be 100% positive. If one single thought, simple, short, negative, will be enough to maculate the whole procedure, and thus the expected result will not be achieved.

To help you stay optimistic and positive, look at these practices:

Find Your Inner Happiness

We all have something that moves us forward, that encourages us, gives us strength and serves as a propulsive energy for our actions. It can be family, love, success, faith, a hobby, travel, etc. Whatever gives you this feeling, enjoy it. Cultivate this daily within you and stick to what keeps you going. Put a reminder or symbol that refers to what makes you happy in a place that you can see daily, so you don't forget and stay inspired.

Manage Your Stress

The way you handle your stress can either save you or bring you down, depending on what it is. Even at lower levels, stress can cause physical and psychological problems, such as headaches, exhaustion, high blood pressure, gastrointestinal problems, feelings of disability and depression.

Everyone has different ways to relieve stress, so find the one that works for you. Singing, painting, dancing, writing, exercising, listening to music, and meditating are some of the effective and popular ways to combat discouragement. Always reserve a space on your calendar for some enjoyable activity.

Stay Motivated

Often, when we go through a long process, such as having our own business, we forget the reasons why we are doing certain things. Always remember what motivated you to start, what goals you've already achieved, what you still want to win, and what your biggest reward is. And then stay focused.

Success requires time, persistence and confidence. Many people try a thousand times before they can do it. Remember: even if you've tried several times, the next one may be the right one!

Prepare for Everything, Including Good Things

We cannot predict what will happen, so we must always be prepared. Yes, bad things can happen, as well as good things, and you have to be prepared to take advantage of them. Have an open mind, and don't let negative events knock you down. And if that happens, get up! You will encounter obstacles and make mistakes, so accept them and learn from them.

You will also find joys, opportunities and various wonderful situations. Also, make sure you are ready to take advantage of the opportunities, live your dreams and make the best of them.

Build a Positive Network of Contacts

We tend to approach people with the same vision and attitude as we do, and this can be both good and bad. If you have a negative view of the world, you may end up approaching people who think the same way, and even if they don't want to, they will disappoint you because they can't see a solution either.

On the other hand, if you get along with people who are more optimistic and confident, they will help you to always see a positive response, solution or action. Of course, you don't have to take people out of your life, but create a network of contacts you can trust and find motivation!

Accept

Yes, we have to accept that the problems reside in our thinking. It is a necessity to say yes to the challenge of improving our thinking. Sometimes our ego and pride prevent us from committing to learning; we also need to get rid of them to start regular practice. So, ask yourself again and again, do you fully accept that you were once an unthinking thinker? If you consistently answer yes, then you are ready.

Change Your Perception of Things

In every situation, we are the ones who give it meaning. Your current state can be transformed by the way you see it. You have the power in your mind to make your life more fulfilling. A problem is only a problem when you see it as a problem. You can give it negative or positive definitions. We are sad when we could be happy. We are frustrated when we could be satisfied. Changing our perception of things will redefine negative thoughts into positive ones, problems into blessings, and regrets and mistakes into opportunities for growth. The exercise consists of establishing a specific pattern for us.

Value and Respect Other's Ideas

Critical thinking is not always about thinking about your interest and will, because that is something different called ego. A true and developed thinker values and respects the ideas of others sincerely. It is a form of humility and another aspect of critical thinking.

- Learn to listen because the ideas you were looking for can be picked up from the person you are talking to.

- Don't prejudge. A person may be dressed in rags but still have rich and brilliant thoughts in his mind.

- Even if you find their ideas conveyed irrational or meaningless, you still learn to respect and appreciate them. No idea is ever wrong or right. It only depends on one's perception.

So the next time you exchange a conversation with someone, and your subconscious mind begins to reject the thought, discipline yourself. Appreciate, value and respect your neighbor's idea.

Assess the Consequences of Actions or Ideas

Look before you jump. Yes, it's also a way to develop your critical thinking skills. Always evaluate the consequences of your actions and ideas. You have heard in the media many stories that ended in tragedy simply by explaining this lesson. In fact, most failures occur because actions and ideas are not evaluated before they are performed. Regret always occurs in the end, and none of us would want to regret it in our lives. We are solely responsible for our decisions, and when taken for granted, they could cause harm to many.

Make Reasoned Decisions

Excellent decision making is characteristic of critical thinking. Decisions must not only be made promptly, but they must also contain acceptable reasons. A good decision is not made in an instant; it must include supporting details that make it sufficiently reasonable. And decision making is part of everyday life, so critical thinking must always come into play. Was there ever a time when you made quick decisions, and later regretted that particular decision? If you had spent more time evaluating that decision, things would have turned out better. We don't want this to happen again. So the next time you find yourself in a critical decision-making situation, make a note of three or even five reasons why you should consider the decision. If you find yourself without reasons, then it may not be a good decision after all.

Think Independently

Letting others do the thinking for us discourages our minds from generating wonderful ideas. In the long run, it will be a bad habit. It is degenerative. And if you are this kind of person, start thinking for yourself.

Except when it comes to gathering information, don't ask others until you come up with an idea of your own, an idea produced by your brilliant mind. Only when you come up with one can you consult others and ask for their respective ideas. Never be tempted to let others do your thinking for you, no matter how difficult the question, no matter how good the other person is. You are brilliant. You can do it on your own. Think independently.

CHAPTER 16
EMOTIONAL INTELLIGENCE
AND CRITICAL THINKING

Emotional intelligence is important for decision making because it can predict the success of a business, the happiness of employees and the quality of all relationships in an organization.

When making decisions as a critical thinker, it is necessary to look at logic, and from this logic, apply your rationality and reasoning to arrive at the right answer. With emotional intelligence, this becomes easier. Emotional intelligence affects the following:

Self-Management

Your decision making can be clouded by emotions that are not kept under control. With emotional intelligence, it is possible to better manage your emotions. It will give you more control over the decision-making process. Also, when you have to adapt your emotions and reactions, you can do so to make sure that your response to a problematic situation helps solve it, rather than accentuating it.

Self-Awareness

Emotional intelligence makes you more aware of your emotions, and also helps you understand your reactions. When you understand your reactions, you are better able to identify the triggers that can make your reactions irrational. As a critical thinker, this is necessary because arriving at well thought-out decisions requires a stable mind.

Empathy

Being able to connect with others at their level, discerning their feelings, as well as paying attention to their emotions is another result of emotional intelligence. The critical thinker can use this type of feedback to help relate to them more effectively, and also create mutually beneficial solutions.

Motivation

A significant aspect of critical thinking and its possible success is internal motivation and commitment to the whole process. Motivation is also important in emotional intelligence, as it helps you gather those emotions that motivate you to take a specific action and to see a scenario through to the end so that you can achieve a specific goal.

Social Skills

Great teams can come together because of emotional intelligence. It is because people are better able to relate to each other, as well as develop their relationships and work as a team. When you have to use your critical thinking skills in a group, having people who are all on the same page is an excellent advantage.

Conflict Resolution

Critical thinking can be used to solve a number of problems, as well as to develop an argument. When you argue using critical thinking, you are aware that there is a point of view that exists outside your own, that you have a purpose for the argument and an audience, and that it is essential to have a central theme that you are addressing in order to address it with information on key concepts. Logically, this makes excellent sense, although when you introduce some emotion, you may end up with irrational solutions. When emotions are not well controlled, they can cloud judgment.

However, with emotional intelligence, it becomes possible to control these emotions, mainly because of empathy and being able to see things from various perspectives. This insight means that conflicts that arise in discussions can be avoided and desired outcomes can be better negotiated.

Negative Self-Talk: Ways to Silence Your Inner Critic

What is negative about internal dialogue?

We spend a lot of time thinking that we are not good enough, intelligent, creative and thin.

We imply that we are not worthy of the things we want.

Or that the things they want to have and witness will never happen, and even if they do, it will be frustrating.

If we believe something is possible, we will strive to achieve it with greater probability. We won't bother even if we think it's unlikely.

If we believe that we are a good person who deserves to live a life that we love, we will create that life. But if we think we are inadequate or not capable enough, we will inadvertently sabotage our efforts.

Studies show that your thoughts naturally affect your body as well.

We show that your emotions directly affect your blood pressure, muscle tension, temperature, breathing rate, heart rate and how much you sweat on your palms - these are some very important natural reactions to our thoughts!

Negative Self-Talk Examples– and How to Overcome Them

"Focus on negative emotions."

When you are so busy with the bad things in the world, you can't see the good things.

But the fact that not all of life is bad is not good either. Both are a combination. For almost everything, there is a positive and a negative side.

And when you can choose what to focus on, why not focus on the positive?

Catastrophic prognosis.

It's when you think the worst outcome in any situation and are convinced of the inevitable, usually without real facts to back it up.

The reality is that we don't know what the future holds, and history shows the rare occurrence of the worst-case scenarios. So why think about something that hasn't happened yet and probably never will?

It's probably better to focus on what's happening right now and think about it as the work at hand.

Reading the sly mind is the fourth form of negative thinking.

It happens when you convince yourself that you know what someone else is doing, and that is always negative.

Have you ever talked to someone in your head?

Can you imagine saying all kinds of horrible things that frustrate you and make you angry and hurt or embarrassed?

This is mind reading... you don't know what this person is thinking. But you ask yourself to do it, and you let this false belief negatively affect your friendships.

Keep in mind that you are not crazy. The only way to find out what someone else is thinking is to ask them and have an honest conversation about it. It's how you create relationships that are deeper and more important.

The guilt fades away.

It has been observed that people waste their entire lives because of their feelings of guilt about something they did decades ago: divorce, loss of family due to alcohol or drug addiction, car accidents, failure of troops under their control in battle, incarceration, and insisting that someone else's death and suicide could have been avoided if they had acted differently.

The truth is that everyone has done things they regret, including me. You shouldn't let that determine you.

You have also done many wonderful things in your life.

When you focus on the good things and continue to see yourself as a fundamentally good person who has made many mistakes but is also capable of great things, you will reopen to a future of unlimited opportunity.

Stop bad-mouthing yourself today!

Whenever you think a negative thought, say the words gently and gently, "Cancel-Cancel," and then deliberately change it into a positive thought.

CHAPTER 17
CRITICAL THINKING
IN THE PROFESSIONAL WORLD

Business is not the only profession where critical thinking is necessary. Critical thinking is essential to any profession you can think of. Retail? You will need to use critical thinking skills to solve problems on a daily basis and try to meet the needs of your customers. Journalism? You use critical thinking to evaluate the news value of a story and determine whether a story that seems simple on the outside has a deeper impact. Professions? This involves using a unique set of skills to create or fix things and solve problems as they arise.

There are some specific ways in which critical thinking is beneficial to any profession:

Producing new ideas: Collaboration is a key factor that helps any company stay afloat. There are few professions in which you don't have to work with others at some point to come up with new ideas that benefit the company. Critical thinking produces new ideas because you enter with an open mind and don't judge or dismiss your co-workers' ideas before you hear what they have to say. Your ideas join those of others to improve them, and vice versa, and the group looks beyond conventional solutions to address problems efficiently.

Encouraging teamwork: When everyone is involved in the critical thinking process, the workplace becomes more efficient and organized because everyone is thinking to the fullest extent. Especially if the workplace is diverse, everyone contributes their own experiences, and someone may contribute something that others would not have thought of before just because they have not had that same experience. Critical thinking promotes tolerance in the workplace and gives everyone the opportunity to have an impact on the future of the company.

Lawyer

Critical thinking is immensely important in this profession, as lawyers have to make decisions in their cases that will have a direct impact on their clients' future. It involves using careful judgment and judicious assessment. Lawyers must be able to question and analyze what they hear, what they see, what they read, what they feel, and what they think. Lawyers understand that they should not take first impressions at face value and go deeper with more thoughtful analysis.

Lawyers can make distinctions that the typical person would not see; they easily detect ambiguity. Conversely, others see things very clearly; they can look at issues from all sides without actually stating their position, can manipulate the facts to argue any point persuasively, and are often better at analysis than decision-making.

Law is a growing industry, and there are many different fields of law. However, no matter how different the field of law, the ability to think critically is equally essential to each of them.

Civil Rights Law: This field aims to find a balance between government and individual freedoms. Although it is a small field, many lawyers who practice in other fields assume a secondary practice in civil rights law for free or without charge. These lawyers often work for non-profit organizations, public interest firms, and law firms with diverse practices.

One of the most famous civil rights cases was Brown v. Board of Education, which found that racial segregation in public schools in the United States was unconstitutional. The lawyers who supported Oliver Brown, the African-American father who led the prosecution of the lawsuit, would have had to use critical thinking to gather the key points of his case to argue his case against school segregation in a persuasive manner.

Corporate Law: These fields of law focus on helping clients conduct their business affairs in a manner that is consistent with the law as well as efficient. Their responsibilities include preparing the initial articles of incorporation for businesses and handling a corporate reorganization under the provisions of the federal bankruptcy law.

A famous example of corporate law was the case of Dartmouth College vs. Woodward, in which its employees deposed the president of Dartmouth College, and the New Hampshire legislature then attempted to give the state governor the ability to appoint trustees for the college. However, the school was a private institution. The original charter of the school was created before the state established the nature of public versus private charters.

In the case of the attorney representing the case, it took critical thinking to use deductive reasoning to argue the case that the school is a private entity and the time of creation of its charter.

Criminal Law: Focuses on fundamental issues of law and personal freedoms. Criminal lawyers defend the basic rights that are crucial to the preservation of a free and fair society. The two main types of criminal lawyers are defense attorneys, and prosecutors and district attorneys.

A high-profile criminal case in the United States, called the Central Park Five, involved five African-American teenagers accused of raping a white woman in Central Park, New York. Although the boys were wrongfully convicted and imprisoned for many years for the crime they did not commit, the lawyers representing them would have been responsible for proving their innocence. From the standpoint of critical thinking, they would have used critical thinking to see the distinctions that would have pointed to the flaws in the argument that the boys were guilty and could have used analogies with other cases to prove their innocence.

Doctor

Critical thinking is especially important as a physician, because the lives of your patients are literally in your hands. The decisions that physicians make are the difference between the life and death of their patients.

They determine what medicine their patients need to keep their ailments at bay, the best types of treatment for various diseases, and whether or not surgery is necessary to improve their condition. Therefore, critical thinking is essential for a physician to make effective decisions.

Although there are so many innovations in modern medicine that include technology such as robots and high-performance computing, as well as things like molecular biology and DNA analysis, the power of critical thinking will always be important to medical practice.

One of the most important steps in treating a patient is to properly diagnose the patient with any medical condition so that the physician knows how to proceed with the treatment process. Cognitive errors cause many medical errors. According to Jerome Groopman, a member of the American College of Physicians (ACP), and endocrinologist Pamela Hartzband, in an article for the ACP Internist medical journal, medical studies have shown that diagnostic errors occur in about 15% to 20% of all cases. In addition, about 80% of these cases are the result of cognitive errors.

Critical thinking benefits physicians in several ways. It helps them avoid medical and clinical errors and identify better alternative options for diagnosis and treatment. It also increases productivity and leads to better clinical decision-making. It also helps them to work in resource-constrained settings, enabling them to think outside the box and deliver quality work. It brings innovation through creativity, helps avoid litigation, and serves to develop confidence in their practice.

Physicians must be experts in the art of meta-cognition, or the ability to think in their minds. It provides them with an understanding of how information can be misinterpreted or misleading, and awareness of this is more likely to reduce their own prejudices and cognitive traps.

Making a correct diagnosis also involves organizing the information of the patient's symptoms, signs, and laboratory findings into a pattern, and applying it to a template of a typical case in the physician's mind. With the help of medical textbooks and evidence-based protocols, physicians use critical thinking to analyze their patient's symptoms and determine the likely diagnosis in typical cases.

However, cases are not always easy to decipher and may contain misleading information. In this case, critical thinking becomes even more important in attempting to determine the exact diagnosis or to return to their analysis if they are indeed wrong. This resilience is a characteristic of critical thinking that is necessary for physicians to possess.

A perfect example of critical thinking in the field of medicine comes from the popular TV show House M.D. This show follows the main character, Dr. Gregory House. His superb critical thinking skills help him solve the medical mysteries in his hospital. Most of the time, his team is unable to reach out on their own because House has the ability to see things from a unique angle and analyze his cases in depth to arrive at the correct diagnosis.

Although Dr. House is quite cynical and has many personal demons, there are some key critical thinking skills he uses in his diagnosis that are important to any physician:

Taking risks: Dr. House is constantly taking risks with his cases. Often, everyone on his team thinks one thing is wrong with his patient, but

House insists it is another. He follows that gut instinct to follow his suspicions. If he didn't look beyond the surface of the patient's symptoms and risk what everyone else is saying many times, he wouldn't be able to diagnose his patients with the right disease.

He does not always follow the rules: One of the most defining characteristics of Greg House is that he doesn't follow the rules. Sometimes that gets him into big trouble. But sometimes, he embodies a special trait that any doctor could promulgate in his real life. We must be careful not to break the rules, but sometimes it is necessary for critical thinkers to follow their instincts in doing so.

He understands the importance of precision: Precision is critical in the field of medicine; one false step can be the decisive factor in a patient's life. Dr. House went to great lengths to ensure that his diagnosis and the administration of treatment to a patient were accurate, and when he was wrong, he immediately returned to the drawing board. He never settled for the obvious answer, like the other doctors who insisted that numerous illnesses were the result of lupus, until it once turned out to be lupus.

He knows the dangers of overanalysis: We know that data analysis is an important step in the process of critical thinking. Overanalysis, however, is when things can start to get out of hand. The mind gets tired, restlessness begins to set in, and the critical thinking train begins to fall off the track. While Dr. House spends a lot of time thinking about his cases, he also knows when to take a break and go back to his cases, skills that can be useful for anyone.

CHAPTER 18
CRITICAL THINKING AND LEADERSHIP

One might assume that our leaders in government, business and the non-profit sector are strong critical thinkers. Unfortunately, this assumption is largely incorrect. While many leaders have at least some of the qualities of critical thinkers, few possess all of them. However, if one aspires to reach a leadership position at some point, or if one is already a leader within a field and wishes to improve his or her leadership skills, he or she could benefit significantly from studying and applying critical thinking skills in his or her life.

One of the most important characteristics of a successful leader is that he or she constantly strives to learn more about himself or herself and to seek his or her own improvement. Leaders work hard to look inward, or in other words, to do the introspective work as one of the most important tasks of a critical thinker. Leaders must know their strengths and weaknesses so they can capitalize on what they do well and work to correct areas where they fall short. Leaders, like critical thinkers, understand that introspection and reflection are life-long processes that must be done routinely and honestly in order to stay alert.

The second skill a leader must have is that he or she must be competent in the use of the tools and skills he or she has. In other words, a strong leader must know how to do things daily, using the skills he has acquired throughout his life and training, as well as the tools available to him, technical and otherwise. Leaders, like critical thinkers, must know what they need to do the job. And, just as importantly, they must know where to look to get what they need to fulfill that specific mission. As critical thinkers, leaders are not afraid to consider various perspectives to solve the often complex problems they must address. They will seek the opinions of others and then take the time to examine the quality of each perspective, taking the time to separate fact from opinion. Then, and only then, are leaders able to put themselves in a much stronger position to begin tactfully preparing a strategy for solving the problem.

The third principle of a strong leader requires that leaders develop a sense of responsibility among their subordinates. Leaders who participate in the critical thinking process understand that team building is a very important function of leadership, and the best way to achieve that goal is by working to instill a sense of partnership among those being led. This is achieved by understanding the team's mission, as well as taking the time to learn about the individual strengths of each team member and what they can bring to the team. The leader must then facilitate communications between team members that focus on sharing information and breaking down barriers to honest communication.

A fourth principle is that leaders must be able to make good decisions quickly. This is undoubtedly one of the most important tasks of leadership. As we have learned from studying the decision-making process in our examination of critical thinking processes, making a decision begins with a clear and accurate statement of the problem. Then, leaders must figure out how and where to gather the information needed to begin thinking about possible solutions to the problem. Once the information has been gathered, leaders must separate facts from perspectives and carefully consider each piece of information on its own merits. Once the evidence has been evaluated, the leader must construct possible solutions and consider the likely consequences, or implications, of each possibility. The leader can then move forward with a decision and take action. It is the same process that critical thinkers follow when they address problems.

Timely decisions are important because leaders are often asked to make difficult decisions in a very short time. Even when time is short, it is important that leaders, and critical thinkers, do their best to keep their mission in perspective and work as quickly as possible, while working to minimize the possibility of compromising the foundations of sound decision making.

The fifth principle of leadership requires that leaders always focus on setting a positive example. Leaders and critical thinkers set the best example by giving examples of integrity and discipline. Leaders who practice the principles of critical thinking are in an optimal position to positively affect those they lead because, through example, they have the opportunity to motivate people to be both strong critical thinkers and strong leaders! Leaders lead by example by behaving the way they want their subordinates to behave, and they are wise to remember that their position as leaders carries with it an awesome responsibility to teach as well as to lead.

The sixth principle of leadership requires leaders to know the people they lead and to care for their well-being, which is aligned with the concept of empathy. Leaders are, at least in part, responsible for those they lead. That accountability role can certainly be enhanced in a military environment, for example, but all leaders are at least partly responsible for educating, training, or helping their subordinates move from point A to point B in some way. A strong leader seeks to understand those he or she leads from their perspective as much as possible, and works to achieve this by holding individual or group meetings with them and actively listening to what they say. Contrary to popular belief, a leader is not the only person who speaks. On the contrary, good leaders understand that to understand the perspectives of their subordinates, they have to ask open-ended questions and then pay close attention to the answers.

The seventh principle of leadership reminds leaders to keep their people informed. Effective communication is critical in leadership roles, and leaders must ensure that the messages they convey to their teams are clear and accurate with minimal or no use of vague or ambiguous terms or phrases. Communications must be delivered promptly. When preparing communications, it is important for the leader to be aware of his or her biases, which may influence what he or she says or how he or she says it. He or she should also consider the possible biases of his or her team members and how those biases may influence their interpretations of the message he or she is presenting.

The eighth principle of leadership advises leaders to seek accountability and to take responsibility for their actions. In terms of critical thinking, this principle addresses the goal of self-direction and self-responsibility. Leaders and critical thinkers have the responsibility to offer their talents and skills when they believe it is appropriate to do so, and not wait for information when they need to solve a problem. They find out where to look, and then collect and analyze the data in a timely manner. They also take responsibility for their shortcomings as well as their successes.

A ninth principle of leadership requires those who lead to ensure that their assigned tasks are understood and that their team members receive the supervision they need to carry out the tasks successfully. This principle addresses the need for clear and accurate communication and the need to understand the perspectives of those who are responsible for doing the work.

CHAPTER 19
DEVELOPING CRITICAL THINKING SKILLS IN YOUR CHILD

You will notice that most of the children in honors, AP or other advanced placement classes are usually children who have developed their critical thinking skills. Although they were born with many of their intellectual abilities, many of their skills were also taught and mastered. Therefore, any child can develop their critical thinking and improve their understanding of the information they receive in school and outside of school.

Activities to support your child - Don't just encourage children to spend all their time watching TV or playing video games during the long summer vacation and delegate their work to them. Allow your children to work on developing their critical thinking skills. Here are some examples.

1. Read and discuss a book together - Have your children read a book appropriate for their age and reading levels and then write a review of the book indicating what they liked and why. The "why" is most important because it encourages your children to think more objectively about the why of their opinions. You should also have read the novel. Make sure the author discusses several components, i.e., the information presented and the different methods used by the author, such as symbols, metaphors, prefigurations, moods, etc.

2. Assign your children an argumentative research paper, and then change it - Have your children choose a semi-controversial topic (you may want to choose the topic for them), then write your children as logically as possible why they are in favor, and then write another paper explaining why they are against it. When your children have finished writing both papers, let them show what they have discovered during their writing. Then work together to improve both papers - give constructive criticism while acknowledging the positive.

   a. Make sure your children remember that there are different ways of looking at things and that they should learn to take critical information and not allow emotions to dictate their opinions.

b. Objectivity is important for being a rational thinker; emotions also impede our analytical thinking.

c. The best arguments are those in which the writer can predict what the opposing party is going to argue and therefore can carry out these arguments.

3. Analyze a Work of Art - Have your children analyze an important work of art. Ask your children questions about this work so they can think critically and look at art differently. What is the point of view? Was the painting effective for the desired point of view? Why not? Why or why not? Read the subtitle that accompanies the artwork or any other relevant information so that the artist and his work are better understood.

4. Analyze the source - Write down your child's research work. When reading, your children evaluate what the writer's point is - Is the writer trying to persuade you? Take note of the sources given by the author, considering if they are accurate and why. Also, note any inconsistencies or contradictions contained in the post. Is the article based primarily on opinion, or does the writer give you enough objective and factual information to prove his point? Help your children analyze the information presented in a critical and objective manner; let them know your thought process as you analyze the article.

CHAPTER 20
NUTRITION AND SPORT AFFECT RIGHT THOUGHTS

Aggregation evidence recommends that diet and lifestyle can take a significant role in delaying the onset or end of movement for age-related wellness problems and can improve individual ability. Exercise has been advanced as a potential aversion to neurodegenerative disorders. Exercise will impact understanding, and expands the neurotrophic factor inferred by the mind, a basic neurotrophin. It has been recognized that some segments of the diet have an impact on psychological abilities. Explicitly, it has been explained that polyphenols apply their neuroprotective activities through the ability to secure neurons against damage incited by neurotoxins, the ability to quell neuroinflammation, and the potential to improve memory, learning, and psychological ability. Dietary components can influence various forms of the mind by targeting synaptic pathways, synaptic transmission, layering smoothness, and signal transduction pathways. Flavonols are a piece of the flavonoid family found in different organic products, cocoa, wine, tea and beans. Although the cellular reinforcement impacts of flavonols are established in vitro, there is a general understanding that flavonols have increasingly complex activities in vivo. A few cross-sectional and longitudinal investigations have shown that a greater intake of flavonoids from food could be related to higher subjective development. Whether this reflects a causal affiliation remains to be clarified. Some think they have tried to "control" the mind to delay focal exhaustion. Most studies have shown that under typical ecological conditions, these intercessions are difficult to perform. Evidence is being gathered that rinsing the mouth with a sugar arrangement will improve the continuity of performance. There is a need for further controlled research to investigate the conceivable effect of diet and eating on mental work.

Presentation

Physical movement has been associated with a decrease in various physical and mental problems. Currently there is sufficient evidence that physical movement decreases the occurrence of cardiovascular disease, malignancies of the colon and breast and adiposity, but also diseases such as Alzheimer's, pain and stress. Livelihood has traditionally been seen as a way of giving vitality and building materials to the body. However, its ability to prevent and insure against disorders is beginning to be perceived. Food and exercise are thus used as intercessions to reverse these conceivable negative impacts on well-being. Current information shows that general well-being, but also mental work, is affected by exercise and healthy intercessions. This article will describe how exercise and eating can affect mental health (mind) performance and understanding.

Mental Health, Exercise, Nutrition, and Cognition

There are strong signs that young people are becoming progressively stationary and unfit, and that these lifestyle factors are identified with an earlier onset of some incessant infections, for example, type 2 diabetes and weight. A few cross-sectional and longitudinal studies have confirmed a relationship between overweight and poor school performance. Oxygen-consuming well-being has also been linked to academic insight and achievement. Some studies have recommended that children's subjective ability and school performance may be influenced by their overall physical condition.

For example, unsaturated omega-3 fats provide building blocks for the mind. They are essential to support the occasions of intercellular decay, and thus, emphatically impact the synaptic capacity. Either way, abstinence from foods high in sugar, saturated fats or high in calories is considered detrimental to neural function, as they act to raise oxidative pressure levels and to decrease synaptic flexibility and psychological abilities. Mental work is subject to a satisfactory diet, and the transitory varieties in the addition and synthesis of supplement consumption in healthy people have an impact on the proportions of intellectual capacity. Studies have indicated that eating breakfast is related to some beneficial results for the mental work of well-maintained young people. Exercise seems to cooperate with dietary mediations, extending favorable results on brain functioning and decreasing the adverse effects of a high-fat diet. The overall evidence seems to show that established systems that rely on exercise and diet management may infer a maximum advantage for the advancement of neuronal well-being. In addition, it has recently been decided that the impact of a morning meal on the complex mental capacities of young people (matured 8-11 year olds). Brain action was estimated by electroencephalography while the children addressed fundamental issues of expansion after a rapid medium term and again after having eaten or skipped breakfast. Reinforced children indicated a critical increase in correct reactions, while young people who continued to fast did not. Together. The findings recommend that the action of the neural system involved in preparing numerical data is virtually improved, and performance is improved in children who have eaten breakfast, while a more remarkable mental effort is required for this scientific speculation in children who skip breakfast.

Tests of cross-sectional considerations have reliably demonstrated direct age-related decreases in subjective abilities, e.g., speed of preparation, transient memory, working memory, and long-term memory. Age-related decreases in perception have been associated with changes in the structure of the mind and work, and physical movement can take on a focal role in improving age-related psychological distress. Subsequent meta-research on the effects of physical activity on the intellectual maturation of human beings has indicated that oxygen-consuming exercise had general and particular effects that were beneficial to the personal capacity of more experienced adults. These findings recommend that, although intelligent execution decreases integrally and directly with age, vigorous physical action and well-being can serve to insure against age-related loss of individual capacity, and the best advantages are inferred for forms that require extensive official control measures.

Nutrition and Cognition

The brain is a metabolically dynamic organ that represents a high level of total metabolic rate. Just as it influences the engineering of the brain, livelihood can also influence minute-to-minute work. Non-intrusive imaging methods have clearly demonstrated that, basically, weighted feeding can adjust neural movement in specific regions of the mind known to be occupied with the subjective controls of appetitive practices, and can cause physiological reactions, e.g., salivation, gastric corrosion, and insulin discharge.

Recently, an interest has developed, supported by several epidemiological and trial ideas, in the valuable conceivable effects of polyphenols on the well-being of the brain. Polyphenols are abundant micronutrients in plant-determined foods and are incredible cancer-prevention agents. Foods that grow in the soil; for example, tea, red wine, cocoa and espresso are important dietary sources of polyphenols. Polyphenols have been shown to apply their neuroprotective activities through the ability to secure neurons against damage caused by neurotoxins, the ability to quell neuroinflammation and the possibility of improving memory, learning and intellectual capacity. Despite considerable advances in the understanding of the science of polyphenols, they are still mistakenly considered to be simple cancer prevention agents. In any case, ongoing evidence recommends that their important impacts include decreases in oxidative/provocative pressure, increases in defensiveness, and neuro-hermetic effects, leading to the declaration of qualities encoding cancer prevention agent catalysts, neurotrophic factors, and cytoprotective proteins.

Polyphenols have been associated with a decreased danger of creating dementia, and improved intellectual display in ordinary maturation and improved psychological progression. Letenneur and others conducted an imminent associated examination over a 10-year period among subjects with 65 years or more of experience in investigating the connection between cancer prevention agents, psychological decline, and dementia. A total of 1,640 dementia-free subjects in a pattern in 1990 and with reliable dietary assessments were rethought multiple times over a 10-year period. Subjective work was studied using three psychometric tests. Data on flavonoid intake was collected at the baseline. After alteration by age, sex and educational level, flavonoid intake was related to better subjective performance on the indicator and to higher long-term exposure progression. Subjects in the two higher quartiles of flavonoid intake would be advised for psychological improvement than subjects in the lower quartile. After ten years of development, subjects with the lowest flavonoid intake had a totally horrible performance in the psychometric tests, considerably after the modification for some other possible confounders. In a cross-sectional examination, Nurk and others analyzed the connection between the intake of three regular flavonoid-containing foods (chocolate, wine, and tea) and intellectual performance - more than 2,000 members (aged 70-74; 55% female) recruited to the Hordaland Health Study, based in Norway, experienced intellectual testing. Members who consumed chocolate, wine, or tea had fundamentally better average test scores and a lower prevalence of poor psychological performance than individuals who did not. Members who spent each of the three items covered had the best test scores and the lowest dangers of poor test performance. The relationship between admission of these staples and discernment was subordinate to serving, with the most extreme impact on admissions of 10 g/day for chocolate and 75-100 mL/day for wine; however, they were around directly for tea. Most of the intellectual capacities tested were affected by the admission of these three foods. The impact was more articulate for wine and humbly more fragile for chocolate consumption. Thus, in the old, and routine eating high in some flavonoid-rich foods was related to better performance in a few intellectual capacities in a subordinate portion.

Evidence under development proposes that dietary flavonoids may improve human memory and neurocognitive performance through their ability to secure impotent neurons, improve existing neuronal work, and enhance neuronal recovery. Long-term potentiation (LTP) is generally considered to be one of the significant systems of securing hidden memory, binding, and capacity in the brain, and is known to be controlled at the subatomic level by the enactment of various neural signaling pathways. These pathways incorporate the phosphatidylinositol-3 kinase/protein kinase B/(Akt) pathways, protein kinase C, protein kinase A, calcium and calmodulin kinase, and the mitogen-driven protein kinase pathways. The developmental test proposes that flavonoids apply impacts on LTP, and subsequently, memory and subjective performance through their communications with these decaying pathways.

CHAPTER 21
IMPROVE YOUR DECISION-MAKING SKILLS

If you need to improve your decision making skills, you need to step out of your comfort zone a bit. Remember that when you show something new to your brain, it is stimulated, and it will end up being a very oiled machine. I urge you to try to improve your decision-making ability, because your choices are important. These are just a couple of mutual goal-setting programs you can use to improve your skills.

Art and Culture

If you want to improve your decision-making ability, you must improve your mood and your ability to concentrate. You can do this by practicing some kind of art. Try to spend three one-hour blocks a week learning something new like painting, playing an instrument, or even building a model car. Although it may seem slow, taking the time to expand your horizons increases brain activity and helps you make decisions. The best decision making skills are gained by trying something you never thought you would do because you are activating your brain.

Language Skills

Working on something technical like programming or studying a foreign language. If you immerse yourself in one of these skills, you will greatly improve your decision-making ability because you are exercising your brain.

Surround Yourself with Different Age Groups

Communication with the elderly helps you to be careful and plan a better future for yourself, and with the young, you can keep in touch with achievements, failures and dreams.

Try not to eliminate any age group from your social group. Interacting with people from different backgrounds and age groups will help you make decisions. You will come back from the struggle with your peers and weigh the pros and cons of the decisions you are about to make.

Exercise

Whatever sport you want to practice that makes you feel comfortable and fun, do it! You'll meet new people and stay in shape at the same time. A healthy body is a healthy spirit. As your body becomes thinner, your mind will also become more intense. And so are your decision making skills.

Cook Experimentally

If you are not already cooking, I encourage you to try it. If you are used to cooking, try to open your gastronomic horizons and do something new. Spend a Saturday morning baking something you haven't cooked before, or surprise your family with an incredible lunch or dinner. You will discover that when you cook, your mind will think about the decisions you have struggled with.

Pros and Cons

This is the most basic of the basics. Record the advantages and disadvantages of your choice and think about them. In case you need to seek advice from people who have experienced what you are experiencing, be sure to do so. In any case, at this point, make your own choice. Your life and your choices are important.

How to Make Better Decisions

So you know how to make decisions, but what about making better decisions? We all want to make decisions in our lives and make them happen. However, we want to make the right decisions and not end up badly. Well, you will make mistakes, but you can minimize the number of mistakes you make by following some of these tips. Let's take a look at some of these methods to help you make better decisions in both your personal and professional life.

Cost-Benefit

Before making a final decision, you should weigh the pros and cons to make sure you have made the best possible choice. It requires a cost-benefit analysis as if you were in business. You want to consider the outcome of every possible decision you might make, both positive and negative. It will help you see the opportunities and the things you might lose when you prefer one decision over another.

Narrow Options

To simplify the cost-benefit analysis, narrow your choices. When you have presented more options, you will find it difficult to make a final decision. More options will result in more regrets, as you will consider all the lost perspectives and stress about whether you could have made a distinctive and more cheerful choice. Therefore, reducing them will give you some peace of mind.

Stop Sweating the Little Things

If you are worried about what to watch on TV or what to eat for lunch, remember to keep everything in perspective and have time to make decisions. It's all about assessing the importance of the decision, and if it doesn't affect you or others significantly, don't waste time arguing about it.

Investigation

This may seem obvious, but if you are making an important decision, such as buying a car or a house, take the time and effort to fully inform yourself about the next purchase or choice. This can mean the contrast between satisfaction and dissatisfaction.

Well-Informed Views

If you have difficulties, get an educated opinion from someone you trust. This can give you confidence that you are making the right decision. Updates are consistently helpful, so consistently look at the reviews and ask your loved ones what they would do if they were in your place.

CHAPTER 22
TYPES OF CRITICAL THINKING

The term "critical thinking" is actually incredibly broad. So far, we have discussed it in terms of elements common to several different forms of it. In this chapter we will see the different types of critical thinking.

Logical Reasoning

In its formal sense, logic is a system of rules according to which conclusions or findings can be drawn. In other words, logic dictates how facts and conditions can be used to obtain a new understanding.

For example, if we start with the actual statement that "A beagle is a type of dog" and then add the fact that "The Rover is a beagle", we can conclude that "The Rover is a dog". However, if we are told, "Scruffy is a dog", the laws of logic do not allow us to conclude that "Scruffy is a beagle". All beagles are dogs, but that does not mean that all dogs are beagles, so we cannot say anything else about Scruffy.

Note that the above logical example does not show any proof of any of its statements. The facts we started with (hereinafter "facilities") are true for reasons of argument. That is why critical thinking requires proof and logic to ensure that rational statements reflect reality.

Logic is a discipline in itself. For now, we will cover the two types of logical reasoning that cover most arguments.

- Deductive reasoning or deduction guarantees the truth of a conclusion based on its premises.

All humans are mortal, and Andrew is a human. Therefore, Andrew is mortal.

It has been established that to be human means to be mortal, so if we know Andrew is a human, then we know he is a mortal.

- Inductive reasoning shows that something is probable but not definitely true according to its premises.

August has been the hottest month of the year in this region since we started recording temperatures, so this year will probably be the hottest month.

There is an established record that August is the hottest month of the year, so it is probably the hottest month of all. However, there is no law or scientific rule that says it has to be the hottest month, so it is possible that another month this year could be even hotter than August.

Note that deductive reasoning begins with a general statement - in this case, a statement about all humans - and uses it to reach a specific conclusion, i.e., a conclusion about the specific case of Andrew. On the other hand, the inductive uses a specific observation - in this case, what we know about August in the past - to make a general statement that is likely but not necessarily completely true, namely, that August is the hottest month of all.

Scientific Reasoning

The scientific method is the way in which scientists and many other scholars and critical thinkers use experiments and It is a general way of thinking that, although it is mainly related to experiments in the natural sciences such as biology, chemistry and physics, it is also widespread in the social sciences, as well as in philosophy and other disciplines.

A question with the scientific method begins with, for example, "How can I use electricity to make something work," or "Why do people get this disease? The person who wants to answer your question provides a "hypothesis," an educated assessment that believes it is possible based on what he or she already knows. They will then conduct a test in the form of several experiments or collect data related to the problem. They may experiment with different patterns of electricity use, compare the health records and habits of patients living in the infected area, or simply test different brands of detergents. They then analyze their findings to reach a conclusion.

The experiments are often reproduced in test results under different conditions. For example, if the experimenter finds a correlation between people suffering from the same diseases in a certain area and ingesting a chemical in the water, he could perform an animal experiment using those chemicals or find another population. Show a similar correlation and analyze it.

As already stated, no scientific theory is concluded to be one hundred percent accurate, and no experiment or test can prove the absolute truth of any proposition. That is why scientists and others continue to test, experiment and then re-examine things so that they can claim with overwhelming probability that their conclusion is correct. Evidence may never be perfect, but imperfect evidence is not the same as lack of evidence.

The Psychology of Critical Thinking

Critical thinking in psychology is defined as the habits and skills to perform activities or exercises of reflection and criticism, focused on deciding what to believe and what decisions to make. Critical thinking is an important tool even in psychology, and is taught in psychology classes. Many students who come to university have already formed theories and opinions on the subject and on life in general. When they are confronted with university work, they are surprised to discover that it is not what they thought it would be. Some students choose to cram textbooks to help them with exams, forgetting that learning involves more than that.

For these reasons, psychology teachers decided to teach critical thinking by approaching it systematically, with purpose and development. The proposal was to teach critical thinking skills in 3 main domains of psychology: practical (functionality), theoretical (development of scientific explanations of behaviors), and methodological (testing of scientific ideas).

Practical Domain

Practical critical thinking is expressed as the long-term goal of psychology teachers, even if they do not spend much time teaching critical skills to students so that they become better consumers or careful judges of character, etc. Accurate interpretation of behavior is essential, but few teachers spend time teaching this to students and helping them understand how their thoughts are not invulnerable.

To instill in students the ability to think critically, the practice of accurate description and behavior is encouraged, giving students ambiguous tasks, for example, as students to differentiate the behavior they observe from the inferences they find in the behavior. With this exercise, students will discover that descriptions of behavior are consistent across observers, but the inferences will vary widely. They realize that the way they interpret is biased and personal because of their preferences and values. Because of these large differences in interpretation, students are likely to learn not to rely too heavily on their immediate judgment or conclusions that they should be more tolerant of ambiguity and be willing to give alternative interpretations, since they need a good understanding of procedures in science, effective control skills, and legitimate forms of evidence. With this, they are less likely to be victims of multiple claims or off-base conclusions about the behavior we all face.

Theoretical Domain

Theoretical and critical thinking is helping a student develop an appreciation of science to explain behavior. This means that one not only learns the content of psychology, but how to organize psychology into concepts and why it is organized into concepts, theories, principles, and laws. The development of theoretical skills begins in the introductory class, where the main objective of critical thinking is to apply and understand concepts adequately. For example, when students are introduced to the principles of reinforcement, challenge them to find examples of the principles in the news or to create stories that demonstrate the principles.

Intermediate level courses require a major breakthrough in which students move from applying concepts to learning how to apply the theories. For example, provide a case study that is rich in abnormal psychology, and then ask students to interpret it and make sense of it from different perspectives by using the accepted and existing frameworks in psychology to explain behavior patterns.

At advanced levels, students may be asked to evaluate the theory by rejecting the least useful or selecting the most useful. For example, students may argue different models for discussing drug addiction in physiological psychology by evaluating the strengths and weaknesses of existing frameworks. They can choose the theories that work best by justifying their conclusions based on reason and evidence.

Graduate and honors courses go beyond evaluating theory and encourage students to create or devise original theories. Students choose a difficult question about behavior and construct their explanations based on behavior theory. This type of challenge requires them to synthesize and include the output theory, as well as provide new knowledge about the behavior.

Methodological Domain

Many departments offer students the opportunity to develop their methodological critical thinking skills by applying various research methods in psychology. Beginning students first learn what the scientific method entails. The next step is to apply their understanding of the scientific method by identifying elements in existing research. For example, a detailed description of the experimental design will help the student practice differentiating the dependent variable from the independent variable and understand how researchers controlled for different explanations.

The next step in critical thinking about the objectives of the methodology includes assessing the quality of existing research and critiquing the conclusions of the research results. Students may require encouragement from teachers to overcome the fear they sometimes experience for anything printed, even their textbooks. Asking students to conduct a critical analysis of a sophisticated design may be too much for them. They are likely to do much better when given poor design assignments so that they can cultivate the critical skills as well as the confidence to handle more complex designs. After this, students will be able to develop their research designs in their methodology courses. When students are asked to conduct their independent research, whether it is a comprehensive study of parental attitudes, a well thought-out experiment on the study of the association of sarong, or a study of the behavior of a museum pattern, it engages students in critical thinking skills and allows them to practice with conventional writing in psychology.

After students complete their work, have them evaluate the strengths and weaknesses of their work as this will help them develop their critical thinking skills.

There are many ways and areas of critical thinking and reasoning that can be applied. Different disciplines and areas of life require the application of critical thinking processes to form the best decisions and conclusions.

CHAPTER 23
CRITICAL THINKING TO SOLVE PROBLEMS

The use of critical thinking techniques allows you to separate complex problems and understand each element, as well as the effects of your ideas on the problem. Most of us can recall from our days in school that much learning once depended on memory recall. However, when it comes to problem solving, this approach can be a problem. To solve a problem, we not only need to know the facts and information, but also to be able to apply them in relation to a situation. This is where critical thinking skills come into play.

Step-by-Step View of Critical Thinking as It Is Applied to Problem-Solving

Identify the Problem

To try to solve a problem, you must know if there is a problem. This means taking the time to look at a situation and see if it is a problem worth rectifying, or if there has been some kind of misunderstanding. When a problem is found, you must identify exactly what it is in detailed and specific terms.

Analyze the Problem

Once you know what the problem is, look at it from many different points of view. This will help you answer questions like: Can it be solved? Will you be able to solve it yourself, or will you need the help of others? Is the problem real, or is it only perceived that way?

Great Idea

In this step, you will analyze your options for solving the problem. Each problem can be solved in more than one way. Make a list of all the solutions you can think of, writing down what you come up with. Then cross off your list to the best and most appropriate solutions possible.

Decide on a Solution

Take another look at your list of possible solutions and take your time to decide which one is best for the problem you are facing. To take action

Now that you have carefully reviewed the problem and decided on a solution, it is time to put your plan into action.

Every problem you solve is an opportunity to improve your critical thinking skills. Instead of viewing problems that may arise as challenges that cannot be met, use this step-by-step system to break down the elements of even the most complex problem and find a method for dealing with it. Over time, you will see that not only your thinking skills, but also your problem-solving skills will be developed.

Strategies to Improve Problem-Solving and Logical Thinking

Delve into the Question

Starting with a broad question will make it difficult to find the right answer, especially when you are thinking critically. Critical thinking requires you to examine a large number of variables, after which you can come up with a solution. Here's an example of how you can break it down.

Make Use of Diagrams

A picture says more than a thousand words, and a great diagram can help you accentuate your logical thinking. One great mind embodying an excellent critical thinker was Steve Jobs of Apple. When sharing information in a presentation, he engaged the audience and helped them conclude by using illustrations and diagrams in his presentations.

Try Logical Games

Some games are purely based on logic if you want to reach a solution, like chess and Sudoku. Chess is a game to play with another person, as you learn to understand how other people think and how their thoughts affect their judgements. You also develop strategy and problem solving skills as you progress on the board in an attempt to win the game.

Sudoku is a great game to play alone, as it helps you find different ways to reason. Through this game, you will learn how to solve a problem by eliminating certain variables and using the information you have available to help you find a viable solution.

Consider Your Assumptions

You will be surprised by the amount of assumptions you make before reaching a decision. Assumptions are not based on truth or on something that should happen, but are our opinions about something that could happen if we take a certain action. When seeking to improve problem-solving skills and logical thinking, it is necessary to discern when thoughts and actions are based on assumptions rather than facts. This means that you should be able to analyze the problem.

Choose the Right People Around You

When you have smarter people around you, it is easier to learn something from them, which will help you improve the way you do things, as well as develop your critical thinking skills. Their intelligence will require you to find logical ways to interact and communicate with them, which will also help develop the way your brain works.

Read Logical Books

Read, read, and read some more, and you will be surprised how quickly you can elevate your logical reasoning. Don't read any books. Focus on the ones that make you think, and these books fall mostly into the category of Mysteries and Thrillers. As you read these books, work to find out what might happen at the end of the book. You may need to identify a villain, find out what happens with an attack, or simply solve some kind of mystery. By looking at all the variables, you'll find that making a calculated guess is not only possible but gets easier over time. To perfect this skill, you must keep reading and practicing.

Investigate Everything

Whenever you get some information, take the time to do some thorough research to determine if the information you have on hand is good or not. This applies to all information, regardless of who the source is. When you go to investigate this issue, your brain begins to analyze the information differently. You will begin to see gaps in the information and make judgments based on everything you have been given. This is particularly true for negative news that may be more sensational than objective.

Problem solving will be much easier, as will critical thinking to address the problems.

Use Intuition and Critical Thinking for Better Problem Solving

Intuition is very important when it comes to finding the best strategies to deal with a particular situation. Why? Because these thoughts are often what you have learned through experience, which makes them very ideal tools for problem solving.

They are products of true, justified beliefs or things that you already know are real. You consider them hunches because pieces of information are still missing, and your mind immediately tells you that it would be a good idea to try to follow them. Combined with critical thinking, your insight becomes invaluable when it comes to observing and solving real-life puzzles. Here's how you can do it.

Think About Where Your Intuition Came From

Since intuition is an essential knowledge, it is necessary to know where you got it from to know if it is appropriate for the situation. For example, if your e-book reader doesn't turn on, you have an intuition that it has no power. The reason you have that thought is that you have experienced that this particular device, or any electronic device, does not turn on when it is not charged. The most obvious solution is to plug it in and charge it.

Test Your Hypothesis

If your intuition tells you that your ebook reader didn't turn on because it has no power, there are many reasons why this happened. It may be because it's not charged or because it's broken. These lines of reasoning are all intuitions, but since there are two reasons available, you should be sure to test them to find out what is wrong. What it will do next is charge it, and if it still refuses to turn on, then you have reason to think that it's probably because your device broke.

Try to See If You Explored All the Available Options

From the example above, do you think the above ideas are complete so that you can reach the right conclusion? Probably not. You didn't mention the possibility of checking if the device has its batteries and see if the problem can be easily solved just by changing the battery. Again, you should try that to see if that additional information is correct.

Go outside the Scientific Method

The previous steps spoke of a concept that has been learned in elementary school, which is the scientific method. However, intuition does not only take place in situations involving physical objects. It can also occur during moral dilemmas, in which you must carefully weigh situations related to your values. Just as when thinking about whether you should sign a document that allows you to get a job in a large company known for land grabbing, you should check what your moral intuition tells you. You may not be able to prove them empirically, but your argument would be largely derived from the set of values you hold. If you firmly believe that it is morally wrong to cause trouble to a poor family for the sake of advancing the enterprise, then you know that it would be wrong to accept the deal.

CHAPTER 24
PROBLEM SOLVING TECHNIQUE

Have you ever been in a situation where you thought, "I wish I didn't come to that conclusion so quickly," "maybe I didn't solve the right problem," "maybe I acted too quickly without all the necessary information," or something like that? Well, we've all come across such situations. And therefore, it is essential to understand how to solve a problem.

Finding the Right Problem to Solve

Well, do you find it surprising that we are starting with this step? It's a simple but crucial step. Think of all the time, energy and resources we end up devoting to problems that don't necessarily need all that attention. Ask yourself a simple question: "Is this the right problem to solve? Most of the time, the usual approach to solving a problem turns out to be reactive. We wait for a problem to arise before we think of a solution. The first step towards practical problem solving is to start being proactive. Find a problem and address it before it can arise. Look at all the likely problems that may arise and try to solve them one after another.

Defining the Problem

Combining the problems that are valuable to solve and then defining what you are trying to solve will help dramatically improve your problem-solving efficiency. Attitude is the key to determining a problem. Try to look for an opportunity in every obstacle you face. Look for the positive side. It is very important, and it helps you define the problem in such a way that it will help you focus on the potential that is available in each situation you encounter. Start starving your problems and start feeding all the opportunities you have. Well, you may not see it right away, but every problem is a learning opportunity. When you stop thinking of a problem as an obstacle and instead see it as an opportunity, you will be able to deal with it effectively. So, try to frame your problem with a positive attitude, and it won't seem so terrible anymore.

Analyzing the Problem

The analysis involves the process of discovering the facts and finding out all the relevant information about the situation you are in. You can even make a checklist of the different bits of information you will need and then go and collect it. You will need to dig deep and try to analyze what is the problem and what is not. A critical aspect of this step is making sure you involve the right people. You can make use of these three simple questions as you select the people who can be brought on board to help you solve the problem.

- Who knows? Who are all the people who know the situation and have information or something of value to contribute?

- Who cares? Who are all the people who would care if something is done to rectify the problem at hand?

- Who can do it? Who can help you find a solution?

These questions are fundamental and can be useful when trying to identify all those who can help solve a problem. The analysis often requires a detailed examination of a given situation, and this step should not be omitted at any cost. If a situation is not thoroughly analyzed, you never know what it is and what it is not. When you do not have this basic information, it becomes quite difficult to think of an ideal solution.

Developing Possibilities

Once the problem to be solved has been understood, the next step is to take some time and find creative solutions to the problem. It is essential not only to recognize the ideas you come up with, but also the ideas that others propose. You cannot be a good leader if you do not listen to what others have to say as well. First you will have to find the right problem to solve and then think of all the opportunities that problem can create. But how exactly will you be able to focus on these opportunities? There will be more than one solution to solving a problem. The idea of this step is to have you brainstorm on your own or with others to come up with different possibilities. There will always be many alternatives to choose from. It is an important skill to understand the various alternatives that are available to you.

Selecting the Best Solution

The next step is to find the best solution for the problem in question. There will be specific constraints that must be taken into account, and all likely solutions must be thoroughly evaluated. There are three simple steps you can follow while selecting a solution.

The first step is to evaluate the operational validity it offers. Are you able to act on this idea, or is it just something you talk about? Will you be able to do something immediately to bring about the future you really want? Can this solution be implemented efficiently? The second step is to check its economic validity. Certain solutions are good, but when you begin to see their economic viability, you frustrate the purpose of trying to solve the problem. The investment you are making to solve a problem should not be greater than the result you expect. If this is not the case, then you should certainly evaluate other solutions. The third is to think about the personal commitment you will have to make. Do you honestly believe this idea will work, and can you attest to its viability?

Take some time and think about these questions. All the alternatives would not answer all three questions. If you find a solution that answers positively to all three questions, then you have your final solution that needs to be implemented.

Start Implementing

This is the most crucial step. If you don't execute an idea, then there's no point in even thinking about solving a problem. However, before you execute a particular idea, make sure you have carefully defined the problem and the result you want, the problem has been thoroughly analyzed, all the information you will need is available, and you have in fact chosen the best course of action available to you. If the idea you have focused on does not answer any of the above points in the affirmative, then retrace your steps and make the necessary changes.

Evaluate and Learn

When you have completed all of the above steps, you will need to evaluate the work that has been done. Check if the desired results have been achieved. If not, then check what went wrong. Make a list of all the things you can improve next time. Every opportunity to solve a problem will teach you something. Be open to learning and evaluate everything yourself.

CHAPTER 25
SKILLS FOR CRITICAL THINKING

Has anyone ever told you that critical thinking skills are essential to creating a successful career for you? You have probably heard this before. But do you know anything about the skills you should develop to do this? If you start looking for critical thinking skills online, you will find over a million results that provide different information. Well, that's not helpful, is it? You don't have to worry about that anymore.

Interpretation

It includes not only the ability to understand the information presented to you, but also your ability to communicate its meaning to others. You will see yourself in situations where you will need to make use of this critical skill. Interpretation skills will help you better understand the information that has been presented to you, and will also help you decode it. Doing this will provide you with some clarity.

Application exercise: Make a list of 10 facial expressions that can be equated to different emotions. For example, a smile means happiness; a frown can mean confusion and so on. Try to analyze the different emotions that you can measure by looking at the expressions of others.

Information Seeking

Critical thinking is about taking the facts and combining them with what you know to create a perspective. This perspective helps you decide based on what you have learned and any other factors that come into play. The importance of logic in critical thinking makes the search for information a large part of the critical thinking process. This is especially true since the knowledge you have affects your perspective, as well as the variety of options available to you.

Application exercise: Imagine that your boss comes to you with a big project - working with the budget department to implement an energy saving plan for the company. The goal is to maximize profits while spending as little as possible on equipment and energy-saving alternatives.

As the field of energy technology is expanding rapidly, this is something you'll want to investigate before you dive in. Conduct the research and come up with an energy saving plan that is effective but cost efficient.

Stimulating Thinking

There are opportunities around you that you can use to practice critical thinking throughout the day. For example, when your co-worker asks you to complete his or her homework over the weekend, you need to think critically. Consider whether you would be sacrificing something, such as plans you had made earlier. Then, think about the co-worker and whether there are any benefits. There are times when you can (and should) help others without expecting anything in return, but it should not be a one-sided relationship. Be kind, but don't be afraid to say no, whether you have plans or just want to relax over the weekend. Responding to them should not be an instantaneous response - take the time to think critically. By taking advantage of situations like these, you are getting the practice you need to be "good" at critical thinking.

Application exercise: One of the easiest ways to stimulate critical thinking is to ask yourself questions about a scenario. Asking things like "What is my point of view on this topic" and "Why do I believe that? Answer these questions and identify your reasoning for your point of view and consider any alternative perspectives that may exist. This process can be applied to any scenario in your life to create a critical thinking situation.

Analysis

Being able to connect the different pieces of information that have been provided to you and determine the intended meaning of those pieces of information is known as analysis. This skill gives the user the ability to read between the lines and will help them understand the real meaning of something. Analysis is an easy skill to acquire, but it takes time to master.

Application exercise: If you are interested in starting to practice this skill, then try to understand the meaning of this Chinese proverb "Be the first in the field and the last on the couch". Do you understand what this proverb is trying to convey? We will all have a different interpretation, but this proverb is essentially talking about hard work.

Non-Judgment

Critical thinkers need to see different perspectives without being critical. Critical thinking requires you to consider different points of view in an objective manner, assuming knowledge without emotionally charging it or manipulating it to fit your schedule. It is easy to let emotions cloud judgment, especially when you are passionate about the subject. However, if you let prejudice cloud your viewpoint, you can never be sure that the conclusion you have drawn comes from the facts or the emotions of the situation.

Application exercise: Practicing attention helps you learn to recognize your thoughts without letting them cloud your judgment. Start by bringing your mind to a state of concentration and relaxation. Sit in a quiet room and breathe deeply, paying attention to the feeling of your belly falling and rising. Once you feel relaxed, open your eyes and choose a point of focus. You may observe a beetle on your window sill, look at the wood patterns on your desk, or look at a painting on the wall. Look at the chosen point of focus and observe it without analyzing or judging it in any way. If you think of something, observe the thought without becoming emotionally attached to it. Concentrate on your breathing again until your mind clears and returns to your main point of focus.

Inference

The ability to conclude by understanding and recognizing the different elements presented to you is known as inference. Most people tend to reach a conclusion without considering all the available information. Doing so will lead to erroneous assumptions and, in turn, can affect your ability to make decisions. Think of a scenario where you are the manager of the company, and you are looking at the sales forecast. You will notice that sales are down. It is essential that you take into consideration additional information to determine the exact reason for the decline in sales. There may be internal and external problems that have led to a decline in sales.

Application exercise: Select a crime show and watch one episode per week. Watch and observe the different clues they drop and see if you can figure out who the culprit is on your own before the program ends. It will help you with your inferential skills.

Evaluation

This refers to the ability to be able to evaluate the credibility of a statement or information presented to you. This skill is useful when measuring the validity of the information at hand.

Application exercise: There is a very easy way to perfect this skill. Just open your laptop and look for skill assessment tests and voilà! You will have many tests to choose from, and this will help you develop your assessment skills.

Explanation

Explanation is the ability to restate information in a way that adds clarity and perspective. This is necessary so that the information can be properly understood. For example, think of a scenario in which you have to make two presentations about an idea for a new product, one for the company's board of directors and the other for the product engineers. Both parties will be eager to hear what you have to say. However, the way you present the information to these two groups will be significantly different. The board will probably be interested only in the high-level idea, while the product engineering team will be interested in the specifics of the product. Their ability to explain your idea with the audience in mind is the quintessential way to ensure that the information is not only well received but also well understood.

Application exercise: A very simple way to perfect this skill is by explaining a rather complicated concept to two different people. You can use your children and your spouse for this. How you explain a particular concept to your spouse will be different from how you explain it to your children. The goal is quite simple - the audience should understand what you are saying.

Communication

A commonly overlooked skill in the art of critical thinking is communication. Even the most intelligent and introverted individuals have to communicate to succeed in critical thinking.

Communication is useful at many stages of the critical thinking process. During the information-seeking stage, you may need to talk or communicate with others to ask them about the research they have done or their knowledge of the topic you are studying. Communicating with others can also help you learn about other perspectives or ideas that are relevant, which is important for making decisions. Even after you have finished researching your ideas, it is important to use communication to share what you have learned. That's right, whether your idea was a success or not, sharing allows everyone to learn from your thoughts and ideas.

Application exercise: Next time you think critically about an idea, take the time to research it thoroughly and come up with different perspectives. Use what you have learned to create a PowerPoint presentation as if you were going to give a slide show and explain the idea and the different perspectives that exist.

Creativity

Some people overlook creativity as an important trait, especially for something like critical thinking that focuses on logical thinking. Still, critical thinking requires creativity when thinking up alternatives and solving problems. It is essential and as simple as knowing when to step outside the box and come up with an unconventional solution. Being creative broadens your perspective and gives you a greater understanding of the world's possibilities.

Have you ever noticed that children are more in touch with their imagination than adults? As we age, we are often told to focus on logic and complete our studies. It can be beneficial to intelligence - but intelligence is not worth anything unless you have the skill and creativity to use it. Over time, focusing our brain on the creative side of things causes our mind to disregard creative ideas before we have them consciously. It means that even though our minds are still capable of creative thinking, we are not receiving the ideas in our conscious mind. It's like a phone call over an unserved line - the connection with that creative thinking cannot be completed.

Application exercise: Encouraging creativity in your life is as simple as getting into the habit of trying new things. Take a dance class or order something new at a restaurant. Creative thinking can also be benefited through creative acts, such as sewing, making crafts, painting, writing, playing a musical instrument, singing, or any number of other activities.

CHAPTER 26
STEPS OF THE CRITICAL THINKING PROCESS

These steps can be used by anyone, regardless of the field or industry in which they work. The steps follow a sequence that takes you from understanding your problem to implementing the best possible solution. There are several tools you will learn to use as we go along.

One thing you should understand about critical thinking is that it is a process. It is the reason it is so effective. You are supposed to go through a particular process so you don't end up jumping to biased conclusions and doing something you will regret.

Six steps are needed for the critical thinking process.

Step One: Knowledge

The first step is to acquire enough information about the problem you are facing. You can do this by simply asking a series of open-ended questions. The two most important questions are: "What is the problem I need to address" and "Why do I need to solve it? With these two questions, you should be able to generate a clear vision and gain a deeper understanding of how to start solving your problem.

For example, Company X has been marketing one of its products for some time without much success. Customers are simply not buying the product as expected. By asking the two questions above, we can begin to move toward a solution.

The problem that needs to be addressed is that the product has low market penetration. It is a problem because the company is spending a fortune manufacturing and marketing the product with minimal returns. In other words, they are losing much more money than they are gaining.

Step Two: Comprehension

Once the problem is identified, one must begin to assess the situation and gather all relevant data about it. Your goal should be to increase your understanding to eliminate any potential blind spots and ultimately make the best possible decision.

There are many research methods you can use to collect your data. Which method you use will depend on the complexity of the problem, the type of data you need and the time you have available to solve it.

From the example above, company X can use online questionnaires to capture its target market. They can also call the retailers who stock their products and get their opinion on the problem.

Step Three: Application

It is typically a continuation of the previous step. You are still trying to better understand all the information you are receiving. The only difference is that you are now linking each bit of information to the number of resources needed to solve your problem.

For example, Company X may discover that its product is not easy to use. This means they must redesign the product and make it easier for consumers to use. They may also find that their target market considers their product to be a little more expensive than others, and this may require a reduction in price. They may ultimately have to look for cheaper raw materials in the process. Another reason could be that one of your competitors is offering after-sales service, and this is driving customers away from them.

As you can see, Company X could be facing only one of these scenarios or maybe all of them. The best way to analyze all these situations is to create mind maps. It will help build a link between the main problem, the reason for the problem, and the potential solutions.

Step Four: Analyze

By now, he has gathered some information and built the necessary links. It is enough to help you analyze the whole situation from a better perspective. The goal here is to look at each individual situation, including its strengths and weaknesses, and the challenges you may face as you resolve it.

A very effective tool you can use here is the cause-and-effect diagram. It will help you analyze your problem and the different causes. This tool will also be useful in assessing the impact of each cause on the main problem.

As you can see, the cause-and-effect diagram divides the main problem into its causes and then looks at the factors that affect each cause.

Step Five: Synthesis

In the synthesis stage, you have to decide how you will solve your problem and the route you will take to implement the decision. By this point, you have fully analyzed all relevant information using the tools at your disposal.

If you discover that there are multiple solutions to your problem, then you must rank each solution to find the best one. To facilitate your work, you can use a tool known as SWOT (Strengths, Weaknesses, Opportunities, Threats) analysis to identify the strengths and weaknesses of each solution. It will also help you determine the opportunities and potential threats.

From the example of Company X, let's assume that the cause of your problem is pricing. Therefore, you must now determine the best solution to address this cause. You can either lower the price or give customers a complimentary item to complement the original product.

Let's use a SWOT analysis on the price reduction option:

a. Strengths

- Increased product sales

- Improved reputation with consumers

b. Weaknesses

- Customers may associate low price with poor quality

- The cost of production remains the same

c. Opportunities

- There is a growing market for low-priced products

- Sales of other products manufactured by the company can receive a boost

- Customers can change product loyalty and eliminate the competition.

d. Threats

- Some competitors may follow suit and lower their prices as well, thus causing the price to fall into disuse.

This is just one example of how you can use the SWOT analysis strategy as part of your critical thinking process.

Step Six: Action

The final step should always be to put your decision into action. In the Company X example, these action steps can be implemented by a special team or through a specific project. An action plan will need to be developed to ensure smooth implementation.

These six steps described above form the basis of critical thinking skills. Whenever a problem is faced, it is necessary to avoid making decisions based on emotion or prejudice and to approach it with a critical mind. This process can be as short as a few minutes or as long as a couple of days, but this will depend on the complexity of the problem.

Evaluation

However, when you have finished executing your plan, it is time to evaluate its effectiveness. While sometimes this is quite simple, like knowing you succeeded when your children suddenly became quiet, other times it will require you to dig in and make sure you have solved the problem. You may need more testing, for example, to confirm that the problem is no longer a problem. You may need someone to review what you have finished to make sure it is accurate. You may even have to submit the work and then assume that it will be evaluated before you find out if you did it well in the first place.

If you find that you have failed at some point, then it's time to start at the beginning: find out why you failed and then remove the current solution from your list of possibilities. Find out if failure can provide you with some information other than not trying next time, and if you can provide that information, then use it and don't feel defeated or too defeated - failure does happen, but it is a learning experience. You have eliminated one possible solution from your list, and that only teaches you something! Instead of seeing your failure as a problem, you can use it to learn from it as you continue the process of critical thinking and try to solve the problem.

This process will usually continue until a solution is discovered, or eventually you give up, accepting defeat. However, remember that people are rarely really successful in their first attempts at success in the first place. Think about how many theories are tried and failed before any are deemed appropriate enough to sustain - sometimes failure comes hundreds or thousands of times before success appears, and that's okay. Very few successes come without obstacles or barriers - otherwise, everyone would succeed.

CHAPTER 27
EXERCISES FOR CRITICAL THINKING

Time to Think Critically

Critical thinking is a process, not an easy solution. It takes time and thought. Think of time and thought as an investment in making the right decision.

You may want to write that process down. You might think about all that in your head. Either way, critical thinking involves organizing one's thoughts so that they can be adapted around the facts in question. It also involves making sure that it is your thoughts - aligned with the facts and logic - rather than the assumptions that have been conveyed to you. It may seem like a long process, but the more you do it, the easier and more intuitive it becomes.

Start by Asking How You Will Make Your Decision

What does "the best car" mean? What would "the right candidate" do? What does "help" mean when you say you want to help a friend? It is important to understand the topic, question, issue, or choice before you on your terms. For example, you may want a car that looks good. You might think that a political leader should focus on keeping crime under control (while another voter might prioritize the environment or another issue).

Ask yourself why you want those things. Is a car nice enough for you to admire or to impress others? Is it such a big crime that it's a problem in your community, or is it just something that everyone around you seems to focus on?

Before you start making a decision, be honest about what you are looking for as a result of that decision. Along the way, you may even change your mind. You may realize that you don't want to spend so much money on a luxury car just so other people can admire it. You may learn that the crime rate is much lower than you thought, but there is another immediate and more pressing issue that affects you. The point is to understand why we do the things we do and be honest about the reasons. Critical thinking requires objectivity, even when it comes to ourselves.

Who, and How, Do You Trust Anything?

Now that you have established precisely what is important to you in addressing this issue, you can begin to gather the facts. A "fact", in general terms, is an event or action that is known to have taken place, a thing that is verified as existing in the world, or a piece of information or occurrence that has been verified either through observation, experience, experimentation, or some other evidence-based process. In other words, the facts are true according to some verifiable standards.

Whenever you are presented with a piece of information, such as a description of the features of a car or a political candidate's plan, first consider the tone of the language. Is it too favorable or unfavorable? Do you present things in neutral terms, or do you use excessively colorful or negative language? Do you stick to descriptive statements or make inferences for yourself? In other words, is the language there to educate you, or is it trying to "sell" you something?

Next, consider the source of that information. Is that source speaking from your own experience, or is he or she just basing the information that was collected elsewhere? Does the source have something to gain, for example, in terms of profits or popularity? Does it come from a well-known source, such as a major political newspaper, or a website that you have never heard of? Popular sources can get bad things, and lesser-known sources can get the scoop on things before famous ones. However, in general, those known sources are known because they have established a reputation for reliability.

Analyzing Facts and Applying Logic

Hopefully, they will have gathered enough facts to help them make a decision. The process of applying the facts to the issue at hand is called "analysis. Making sure the facts are consistent with each other and concluding them involves "logic. Philosophers, mathematicians, psychologists, and other scholars have very sophisticated systems for describing and outlining both analysis and logic. For this book, we will stick to less abstract and more "on the ground" examples of analysis and logic.

What do the facts tell us in relation to the questions and definitions we have posed before? What do we know now about the safety of the car we want to buy or the candidate's plan to reduce crime? It may not always be an easy answer to those questions. Everything the candidate says may indicate that he or she is tough on crime. However, the policies he has enacted in the past indicate otherwise. Based on how the candidate has acted in the past, and despite his other rhetoric, it is safe to assume that he will not be tough on crime. This assumption is an "inference," a logical deduction based on some form of evidence.

Critical Thinking Exercises

Critical thinking is the suspension of your beliefs to explore and question issues from a neutral or blank point of view. It also requires the ability to differentiate fact from opinion when evaluating an issue.

Have you ever wanted to analyze and evaluate situations like a master detective? Or even present arguments like an experienced lawyer, but you are not? Are you tired of looking confused and out of place in intellectual forums or in class or in life in general?

Critical thinking is what will help you get out of this mess. Critical thinking is a skill, an art and a practice that gets to the heart of any issue, allowing you to see the big picture and challenge and criticize anything that stands between you and the truth.

Critical thinking, however, is not easy. It requires development and practice before it becomes second nature to anyone. To develop it further requires critical thinking exercises and practices.

There are many exercises that can help a person develop critical thinking skills. In this part, we will discuss some of them.

Critical Thinking for Students

Exercise 1: Alien Tour Guide

This exercise is an attempt to get students to think outside the box.

Suppose they have been given the task of taking a tour of aliens who have visited Earth and want to understand human life. They are mounted on a blimp while viewing the scenes and landscape below. They are passing over a baseball stadium. One of the visiting aliens looks down and is curious about what is going on. He tells her that there is a game going on. Assuming he asks you the following questions, how would you respond?

- What is a game?

- Why do only men play it? Are there no players?

- Why do people seem so excited when they see others play?

- What is a team?

- Why are some people in the seats and others on the field?

If these questions are answered comprehensively, it will become clear that we carry assumptions and values with us. There are reasons why you support a certain team, maybe it makes you feel like part of a community. The sense of community itself is a value that matters to some people and not to others. You may also need to explain to the alien the value of winning and losing. When you reason as an alien tour guide, you will find yourself thinking deeply about the things we do and value, and you may be surprised if they don't sound logical to you.

Exercise 2: Opinion or Fact

Are you always able to differentiate between facts and opinions? If you don't learn the difference between facts and opinions, you will only be reading and seeing things that improve on the assumptions and beliefs you already have.

Critical Thinking Exercises in the Workplace

One of the fundamental skills that a leader or manager must have is the ability to think critically. These skills are essential for solving problems in the organization, dealing with your employees, dealing with your customers, dealing with your business environment like your competitors or even helping you to create a new product. Several critical thinking exercises can help improve your critical thinking skills in the workplace. These include:

Exercise 1: Analyze Your Competitors

Study your competitors, try to describe their strategies and, most importantly, how and where they make money. Try to find out what their customer service group is, how and why they win or lose. Now go back and analyze your organization based on the same thing. Identify the opportunities your organization has over the competition and how to use these opportunities to win. Involve your customer service colleagues or salespeople in the exercise and get their input on the competition's strategies and opportunities. Analyze each piece of information critically and objectively and find a solution. Maybe your problem was how to increase sales. Use the information you have gathered to develop strategies to increase sales in your organization.

Exercise 2: Identify and Adopt an Orphan Problem

There are problems in all organizations that people do not want to be associated with. Identify such a problem and ask your boss to help you deal with it. If it is a problem that affects different departments, you may need to put together a team with members from different departments. Guide the team in analyzing the problem, interviewing all stakeholders, and developing an informed solution. By doing this, you gain visibility as a problem solver and leader, and you develop core professional skills.

CHAPTER 28
HOW TO GET BETTER AT DECISION MAKING

To solve difficult problems on a regular basis, you have to know how to make difficult decisions. This chapter includes tips to help you in the decision-making process. It is a big part of critical thinking in practice.

The First Steps to Better Decision Making

Stop procrastinating: Making a simple choice can be fun, allowing you to accomplish something and check it off on your big to-do list for the day. But when you're faced with greater risks, and have to make a very important business (or even personal) decision, you may be tempted to delay because it's more difficult. However, to be a great problem solver, you should not give in to this temptation.

Take time: Instead of delaying, give yourself a specific part during each day to see the risks, possible outcomes, pros and cons of the possible decisions you can make. Avoiding thinking about it will not make it go away; instead, it will increase your worry and anxiety and consume valuable energy that you could be using to come up with more ideas!

Face things head on: When you are faced with a difficult decision, commit to facing it head-on, with courage. The sooner you develop this habit, the easier it will be to keep it up in the future. You will thank yourself later for taking the time to teach you this skill.

Put your emotions and ego aside: Making decisions can become almost impossible when you become too personally involved in how a choice will affect your feelings and how you see yourself to others. Is there a way to solve the problem objectively? Yes, there is. Just list your options and put your ego and emotions aside for the moment. Think about an example of your business, not having enough income to reach your goals or stay afloat. Is it more beneficial to focus on what will go wrong and how stupid it will seem if it goes down, or to look for the causes of what has gone wrong? These are the questions you might ask yourself in that situation:

- Is there a positioning problem that you don't see?

- Are you pricing your services, right?

- Are you marketing correctly?
- What can you do to solve these problems?

You will always make more logical and beneficial decisions when you look at the facts, rather than your insecurities or fears. Anyone who needs help with their business has a plethora of options to find it if they just stay calm and find those sources. Self-awareness is what makes a businessman truly successful.

Get Professional Insight

The choice you are facing, whatever it is, has probably already been faced by someone else. Even if you think your problem is unique, someone else has probably already gone through it! Fortunately, most successful guys are approachable and willing to help someone who asks them. To find an expert willing to help you with your problem, research influential people related to the topic you need help with and find three to ask for help. Give them the facts of the situation, your ideas and the options you are trying to decide on. You may find it helpful to consult a neutral outside source to be objective in making your choice. In some areas, it is worth doing things on your own, but there is nothing wrong with asking for advice sometimes.

Question What You Find Out

No one has the complete data they need to make an informed choice. Parts are always missing. Still, it's your responsibility to find the right information as best you can. Listening to what your friend says and not considering other sources can get you into trouble, for example. Instead, use quantitative and qualitative information.

Relevant sources: Always look for relevant sources for important data. For example, if you are looking for answers to improve your business, you can look at customer feedback.

No data is better than bad data: You can use industry trends, reports and research, along with expert advice to make strategic business decisions. Most importantly, always remember that no data is better than bad data. Always find data you can trust when making important decisions, and your decision-making skills have already skyrocketed.

Be Prepared for the Worst

Another key to quality decision making is being aware of any risks that may come with your final choices. Ideally, you should be prepared for even the worst case scenario.

Consider each choice: Take some time to thoroughly consider what the worst case scenario would look like in relation to your decision. For example, if you have to fire someone from the company, what could lead you into the worst possible world? They might try to sue, or your team might get angry. There are countless ways to deal with every possible risk that may arise, but you have to be prepared for them!

Feel better about your choice: When you have a realistic view of your possible risks, you can feel better about the decisions you make. Always remember that people make mistakes, so when you make a wrong decision, don't get too depressed. Instead, think about what went wrong, and then write about it to prevent it from happening again in the future. That way, your mistake was not in vain.

More Methods for Improving Your Skills in Making Decisions

Our brains depend on mental shortcuts to make decisions throughout the day. Sometimes, you may not have the information you need, or you may only be able to use a small amount of data to make a choice. In other words, you may have to make decisions regularly using only some data or experience to guide you.

Advantages and disadvantages of heuristics: Methods like these are heuristic (mental shortcuts) and are useful for agility and speed, but are more likely to make mistakes. It is necessary to be aware at all times when making decisions.

Be realistic: When you are realistic and you know that you, like everyone else, can be a victim of mental heuristics and their falls, you can be attentive, looking for more data before making a decision. Remember that everyone deals with this.

The Risks of Ineffective Decision Making and Problem Solving

Consider a typical business situation. You are confident in giving interviews and choosing the best possible option for a position. You know you can effectively delegate and explain what your business is about and how the employee should act to contribute to it. In your opinion, you have effectively given them all the tools they need to be successful on the job, so why do they find it difficult to make even small decisions? You may begin to feel distracted by your employee's apparent inability to make a good decision. Nothing can be done without decisions being made.

Tips for Being a Better Decision-Maker

Decision-making is the core of any successful team. It means that your team has to be full of members who can make decisions skillfully and quickly. If you or your people hesitate too long, you can lose money and morale at work. Our modern world is constantly moving faster and faster, making this increasingly crucial as time goes by. Your entire team needs to be capable and clear about how they make decisions while staying true to the politics of the business as a whole. However, there will always be instances where decision making is difficult and more time consuming than you had imagined. How can you become a better decision maker, and at the same time help those around you to do the same?

Know the mental tendencies: Knowing that the mind always has a preference for quick thinking over critical thinking is a good place to start. But you also need to make sure that everyone on your team, especially you, is aware of the big picture. Following the business example, you would make sure that your team knows your future goals, the reasons for your service or product, and who you are selling to. When you and everyone else agree on the big picture, everyone will know how they fit into it and how they can contribute to the vision.

A clear vision of success: What does success mean to you, and how can you share that vision with your group? Clarity of vision is necessary for good decisions to be made. You can take this one step further and keep everyone aware of how the company fits into the world and what it adds to the lives of its customers. Once you give yourself a balanced mindset and perspective, you can solve anything.

A calm mindset: A calm mindset, especially during difficult times, is the last resort for effective decision making. Once you get a good handle on the skills mentioned above, you can enjoy less stress at work. When you are too stressed, your ability to think, your motivation and even your memory suffer. Prioritize learning how to stay calm during times of stress, and your decision-making ability will skyrocket as a result. This may mean doing meditation, taking frequent walks, or even something as simple as knowing when to take a break from work to de-stress.

When you are a great decision maker, people respect you more, and your life becomes more successful. The union of critical thinking and effective decision making will make you an unstoppable force in all areas of life.

CHAPTER 29
CRITICAL THINKING IN EVERYDAY LIFE

Critical thinking is a skill that can be applied to every area of one's daily life. You may be surprised by the decisions you can, want to, and have made that require you to think critically before you move forward.

You must think critically when you do things like choosing courses for college, as well as the major to follow. Moving to a new place, deciding between two or more job opportunities, selecting a phone and Internet package, and even planning vacations and other trips are decisions people make every day. Imagine how much better you will be able to make those decisions, with the power of your developing critical thinking skills. Yes, critical thinking skills apply to many areas of personal life.

Of course, our personal life is not the only aspect of life where critical thinking is an advantage. Critical thinking will certainly also be useful when making decisions in the workplace.

For example, if you hold a position in the Human Resources section of your company, you will be responsible for conducting a lot of research in the workplace. Deciding whether to suspend or terminate an employee based on his or her actions must be based on critical thinking to ensure that the right decision is made. Conducting interviews and taking witness statements using an objective methodology will help you gather information and formulate an appropriate plan.

Another example of a position where critical thinking is beneficial is marketing. Marketing employees can use critical thinking skills to decide how to sell and package products so that the company can generate the most profit. The use of assumptions will be a stumbling block for someone working in this field. However, by using techniques to conduct research on a target market and its needs, likes and dislikes will help you attract them so that your product can be sold.

Any improvement in thinking cannot take place without a conscious commitment to learning. You can't improve the game of basketball if you don't make an effort to do so, and the same goes for critical thinking. Like any other skill, effort is essential to its development. As long as you take your thinking for granted, there is no way you can release your true potential. The development of your thinking process is gradual, and there are several plateaus of learning that you will have to overcome, and hard work is a precondition for all of this. You cannot become an excellent thinker just by wanting to be one. You will be forced to make a conscious decision to change certain habits, and this will take some time. Be patient, and do not expect any change to occur overnight.

Making Use of "Wasted" Time

How many times have you been stuck in rush hour traffic when you could have easily avoided this by getting out an hour earlier? Aside from all the time we waste doing nothing, we start worrying about unnecessary things. Sometimes we regret the way we operated in the past, or we simply end up daydreaming about "what could have been" and "what can be", instead of making some effort to achieve results. Well, you have to realize that there is no way you can make up for all the time you lost. Instead, try to concentrate on all the time you have available to you now. One way you can develop the habit of critical thinking is to make use of the time that would normally be "wasted. Instead of spending an hour in front of the TV flipping through channels and getting bored, you can use this time or at least part of it to reflect on the day you had, the tasks you accomplished, and everything you need to accomplish. Dedicate this time to contemplate your productivity. Here are a couple of questions you can ask yourself:

Take some time to answer these questions and record your observations. After a while, you will notice that you have a specific pattern of thinking.

One Problem per Day

Every morning, you should select a problem that you would like to work on in your free time. Identify the different elements it is composed of so that you can find a logical solution. To put it simply, you should go through the following questions in systematic order: What is the real problem? How does this problem obstruct my goals, purposes and needs in general? These are the steps that will help you solve the problem.

Maintain an Intellectual Journal

Start keeping an intellectual journal where you record specific information on a weekly basis. This is the basic format you should follow. The first step is to list the situation that was or is significant to you, emotionally. It should be something you care about, and you need to focus on a situation. After that, record your response to that situation. Try to be as specific and accurate as possible. Once you have done this, then you need to analyze the situation and your reaction and analyze what you have written. The final step is to evaluate what you have gone through. Evaluate the implications - what have you learned about yourself? And if given the opportunity, what would you do differently in that situation?

Reshaping Your Character

Select intellectual traits such as perseverance, empathy, independence, courage, humility, etc. Once you have selected a trait, try to concentrate on it for a whole month and cultivate it in yourself. If the trait you have chosen is humility, then begin to notice every time you admit you are wrong, every time you notice that you indulge in any form of negative behavior or that you crush those thoughts. Begin to reform your character and begin to incorporate desirable behavioral traits while leaving out the negatives. You are your own worst enemy, and you can prevent your growth without knowing it. Learn to let go of all the negatives.

Dealing with Ego

Human beings are inherently narcissistic. As we think about something, we tend to favor ourselves over anyone else, subconsciously. Yes, we are predisposed to ourselves.

Redefining How You See Things

It means that all those situations to which you attribute a negative meaning can be transformed into something favorable if you wish. This strategy consists of finding something positive in everything you would have considered negative. Try to see the positive side in every aspect of your life. It is about perspectives and perceptions. If you think something is positive, then you will feel good about it, and if you think it is negative, then naturally you will harbor negative feelings about it.

Get in Touch with Your Emotions

Whenever you feel a negative emotion coming on, try to see the mood or rationalize it. Concentrate on the thought process that produced the negative emotion, and you will be able to find a solution to your problem.

Analyzing the Influence of a Group on Your Life

Watch carefully how your behavior is influenced by the group you are in. For example, any group will have specific unwritten rules of conduct that all members will follow. There will be some form of compliance that will be enforced. See for yourself how much this influences you and how it affects you. See if you are giving in too much to the pressure that is being exerted and if you are doing something just because others expect it of you.

You don't have to start practicing all the steps at once. Start slowly and try to follow as many as you can. Initially, you will need to make a conscious effort to make critical thinking work, and over a period of time these skills will come naturally to you.

There is no doubt that critical thinking is a skill that will improve your daily life both personally and professionally in the long run.

CHAPTER 30
USING QUESTIONING IN CRITICAL THINKING

Why do you normally ask questions? There are things you want Why do you normally ask questions? There are things you want to know and understand more clearly. Even the questions you sometimes ask just out of curiosity are good. Don't you feel more enlightened after someone has answered your question?

You may have satisfied your curiosity now if that is all you were interested in, but some time later, the information you got from curiosity becomes useful. By the way, you don't have to ask questions exclusively to other people. You can also ask yourself questions.

General Benefits of Asking Questions

Every time you ask a question:

- You clarify any vagueness that may have existed.
- You clarify any possible confusion.
- You automatically find yourself rationalizing your thinking.

Every time you consider asking questions in the context of critical thinking, you cannot fail to notice its positive contribution to the establishment of the list at that moment. As you might expect, the answer someone gives you when they ask a question is relevant to the particular situation they are dealing with. Your questions provide a direction to your thinking. To invoke critical thinking, you must design your questions in a certain way.

How to Design Questions to Enhance Critical Thinking

Create questions that help build your body of knowledge.

Create questions that help you improve your understanding of the given situation.

Create questions that help you analyze the data and facts you have.

Design your questions in such a way that they help you synthesize the information you have.

So, now you know the kind of questions you are supposed to create. The big question is, how do you do this? It's very simple. There are some things you can do and some things you can't do, and following them will help you create the most useful questions.

Do's and Don'ts in Creating Questions

Make sure the questions you create are not one-dimensional.

Do you have any idea what one-dimensional questions are? Well, they are those questions that require a one-word answer, either yes or no. Does a question like that cause someone's mind to think critically? Surely, it can't.

Plan Your Questions in Advance

You may wonder what the moment has to do with critical thinking, but if you pause to consider it, it is unlikely that someone who makes up questions as the interrogation session progresses will have any useful questions. The kind of planning referred to here involves preparing the questions well in advance so that you do not end up designing the questions in a hurry.

Do you know who has raised this question of serious questioning in the context of critical thinking? It was an educator named Benjamin Bloom, and the style of questioning he proposed was adopted in the name of Bloom's Taxonomy. There are specific meanings that you need to understand in the context of Bloom's Taxonomy, particularly the meaning of knowledge, understanding, and also analysis of issues.

- In this context, knowledge represents facts, and you know that facts are things you can remember. It also includes any opinions you may have, and also the ideas you currently have.

- As for understanding, you can interpret the information you have in some kind of language you understand well.

- When you talk about synthesizing knowledge and also putting it into practice, it means your ability to interpret the information you have in your possession, and then use it in completely new situations.

In general terms, you can consider questioning as that critical thinking tool that puts you in a much better position than before; to understand other situations similar to those you have managed to evaluate during your critical thinking session.

How to Design Appropriate Questions for Critical Thinking

Ask Questions That Court Knowledge

You can ask for anything you want, can't you? However, not everything you ask for will earn you an answer that is useful to your critical thinking process. If you want to design questions that give you useful answers for critical thinking, you need, first of all, to be sure of what you are interested in achieving with the information you get. Do you know how to establish where your interest lies in terms of achieving a goal? To establish where you are going with your critical thinking:

Review how much you know about the situation under scrutiny.

Make an effort to remember the facts of the situation, and the relevant terminology to analyze and understand the situation.

Make a list of all the ideas you know and consider relevant.

Write down all the answers you may have to the questions you have been asking.

After doing this, a kind of preliminary, you will realize that what you are going to gather next is what is relevant to the situation and very useful in your critical thinking process. In short, you will not risk collecting double or duplicate information, or things that are not important to the process. Now that you are ready to design the questions to use in your critical thinking process, do you know how you should frame them so that you can court the best answers?

How to Design Questions to Attract Informative Response

What do you call this or that thing?

What category does this thing or that belong to?

Why do you get this response or that reaction after doing this or that?

How can you explain this or that occurrence?

When are the moments when this or that phenomenon comes to the surface?

Create questions that allow for understanding.

You must appreciate the context in which the information you have received has been provided so that you can do your critical thinking effectively. It is also important that you can gather all the information for analysis so that the information can serve your purpose well. When you get to this, what you intend to accomplish with your questions of understanding includes

Organizing the ideas, as well as the facts in your possession, with the intention of comparing them.

Translating and interpreting those ideas and facts so that they convey something meaningful.

Giving appropriate descriptions of the ideas and facts you have.

Identifying all the ideas you find are of primary importance, and then organizing and arranging them in what you consider to be their order of priority.

Do you know the next step you have to take, now that you have finished establishing what you want to achieve or accomplish? Well, it's time to ask the questions you want to use.

How Best to Tailor Comprehension Questions

How do you imagine this idea compares easily with the other, or how do two ideas contrast with each other?

What possible explanation can you give for this particular look or that different look?

What are the facts, according to you, that support your position?

What is the possible evidence that makes you maintain your position?

Build questions that help with the actual application of knowledge.

Do you know, by the way, why questions are important in the use of knowledge? The reason is that even if you have a lot of knowledge, as long as you do not understand how to use it better, the problem you have been facing will persist. What you lack is the most appropriate technique, which you can use to make the knowledge you have work for you. It is for this reason that you are required to ask questions that are relevant to the use of the information you have.

Examples Regarding How to Design Questions

What possible examples do you think you can give to be solutions for this or that or even that other challenge?

How do you think you can show that you are comfortable and familiar with this or that?

In your personal opinion, what would you say is the best approach when you are trying to handle this or even that?

What, in your thinking, would happen, just assuming things worked out one way or another?

Design Questions That Are Likely to Enhance Analysis

What is available to help with critical analysis? Well, you have the mass of knowledge you gathered, and from that you will derive the information you need. Of course, the information you intend to use in critical thinking must have enough credible material to support it. How precisely can you determine which specific material to use in your critical analysis? Remember that what you have at this point is general information. To be sure of the specific material to be used, you must first break down that mass of information you have.

What you achieve by breaking down your general information.

You can identify the reasons for the various ideas contained in it, and everything else that is involved.

You can point out the causes that are rooted within the mass of information you have.

You are able to draw inferences.

You will be in a position to identify the evidence within that information that you have in your possession.

When analyzing the information related to the critical analysis, the way to frame the questions is as follows:

What possible inference do you make when weighing the different pieces of information?

Where would you put the pieces of information in your possession?

How can you classify this, that, or another idea?

When you identify a single concept, would you be in a position to distinguish the real parts that make it up?

Create queries that seek to evaluate.

Do you know what you are trying to achieve here? It is to validate the opinion you have developed under the same information you have, and also based on the same technique you have used in applying that information. It is the stage where you are supposed to judge what you have observed, and also what you have experienced during the whole process of critical thinking.

How can you frame the assessment questions?

How, in your opinion, should you contrast this particular idea with that other idea?

Which of the two, or even more, do you consider to be best in these particular circumstances?

How, do you imagine, can you rate this person's performance against some other person's performance?

What have you possibly established as the essence of compromising this particular resource or that other one?

If someone asked you what you would have preferred earlier, what would you have offered as a suggestion?

CHAPTER 31
THINGS THAT SABOTAGE CRITICAL THINKING

The first is the "monkey mind," which Buddhists used to describe mental distraction. With this technique, the mind wanders and jumps from one thought to another without direction. Imagine it as a monkey jumping from one tree to another trying to let out its frustrations.

Another technique is the "alligator brain". It is the primitive part of the mind where its main objective is survival. When threatened, the mind returns to its primitive actions such as eating or the fight or flight response. It is fine in a dangerous situation, however, on a daily basis, this only leads to dysfunction.

Finally, one must only allow oneself to be comfortable in a state of mind. If you are comfortable thinking one way, you will not push yourself to think differently or do anything out of the ordinary. Worse yet, you will feel that you cannot think differently in the first place, so you will not try. If you can't break these patterns when you need to, you get stuck in this reduced state of mind.

Apart from not thinking, there are different ways in which people can intentionally sabotage critical thinking. You may have seen people use some of these negative strategies before, or you may have used them yourself in the past. People turn away from these forms of critical thinking and from true arguments of falsehood and even manipulation.

Lack of Respect for Reason

Reasoning is the cornerstone of critical thinking. It is extremely important for forming solid arguments and deriving a conclusion from its premises and arguments. In everyday situations, people cannot accurately use critical thinking skills without a certain level of reasoning.

As man's tool for understanding the world, it is necessary. It is the method of identifying entities through the senses, integrating their perceptions into concepts, acquiring knowledge through integration, integrating that knowledge into the rest of their knowledge, and finally evaluating and manipulating ideas and facts.

Reasoning can be considered the process of thinking. It is defined by clarity, not by visceral thinking or intuition, and requires clear and identifiable building blocks. Furthermore, reasoning is an organized way of thinking since it is systematic and purposeful. It focuses on the fundamentals of the argument and uses clear methods of logic and deduction to conclude.

As a clear way to achieve knowledge and understanding, the ends towards which it is used end up defining the validity of the method of reasoning. Remember that your conclusion is only as strong as the premises and arguments behind it.

Knowing the importance of reasoning for sound thought patterns, it is not surprising that reasoning is so important for critical thinking. However, what happens when someone has no respect for reason?

Suppose someone argues that there is not going to be a big storm. However, all logic points to a storm coming in a matter of minutes: it is dark, it is cloudy, the wind is blowing, and there is thunder and lightning.

Someone who lacks respect for reason would not agree at all. They support their argument by saying that the clouds are passing and that thunder and lightning are not usually a sign of a storm. They continue to claim that there will be no storm, even though all the evidence points to a storm.

Intellectual Arrogance

Intellectual arrogance is when people fill themselves with what they know. Sure, that person can be very intelligent, and that is fine, but when they have a pompous and exaggerated view of their ability and knowledge because of their intelligence, that is when it becomes a problem.

There are some characteristics that point to someone who is intellectually arrogant:

- They know they are the smartest person in the room and they let it be known that they think their opinions are the only ones that count.

- Most of the time, people will not tell them that they are intellectually arrogant, and if they do, then the intellectually arrogant person will not believe them. They must discover this for themselves.

- Recognition of their intellectual arrogance can lead to their downfall. Sustained success can give a person a feeling of infallibility or invincibility. Once that is gone, a person can feel lost.

Intellectual humility, however, is the opposite:

- It is people who are smart enough to recognize that all ideas and opinions have some value and that all issues and problems are multifaceted.

- They possess the ability to work in a group and do not put themselves above others.

- They are not quick to judge others.

- They try to get the best out of each person they meet.

One study revealed some characteristics that accompany a person who possesses an unhealthy amount of intellectual arrogance and how others evaluate them.

On the one hand, they do not see themselves as others see them. They see themselves as extremely humble and would not dare to call themselves anything close to arrogant. However, other people who know them would think exactly the opposite. They have seen arrogance in all its strength from an outer lens, and would say that this person is full of himself.

Another thing that was found is that in the group projects, other team members gave better evaluations to those who felt they were more humble. Perhaps the intellectually arrogant person contributed much to the project. However, the way they felt they were above everyone else in the group and the way they treated others made the rest of the group think little of them and prefer to have worked with less arrogant people.

Finally, people often agree on who is intellectually arrogant and who is intellectually humble, but it takes time. People will genuinely evaluate others based on evidence to support their feelings for them. If they spend little time with someone, they do not have much time to reach a real conclusion about that person. Sometimes, people may find it difficult to determine whether someone is humble or simply shy, or arrogant or simply very outgoing.

You may have worked with someone who is intellectually arrogant. If not, you may run into one someday. Imagine working on a group project.

The intellectually arrogant person in the group thinks only his or her answers are correct. They do not accept any opinions from the rest of the group. They try to name themselves as leaders of the whole operation, but they do not accept others' suggestions on how things should be done. Their arguments are wrong because they do not listen to the reasoning of the other group members.

Therefore, intellectual arrogance completely derails critical thinking. Yes, critical thinkers are intelligent, but that is not their only characteristic. They are open-minded, without prejudice, and open to new views. All this requires a certain level of humility and therefore the intellectually humble person makes a better critical thinker.

Unwillingness to Listen

This is the person that many people have met at least once. The person who does not listen to what you say no matter what. He completely ignores your point of view in favor of his because he does not agree, or he is not interested in hearing anything other than what he wants to believe.

Someone who does not want to listen does not care to hear reasons, even if your argument is much more valid than his. Their arguments are false, and they are fine with it. Either they know their argument is false but are too comfortable in that position to change it, or they are not aware that they are wrong but have held that view for so long that they don't care to listen to another.

There are four key characteristics of bad listeners:

- Interruption: This is probably the easiest to point out. Most people interrupt others, but only to a certain extent. When the person does not want to listen, they constantly interrupt because they do not want to hear what they have to say. Their own opinions are much more important to them because they feel that only they are correct.

- Closed Mind: People who do not want to listen to others are closed-minded. Their perspective is narrow, and they are not interested in learning new ideas. They think of their world view as a circle they are not willing to get out of or expand from.

- Too busy: with someone who doesn't want to listen, they may give their opinion but when it's time to say what they think, they say they are "too busy" to listen. They either turn their attention to their phone or some other distraction or they may even leave altogether. If the bad listeners stay in front of you, you may get an occasional "aha, of course" from them, but in reality, you focus them on something else because they don't care to hear what you have to say.

- Match back: this is the moment when you can tell someone something, a serious story or something that has happened to you, but the person turns it into something about themselves. Share something that has happened to you that may or may not be similar to your own story and then try to give unsolicited advice on how you would have handled the situation. It's a way of making the situation more about them and doing it, so they don't really have to listen to you.

Listening is an important aspect of critical thinking. On the one hand, it allows you to be open to other points of view. On the other hand, you cannot properly evaluate someone's argument if you don't listen carefully to what they say.

CONCLUSION

Just because you have read this book does not mean that there is nothing to learn about it. Expanding your horizons is the only way to find the expertise you are looking for.

This book has been written to provide an introduction to the process of critical thinking to the reader in order to stimulate interest in a practice that can greatly benefit people as they strive to lead a more productive and happy life. Over time you will be able to rely on your own logic and reasoning in any situation, no matter how challenging or difficult. This will allow you to succeed in the workplace and in your personal life.

Use all the strategies this book has taught you. You have learned to think like a lawyer, and after this, you will be a professional problem solver. By following the simple tips given in this book, you can see a positive change in your productivity and efficiency.

When understood and practiced effectively, critical thinking is a powerful tool. It is important to understand more about the event and the mechanism that involves it when developing critical thinking skills. Once recognized, concerns about the successful application of critical thinking skills are likely to dissipate. Critical thinking can turn the reasoning process into simple, compelling, and honest language designed with care and logic. At the same time, experiences and responses can be transformed into theories, thoughts, observations, conclusions, inferences, hypotheses, questions, opinions, premises, and logical arguments.

There are many misunderstandings about critical thinking that continue to discourage people from actively learning how to improve it.

If you have gone through the proper process of understanding the problem, examining all possible options, gathering information for solutions, and evaluating everything, you should be confident that you will be able to stand firm in the decision you are about to make. You are putting your critical thinking skills into practice by going through this whole process. As with other things you do for the first time, it may seem unorthodox, but as you continue to practice these techniques, your critical thinking skills will grow and evolve further.

You need to understand that, in general terms, the ability to think critically varies from person to person depending on their level of exposure to different problems and how well they manage to solve them. The good thing is that you can learn and develop the ability to think critically and make the most of it.

Critical thinking is essential for analyzing information and coming to clear and sound conclusions about any argument you make or any solution to a problem. It requires a process that includes examining the evidence and making judgments about whatever you are thinking.

As important as critical thinking is, you must avoid things like intellectual arrogance, not listening and being quick in judgment or else your whole argument for critical thinking will fall apart as quickly as it began.

There are a number of situations in which you can use critical thinking. Looking back, you were probably in a situation involving critical thinking without even realizing it. However, it is important to understand that it is how you use your critical thinking skills that determines the effectiveness of your critical thinking.

Above all, critical thinking is a state of mind that not everyone naturally possesses. Although schools try to teach critical thinking, it takes consistent practice to train your brain to think critically at any given time.

As with anything, you should strive to be the best thinker you can be. Better critical thinking skills will allow you to face any situation head-on and solve problems with precision and efficiency. No matter where you are, at work, at school, or in everyday situations, you will find that critical thinking is necessary.

Despite the numerous techniques and skills that come with critical thinking, the best thing you can do for yourself is to practice. Practice every critical thinking strategy, assume all the characteristics of a good thinker, and actively monitor yourself to ensure that you are avoiding anything that serves to ruin good critical thinking.

PART 2

ANALYTICAL MIND

INTRODUCTION

Thinking is the culmination of cognitive activities used to process information, solve problems, make decisions, and propose new ideas. Whenever you try to understand your experiences, organize information, ask questions, make connections, plan or decide on a course of action, you are using thinking skills. There are different types of thinking, and they are as follows.

Analytical Thinking

It refers to the ability to separate an idea into its basic components for further examination and the relationships that exist. It essentially refers to the ability to think logically in a stepwise fashion. By breaking down a larger system of data or facts into different parts, it becomes easier to think.

Creative Thinking

Creative thinking refers to your ability to conceive innovative and new ideas. Getting out of the box and freeing yourself from established rules, theories, thoughts and procedures. It is the process of putting things together in a creative, imaginative and new way. Creative thinking is also known as thinking outside the box.

Concrete Thinking

Whenever any factual knowledge can be understood and applied effectively, it is known as concrete thinking. It is about thinking about ideas or even objects as individual elements instead of a theoretical representation of a general concept or a generalization. It is always literal, to the point, and only involves thinking on the surface.

Critical Thinking

Their ability to carefully evaluate and determine the accuracy, authenticity, value, worth, or validity of an idea is known as critical thinking. In addition to objective analysis and precise understanding of the concepts involved, critical thinking also includes reflection, evaluation, processing, and reconstruction of thoughts. Rather than breaking down the available information into small pieces of praise, critical thinking consists of exploring the elements that may influence any conclusion reached.

Diverging Thinking

Divergent thinking is about generating creative ideas by exploring various possible solutions or outcomes to find the best fit. It is about gathering data and facts from different sources and then using logic as well as knowledge to solve any problem or make effective decisions. It usually starts from a common point and then moves outward in different directions or divergent directions involving various perspectives or aspects.

Abstract Thinking

Your ability to use different concepts to make and understand various generalizations and then integrate or connect these generalizations with other events, experiences or elements is known as abstract thinking. It usually involves paying close attention to any hidden meaning. Therefore, it allows you to understand and absorb various theories as well as possibilities.

Convergent Thinking

Convergent thinking is the exact opposite of divergent thinking. One does not start with a common point as in divergent thinking, and instead tries to bring together different perspectives on a singular subject and then logically organizes them to arrive at a single conclusion. Instead of concentrating on arriving at multiple solutions, it is a matter of focusing on a fixed number of possibilities.

Linear Thinking

Linear thinking is also known as sequential thinking. It refers to your ability to understand information in an orderly or prescribed manner. It involves creating a step-by-step progression, in which a response must be derived from a specific step before moving on to another step.

Non-Linear Thinking

Non-linear thinking is also known as holistic thinking. It is your ability to visualize the big picture and understand the relationships of the different components present in the big system. It is about expanding your thinking process in different directions rather than a single direction. Aside from this, you also need to understand the system by understanding the different patterns present within it.

Opposing Categories

All the different types of thought that have been mentioned so far can be divided into different opposing categories, and they are as follows.

Concrete Thinking vs. Abstract Thinking

Concrete thinking is often limited to thinking on the surface, while abstract thinking requires deeper analysis. In concrete thinking, only the literal meaning is considered, while abstract thinking allows for deepening and understanding the hidden or multiple meanings of the various facts and data involved.

Since concrete thinking is one's ability to understand and apply factual knowledge, it only involves those things that are obvious and visible to an individual. Abstract thinking is not limited to the visible or present things and focuses more on understanding the underlying purpose.

For example, a concrete thinker might look at a flag and only see the colors, symbols, or markings present on the fabric. When an abstract thinker looks at the same flag, he or she may be able to see it as a representation of freedom.

Linear Thinking vs. Non-Linear Thinking

Applying information only in a prescribed way is known as linear thinking. It is about creating a step-by-step progression when one step must be completed before the second step can take place. For example, if $a = b$, $b = c$, then by using linear thinking, you will come to the conclusion that $a = c$. On the other hand, holistic thinking is about trying to see the bigger picture to recognize any interconnections of different aspects that result in a larger system. It is about broadening your thinking process in different directions rather than a singular one to understand how everything is interconnected. A linear thinker might be able to visualize the above equation in the form of a triangle instead of a two-dimensional equation.

For example, if a linear thinker were setting up a table, he would start by following the different step-by-step instructions. On the other hand, a holistic thinker will try to mentally visualize what the final product will look like while assembling the table.

Creative Thinking vs. Analytical Thinking

Breaking information down into different parts and examining them, along with the relationships, is known as analytical thinking. It is about thinking logically while analyzing data step by step to solve problems or make decisions. On the other hand, creative thinking is about bringing new and innovative ideas to bear by questioning any established theory, thought, rule, or even procedure. It is not about taking things apart, but putting them together in an innovative way.

For example, if these two thinkers looked at a bicycle, then a creative thinker could look at it and try to come up with different ways to use it or make it faster. An analytical thinker will probably try to understand how it works or any of its flaws.

CHAPTER 1
ANALYTICAL THINKING

Analytical Thinking Is about Making Complexity Easier

The problem is identified in analytical thinking, the problem is defined, and then key information is found from the data that has been collected. When all this has been done, you then develop and create an effective solution to the problems you have identified to test and verify the root cause of the problem and create solutions to eliminate the problems that have been identified.

The word analytical is derived from the Greek word "analyein" and means "to break" and "to loosen". Thus, analytical thinking is roughly taking a problem or task and then breaking it down into smaller elements to respond to the problem or complete the task.

People always think that analytical thinking has always been about logic and that it is about left-brain type skills. But good analytical thinking is actually something the whole brain is active in. You have to be generative while you are analytical.

But how do we do it, and how do we do it in a way that our mind is very open to be able to continue to be generative? Even the people that you would consider the most logical people on the planet are of an extremely generative nature. They are the brain thinkers of an extreme whole. They don't just focus on logic.

Let's use chess as an example, scientists decided to look at the brain waves of chess players, of good chess players, to see if they were very analytical thinkers and if they used mainly their left cortical abilities. And what they found was that they did, and this was quite surprising because everyone in the field thought it would be a much more complete approach to the brain.

When Making a Decision Having an Analytical Thinking Is Necessary

So, think about all the decisions you've made on the route to the parking lot, how much you've been studying for a class, all the big decisions and the little decisions.

Analytical thinking is a lens through which you see a situation; this lens asks you to press the pause button so you can gather information and evaluate alternatives. Let's think about a decision we all have to make at some point, like; where are we going to live? An analytical mindset requires that we begin by identifying the decision to be made.

The first step we want to look at is to gather some information that will help us make a more informed decision. We have a number of tools that we can use to do this. One of those tools is a decision making matrix. So, after we have collected the information, we want to organize the information in the selected categories around our different alternatives.

So, what are some of the options where you might choose to live? We can decide between a two-bedroom apartment, a three-bedroom apartment, and maybe a house finally after we have achieved the decision-making matrix. We look at each alternative and evaluate which one will be best for us. So, now you should think about questions like; what do I prefer? What will work best for my roommates?

Then you can use analytical thinking to make decisions like, "where do I live or maybe where do I work? We can use analytical thinking in any situation we find ourselves in. Many people assume that someone is better at analysis because of who they are, but the reality is that you can get better at applying analytical thinking over time through practice in every decision scenario; in every problem-solving situation and then by reflecting on what you have done to develop analytical thinking.

CHAPTER 2
BENEFITS OF ANALYTICAL THINKING

Improving your systems thinking skills is no small feat; it has several benefits to make you a more effective problem solver: analytical skills make you marketable: this is one of the most measurable and practical benefits of improving your analytical and systems thinking skills.

With improved analytical skills, you would be more marketable, desirable at the same time.

Now, if you already have your dream job, great! Learning these skills will help you shine in the eyes of your employer and allow you to work better in less time.

However, learning to develop systems thinking skills will definitely help you achieve this role you were looking for if you don't have your dream job.

Put a few analytical skills on your resume, and your future boss will be very impressed.

Analytical skills help you to better solve the problem: an effective and imaginative problem solver allows you to quickly address even the most daunting cognitive problems. In fact, when you know how data can be digested, relevant information extracted and a creative solution created, nothing can stand in the way of what you want.

Effective problem solving at home, at work or for a personal project would motivate you to succeed tomorrow.

Strategic thinking is encouraged through analytical skills: What is systems thinking? It is a type of intellectual discipline that emphasizes the rational synthesis of knowledge to generate informed thought and action.

It means that we can interact with knowledge, experience, and even others without our reactivity so often. The more conscious we are, the less reactive we are, we love, we love. And as we begin to think objectively, we pave the way for stronger interpersonal relationships.

Improve Analytical Skills

An ideal way to further improve your systemic thinking skills is to download a brain training application to test your cognitive skills.

You can access several approved applications to develop your analytical skills:

- Brightness
- Raise
- Eidetic
- Wizard
- Happily
- Brain Wave

Learn something new every day: get into the habit of learning something new every day.

Most of us, once completed with education, are much more passive in our research. We read when we need to, we learn new skills, but we never try emotional and cognitive stimulation entirely on our own.

Well, strive to know something that excites your passions every day. Go online and find a topic that has always fascinated you. Talk to an expert in a field you are interested in. Go out and expand your knowledge base the day before by knowing something you didn't know.

Join a book club: reading is a powerful aid to our thinking skills; reading materials we don't normally collect will teach us a lot.

Therefore, not only can you read more by joining the book club, but you can also participate in direct feedback and discussion at the book club meetings. You have the opportunity to discuss theoretical study, analyze metaphors, and unpack symbolism.

You can even make some friends in the process!

Volunteer in new projects: If you are interested in a certain analytical skill, why not volunteer for a project that involves this skill?

Sometimes, we need a little bit of inner drive to get into something different. We can't expect anything in our lap just yet. We should be able to go out and do it ourselves from time to time.

If you want to learn new analytical skills to apply to your arsenal, volunteer for the projects and activities that will get you to training first!

Take an online course: first, you will determine what appeals to you most, if you want to develop your analytical skills.

Keep in mind that you may already have some of the above analytical skills. Everyone has different strengths and weaknesses, so it is important to decide where you are.

It is better to challenge yourself with something you are not so sure about.

Why? If we follow what we already know, we cannot discover something new, nor do ourselves any favors.

If you really want to develop your analytical arsenal, then you have to try something you haven't learned yet.

Maybe you would like to develop your research skills. Maybe you would like to try your hand at data processing and reporting.

If you want, do some work to see what you can find online.

You will take a face-to-face course near here. And you can sign up for distance learning from the comfort of your home.

You will take a constructive approach to developing your analytical skills. So, decide for yourself what you want, and go for it!

Your passion for success is the secret to increasing your systems thinking skills and developing your analytical skills.

You can prepare for tomorrow's triumphs, but only if you find the door to pass through can you take the appropriate steps to open it.

Each of us can do amazing and wonderful things.

So what would you like to do with your future? The person you want to be is a calculated and focused action.

Think about where you want to change the most. Define your weaknesses, define your strengths. Find your strengths, find your weaknesses. And become stronger than you ever dreamed before.

CHAPTER 3
HOW TO USE ANALYTICAL SKILLS

Gather and Analyze Information

In most cases, we fear new challenges because of how others will perceive us. As such, it is primarily the perception others have of us and not the individual's willingness to accept the challenge. For this reason, you should be socially competent in gathering information and analyzing the context of important details to direct your actions. You should learn to understand and respond appropriately to the particular emotions of the people with whom you interact. Go beyond that and be sensitive to the signals that convey that information such as what people's interests are. It is through those actions that you will learn to time the moment to give the person space or continue to engage with them. As you might expect, emotional intelligence is vital to correctly infer what others are feeling; you must be able to identify and label your individual experience accurately. Most men tend to fail at this. By gathering complete information about the context, you are likely to feel confident enough to confront it.

Building Resilience and Adaptability

A common mistake that most writings make regarding ways to improve one's life is to rush to list the do's and don'ts, while overlooking the fundamentals of what builds resilience and adaptability. Human beings are social beings, and the constriction of the social aspects of a human being will generate frustrations, personality problems and challenges related to knowledge. A unique aspect of ideal social attributes is that one must actively participate in social contexts to develop, refine, and apply social skills. Against this backdrop, one must surround oneself with others to create a rich supply of opportunities to observe interactions and improve one's social behaviors. Social interactions allow you to gradually build your resilience and adaptability to new challenges.

Engaging Conversations

Related to this, we are afraid to take on new challenges because of the horrible experiences of the past. If at some point you struggle to join a

166

conversation and it backfired because your comments are uncomfortable or because others simply abort the conversation as soon as you join. New tasks require meeting new people, working in different places and locations. All of these encounters come with diversity issues in terms of gender, sex, ethnicity, religious affiliations, and socioeconomic status. Navigating conversations in places rich in diversity calls requires one to determine the baseline of content and ways to express it. As such, for one to continually improve, one must learn to restrain oneself and respect oneself when participating in conversations.

Conduct experiments with life in search mode. Build frameworks and processes that can simplify your life. Identify patterns and see why some things repeat.

Perform certain types of intellectual tasks - logical thinking, math, etc.

Accomplish Things

Trust is developed in achievement. With this in mind, learn to segment your tasks so that you complete the small modules of the entire task and record satisfaction. When you feel satisfied, you feel more energized and motivated to continue working. When given a new task, find a way to break it down into smaller tasks and then solve or complete the smaller blocks and process the satisfaction by saying, "Wow, I did that!" However, remember that not everyone realizes and feels happy with their success and is said to exhibit the impostor syndrome. The impostor syndrome manifests itself when an individual persistently feels that he is inadequate and unqualified to perform a task, even when he is exemplary in his performance and will blame himself for the failure of others. Another way to achieve success is to set goals, and once these are met, gradually add new ones.

Track Your Progress

The best way to build an improvement is to monitor its progress, and this requires breaking large tasks into pieces. If you don't break a big task into smaller pieces called modules, you won't notice when you're making small gains or getting stuck. Against this backdrop, you're likely to feel depressed about not accomplishing or not making an impact when, in the real sense, you're achieving success. Since achievement is linked to self-confidence, you need to break a task down into modules and track your performance by module. Sometimes it is difficult to break down a task, and in this case, one should try to quantify the task or progress.

Do the Correct Thing

A society lives based on a value system, and individual members make their decisions based on that value system even when some decisions are against the best interests of the person. By aligning oneself closely with this value system, one will earn admiration and receive acceptance, all of which contributes to increased trust.

Physical Exercise

The recommended physical exercise will help improve memory retention, concentration and stress management, as well as minimize depression. Less physical energy means you have depleted your emotional energy, and this minimizes the risk of stress or depression. In addition, exercise helps improve your overall health, making you feel more prepared for an appearance in public and ready to perform a task. For example, mastering the art of deep breathing in and out can help you manage temperament problems. Running is a great way to distract your mind from thinking too much about a mistake you made at work yesterday. Some exercises are related to spiritual nourishment such as Yoga, which can help you meditate and at the same time dispense intense emotional energy.

Communicate Your Opinion and Stand

Most people mistakenly assume that expressing their position and defining boundaries will be taken as rude, but this is not so. Striving allows people to know what is comfortable for you and what can push you to break. In simple terms, exercising your position allows others to gauge your resistance and take it into account when interacting with you. Most people prefer to abandon or give up new positions when faced with situations where they have to communicate their limits. It is a common mistake to want to appear very versatile and gifted as well as humble, but this is a flaw. Learning to communicate your position is important because it shows that you understand your personality and your competencies.

Think Long-Term

One of the biggest shortcomings for most people is the lack of a long-term strategy. The short-term strategy can be misleading. For example, if you see a colleague who promotes himself as the most improved, then you should not wait to get similar recognition in a month or two. The improvement shown by your colleague was probably the culmination of years of commitment and gradual adjustments. Focusing on getting a similar improvement in a few months is short term and costly. Instead, you should think long term and begin to review what your career growth plan is - your assessment of progress against your personal career growth plan and a feedback on where your passion lies. If you are doing a job that aligns with your passion, then you are likely to find the job satisfying and easy. Most people in third world countries can take jobs that are at odds with their hobbies and passions because of a lack of alternative ways to earn income, and for that person, performance problems are largely attributable to the wrong career.

Exercise

Imran is a 25-year-old male student at Ripple Music Company. Imran has all the qualifications required for the job, but due to the increasing need for perfect work and shorter deadlines, Imran has felt that he is not qualified enough. Recently, Ripple Music Company opened a record company subsidiary in Iowa and appointed Imran as operations manager, which is a promotion from his current position. However, Imran felt inadequate to accept the new challenge due to past experiences when supervising other employees who considered him to be strict, and separately Imran felt that he was not recording success with the project even though the company management was satisfied with his efforts. Using the guidelines provided here, design a customized plan for Imran to grow in confidence and address his other weaknesses.

Being More Efficient

Devise Ways of Handling Failure

We all fear negative feedback on a mental and external level. For example, we dislike negative emotions about ourselves or others, such as anger, sadness, and indecision. Since these negative feelings are mostly undesirable in the workplace, we learn to mask them and have poor strategies for navigating these emotions or activities that generate them. For example, short deadlines cause one to break down and show outbursts of anger. Failure in itself is not unusual, nor is it entirely bad, but it is the associated feelings and feedback that create problems.

The proven way to handle failure is to exhibit resistance. One way to build resilience is controlled exposure in which we nurture individual situations that precipitate failure and let the individual get used to encountering failure and then guide the person to build mental resistance. Another way of building resilience is the practice of prevention in which the affected individual talks about failure before others notice it. Anticipation gives the affected person control over negative feedback, which disables the reaction or perception that the report might have had without the affected individual sharing it first.

Another way to build resilience is to learn ways to safely process negative feedback. For example, learning not to take negative feedback personally. Although all of these suggestions seem easy, they are the most difficult to exhibit, as negative emotions occur in situations that we associate with attempts to violate our rights and dignity, and naturally, we return the fire. However, through sustained practice and exposure to situations that provoke your emotions, you will develop ways to process negative emotions safely.

Defuse Disagreements

Any human interaction will trigger conflict. Recently, conflicts in the workplace are increasing due to the continued emphasis on making the workplace diverse. In the contemporary workplace, we have workers of all genders, ethnicities, socioeconomic status, and religious affiliations. The rich diversity makes it complex to have simple interactions like commenting on a new article, and parenting becomes complex. Increasing diversity in the workplace contributes to the problems that lead to conflict. In order to continually improve, one must learn ways to defuse disagreements when they occur. Most people give up or refuse new tasks if they feel unable to deal with the disagreements that occur.

CHAPTER 4
EMPATHY AND ANALYTICAL SKILLS

Being empathetic implies having an understanding of the emotional point of view of others. It is critical to understand the emotions of those with whom we interact because it helps to respond to the situation at hand and instills more useful behavior. This improves cooperation and mutual understanding in the workplace, resulting in personal and professional development of the workforce.

The following tips can help practice empathy, which is an important skill of an emotionally intelligent individual.

Put Yourself in Other's Shoes

Although it's easier said than done, it helps to put yourself in the other person's shoes to understand their point of view and empathize with them. This can be extremely helpful in conflicting situations where, most of the time, the root of the disagreement lies in insensitivity to the feelings of the other party.

When your boss is irritated after a recent breakup, take a minute to think about how you would have felt if you had faced a similar situation in your life. Or maybe your co-worker is annoying because he actually feels very lonely in his life.

Think about it!

Be an Artful Critique

The concept of an art critic, as put forward by Harry Levinson, argues that a critic should focus on what a person has done wrong in a specific setting rather than attacking his character and thus encourage him to act defensively. When a person becomes defensive, all attention in the conversation shifts to an attack and defense mode. This makes the confrontation futile as the recipient thinks his or her mistakes cannot be fixed and therefore becomes discouraged. This skill can be especially valuable to the leadership that takes on the critical task of evaluating employees.

To be an art critic, you must practice the following:

Be Specific

Let people know exactly where they have gone wrong in a specific scenario. Avoid generalization, as it simply confuses the other person.

Offer Solution

Once you have pointed out a mistake, you must move on to possible ways to fix it. Refer to techniques and possibilities that the condemned person may not know about, so that he or she leaves the room with the proper knowledge of how to turn things around.

Be Present

It is more effective to offer criticism in person and in private. People are less likely to become defensive when they are informed of their deficiencies away from the public eye and given the opportunity to clarify.

Be Sensitive

While the entire practice of art criticism revolves around empathy, being sensitive when you offer a critique is to apply it in letter and spirit. Appreciate the fact that the recipient has emotions too and offer feedback in a way that doesn't hurt feelings.

Respect Their Opinion

Always make the other person feel appreciated and listened to when you let them know that you recognize their opinion no matter what they disagree with. Listening to and validating the opinion of others says a lot about your ability to be empathetic and the best part is that you don't necessarily have to agree with someone to be compassionate to them. Respecting someone's point of view simply means that you realize that everyone comes from a different background and has unique experiences that shape their opinions and thoughts.

To give you a practical illustration, in the future, when a co-worker makes a sarcastic comment about your work, simply let them know that you respect their opinion without being offended and they will leave without further comment.

It's that simple.

Turn Around That Self-Focus

This is just another way of looking at the above points, where I try to preach the benefits of recognizing the perspectives of those with whom you interact. When your focus is limited to yourself, you tend to ignore the views of others. This can be detrimental to your development and success as a professional as it may alienate people because they see you as an egocentric person. In addition, an unwavering fixation on yourself robs you of the opportunity to benefit from the valuable opinion of others.

The best way to be less self-centered is to try to listen to people and pay attention to them. Strive not to cut them off during conversations and listen patiently. Recognize that sometimes people may have a better alternative or perspective and may see things differently and more competently than you do.

Practice Humility

Being humble allows you to be more empathetic to people and understand their feelings better. This is particularly useful for leadership, as you need to be humble enough to lead teams effectively while having some firmness in your behavior to maintain authority.

Being humble instills the ability to receive feedback with an open mind, admit mistakes when they are made, and help leadership work alongside subordinates as they improve and learn from their mistakes. Therefore, it creates an environment that supports learning and is forgiving when people are out of line.

The practice of humility connects with all the points I have mentioned above. It makes you put yourself in someone else's shoes, respect their opinion and avoid focusing too much on yourself, all of which can help you advance in your career.

Social Skills: Heard of Networking Before?

It is essentially one's social skill in practice. Just as socializing is the key to our existence in society, social skills can have a great impact on how we do in the work environment. They help build strong and meaningful working relationships, bring out the internal team player, and facilitate networking. They also support effective communication and help leadership form and eventually lead exceptional teams.

Here are some tips on how to work on your social skills so you can excel in the workplace:

Work on Your Communication Skills

Communication is critical to making your social skills shine. In fact, it's the foundation of your social skills, which don't make sense without it. However, don't confuse communication with being a charlatan. Effective communication involves being a good listener, speaking clearly, being inquisitive to ensure that all points have been interpreted correctly, selecting the most appropriate communication channel according to the nature of the message and the ability to appear assertive, but not combative.

Some tips for effective communication include making sure to make eye contact, being attentive (sneaking a phone call every two seconds won't help!) and really listening to what the other person has to say without getting defensive.

Also, since there is a lot of email correspondence going on in a work environment, make sure you work on your writing skills to fill in any gaps and write clearly and professionally.

Regard Others

No one likes to interact with a person who talks about their passions endlessly without giving the other person a chance to switch to topics of mutual interest. This is related to empathy, which is the realization that others also have a perspective and that it is important to keep that perspective in mind. Without this awareness, there can be no meaningful interactions.

When talking to someone, try to redirect the conversation to occasionally ask how they feel about a certain topic and then listen carefully so you can give your opinion when necessary. Don't act like you're talking to robots. Treat others as you would like to be treated yourself.

Your Gestures Count

You may have had an encounter with someone at some point when you thought their body language was a little strange. To give you some perspective, how would you feel if someone presented an electrifying idea with a completely indifferent attitude? How surprising would this be?

What's more, how would you get others excited about your idea when they presented it themselves as if it were none of their business?

Having proper body language is critical in the workplace because people use it as a lens to perceive you. You can be seen as a shy person who hides in the woods or as an extremely confident individual who kills you based on how you behave. This can have a direct impact on the quality and quantity of your social interactions and will determine the type of tribe you will attract, ultimately playing a critical role in your growth and career advancement.

Therefore, it is suggested that you focus on your body language in the office. Watch your facial expressions, maintain eye contact and good posture, keep your arms at your sides instead of crossing them, keep your hands where they can be seen and do not drag your feet while walking.

I will not lie. There's a pretty basic etiquette there.

Customize Your Interactions

Just as you will interact differently with a co-worker than with a boss, you must understand that people must be treated differently. This concept is based on the fact that people have different personalities and come from diverse cultural backgrounds. Furthermore, they belong to different hierarchical levels in the power structure of the organization.

There is also the fact that people have different personalities. This implies that they can be more or less understanding, compassionate, intelligent and conscientious. These factors can have a direct impact on your interactions with them, so it is suggested that you know the person you are interacting with well. This can help you modify your interactions to their specific personality type and prevent you from approaching everyone in a similar way.

Learn Persuasion

You may never have thought about persuasion like this before, but it can help enormously with your social skills. It is the ability to convince people of your point of view based on reasoning that is seemingly infallible. This skill can help you create strong bonds with people and connect with them on a deeper level.

Learn the precious art of persuasion by employing the use of powerful words supported by powerful reasoning, find common ground to explore mutual interests, do favors and offer help whenever you can, and catch the perfect moment to interact with the target individual.

Over time, you will see your social skills flourish and your networks become stronger.

Be Famous for the Right Reasons

While it is quite obvious that people avoid a person with a bad reputation, it is also true that they are attracted to those they believe they can trust and who can provide a valuable opinion.

Be that person. Develop and protect your trust, be a problem solver and face emotionally charged situations with calm and serenity. Also, be the person who tries to find the best possible solution for all involved and who sees the conflict as an opportunity to come out stronger and to know people better.

Over time, you will attract the right people based on your reputation and have a strong network of valuable individuals in your place.

CHAPTER 5
PRO DECISION-MAKING

Do all smart, successful people suffer as much as we normal people do when it comes to making decisions?

Probably yes, but they also have some tactics and secrets that could help them make the right decision, or at least not spend weeks worrying about it. Finding those secrets can be difficult, but we've compiled a list of secrets from experts that could make decision making much easier for you.

Forward Thinking

This is not only a secret of experts, but also a habit practiced by all successful people around the world. As an expert in high-performance leadership, Dr. Paul Schempp puts it this way: "Those who think about the future look for solutions, but those who think about the past look for justifications. As you read this, your eyes are probably glowing. You know a lot of people like that, and you might even be one of them. In fact, we have all been there many times.

When a new iPhone comes on the market, you think about the past and go buy it. You find justifications after making the purchase - my current phone is getting old, it won't have software updates, and so on. You do this instead of thinking ahead and trying to find out how this new iPhone will solve a problem for you. We do the same with the important decisions in our lives. You see managers firing employees because they had an argument. Then they try to justify it by blaming the employee's behavior, instead of looking forward and thinking critically about whether or not that employee was an asset that should have been left to continue working.

As Dr. Schempp explains, great decision makers take their time at first to identify the problem and look for solutions. This helps them make quick and efficient decisions once they have identified the problem and its root causes. In short, a lagging decision maker focuses on the symptoms. Instead of asking why the employee became stressed and raised his voice, he fires him because he went too far. A forward thinking decision maker would ask the employee what is stressing him/her and why his/her behavior has changed. This, in turn, will help them make an appropriate decision about the situation that might actually resolve things.

Leverage Your Core Values

Professor of decision making, Dr. Joe Arvai, on the other hand, believes that the reason many people are unable to make good decisions is that we rarely think about the big picture. We dwell on the smaller points and the subtext. He also sees that people fail to make the connection between the decision being made and their own set of values and beliefs.

He believes that decisions are mirrors that reflect our beliefs and values, and as such, we need to make decisions based on them. "Decisions define who you are as a person," adds Dr. Arvai. He explains that by making your values a basis for your decisions, you will be able to determine your goals and objectives, propose options from which to choose, determine the consequences of your decision, and finally decide whether there are any trade-offs. When you do everything related to your values, decision making becomes exponentially easier, because every choice you make has a solid foundation and reasonable justification.

This brings us back to the importance of critical thinking, as it is the only way you will be able to determine your own values and beliefs. Questioning everything and learning to think critically about everything around you will help you determine a set of core values and beliefs. When you begin to introduce these into your decision making, difficult decisions will no longer be so difficult.

Learn from Your past Decisions

Believe it or not, one of the best secret weapons for better decision making is failing some. But the ones that do fail will teach you a lot. We are programmed to fear failure, and it is often our worst enemy, but is it really? Self-development guru Tony Robbins advocates the importance of learning from your past decisions in order to make better decisions in the future.

He emphasizes the importance of having contingency plans, so you don't lose out altogether. Everyone makes decisions, and not all of them will be the right ones. But successful people always have a backup plan to protect their investment, whether it's time, money or effort.

When you have a safety net, then nothing can go terribly wrong with your decision, even if it doesn't go as expected. When you use your past decisions as mentors, you can better prepare for future ones.

Balanced Knowledge

For the millionth time, we will talk for a minute about knowledge and the importance of knowing all the facts about a decision you are about to make. But can it backfire? Is there such a thing as knowing too much? Well, according to Mikael Krogerus and Roman Tschappeler in a very popular TEDx talk, yes, too much knowledge can lead to confusion and impair your judgment. In fact, these experts say that if you compare the brain scan image of a person who knows too little and another who knows too much about a decision to be made, they would be the same. So, in other words, they are both equally confused and unable to make a meaningful decision.

This may be explained by the problem of "choice overload," where our brain cannot decide because we are faced with too many options. Too much knowledge can put too many options on the table, and in turn, confuse you when you try to make a decision. That's why Krogerus and Tschappeler recommend having enough knowledge to limit your options, whether it's the Netflix movie you're going to see that night or important life decisions. Once you feel you've covered all your bases thoroughly, then you should make the decision.

The experts also explain the importance of not being a perfectionist when making decisions. Learn to be satisfied. You cannot make the perfect decision, but you can make the best decision possible within your abilities, and that is what you should strive for instead of perfection. Was there a better option? Possibly. Could you have done better? If you thought critically about the problem from all angles and did everything right, then probably not. So, don't stop at the idea of perfection and make a decision.

Trust Numbers, Not Gut Feelings

People tend to overestimate the accuracy of their feelings. You see a businessman telling you that it was his intuition that led them to make the deal with an important client, and the gambler telling you that it was his instinct that made them win the jackpot. Poker champion Liv Boeree has a different take on this. She believes that our feelings are great, but not for "the everyday things we have a lot of experience with. This applies to intuition, like knowing whether or not your loved one is angry, without him or her saying so or feeling that the roads will be crowded today.

She argues that logic and analysis - in other words, critical thinking - are much better suited to life's big decisions. Changing jobs, choosing a career, choosing spouses, and all those important decisions are best left to numbers and careful analysis. Boeree adds that our intuition is important, but when making an important decision, be meticulous and thorough. Don't trust your instinct, because it's never enough to make such important decisions.

CHAPTER 6
ORGANIZATION

You may be thinking, is organization really necessary? I've made it this far in my life without it.

You do the work, you manage your house, but you don't really have any system. Everything happens as if nothing happened.

Would it be fair to guess that sometimes things go wrong? Sometimes things go astray. Sometimes it takes you a long time to find a particular document on your laptop, or an item in your house? Sometimes there are innocent misunderstandings among people about who is supposed to be where and when.

Sound familiar?

If so, then maybe integrating a sustainable organizational system will help improve the quality of your life and work.

In short, yes, you need a system.

Problem #1: Not Following Plans and Systems

Okay, let's say you tried to get organized. You accepted that you needed a system. You even implemented a system. And then everything went to hell.

Another problem we have in being organized is following the systems we choose for ourselves. Like buying a gym membership and then not attending, sometimes we install certain software and then never use it. We put a family activity board in the fridge, fill it out, and then never update it. We have problems with tracking.

We can make intricate and detailed plans, but somehow they don't seem to stick. Sometimes we succeed with our systems for a week, a few weeks, or even a few months, but then something changes, and our system is forgotten, discarded.

You can organize your office desk. Put all your pens in a decorative mug. Buy a three-level paper organizer for different types of documents and have small notes ready to scribble on when needed. Three weeks later, when a major client threatens to cancel his account and your team is caught up in a holding presentation frenzy, your desk becomes a war zone once again. Maybe you'll clean it up again in a month when the stress subsides, or maybe not. However, the clean and clutter cycle is not a system of organization.

We need to make systems that are sustainable and adaptable so that we can retain them through the ups and downs of our lives. A good system helps you navigate through a stressful or chaotic situation and does not force you to abandon it in times of stress.

We need good systems, and we need to commit to them.

Problem #2: Staying Organized Is Super Stressful

If you were stressed, it may be the reason why you have not been able to commit to a sustainable system of organization. Some of us believe that maintaining the organization is inherently stressful.

That is not true. Let's compare a system of organization to a haircut.

If you get a haircut at a terrible salon, you will sit in the chair and watch in horror as your hair is cut and destroyed. You will be stressed and sorry, and you will swear never to trust anyone with your hair again.

On the contrary, if you go to a salon you trust, cutting your hair can be a fun and enjoyable pampering and beauty experience.

If your system is bad, it will cause you stress, but a good system can reduce your stress.

If you think being organized is stressful, you've probably been a victim of bad systems, but that doesn't mean you can't start over with better systems.

Besides the fact that thought systems are inherently stressful, there is another similar myth. "I just don't have time to do it. "I'm too busy to be organized." "There's too much to do."

At this point, you can probably see the flaw in this thinking. A bad system would be a waste of time, but a good system will give you back your time. A good scheduling system reduces administrative work, a good communications application reduces time spent on bad communications, and so on. Good systems are good because they take some of the work out of you, and allow you to concentrate on the meat of whatever it is you are doing.

Proper filing systems and documentation protocols save countless hours of searching for information, documents and notes. If you find your system stressful, try a different one. But don't give up on organizational systems altogether.

Problem #3: Organized People Are No-Fun Tight-Asses

The last reason we don't want to be organized is because we think organized people are not fun.

We want to be the carefree, carefree, open-minded friend, not the folder hug, the big glasses, the friend who is not fun.

But there's no rule that says organized people can't be carefree. Of course, they have functional systems to manage their home, work, life and time, and they're also fun and open-minded.

We tend to want to box people into easily sorted boxes, but that simply doesn't reflect our complex reality. Lawyers can be dancers, accountants can be poets, and you can be organized while being fun (to say nothing of your ass).

Target Results

Target #1: Enhanced Learning and Working Capacity

So now you know why we are not all wizards of the organization.

But why should we be?

First of all, we should get organized because it will help us do more things. We become much more efficient and effective when we have the right organizational systems.

Instead of having to do mundane and repetitive tasks, we can focus on what is important. Organization helps us to clear our minds and spaces of unnecessary information clutter, leaving room for a greater capacity to learn and work.

Let's take something as simple as a WhatsApp family group. Instead of having to call three different family members to ask them what they want for dinner, you can post it in one place and have everyone respond, as they see it, from their phones. This is a functional organizational system that helps you be more efficient.

How about a low-tech example like a calendar manuscript? Elementary school students are told to write all their upcoming homework, assignments, and tests in an agenda planner. Their parents know that after school, instead of pulling out all of their child's writing and looking for teacher comments or assignments, they can look in one place and have all the information they need readily available to them. That's a system of organization that reduces stress, saves time and minimizes communication errors.

Today, we tend to think of systems as high-tech software that we have to learn to use, but it doesn't have to be that way. An organizational system is any process that helps to organize people, activities, space or time.

Target #2: Enhanced Self-Control

Secondly, when you are an organized person, you tend to have more self-control. This stems from the feeling that you have control over the situation and therefore have control over yourself.

Sometimes life gets away from us and we become stressed, overwhelmed and feel like we are being reactive and cannot keep up with everything we are supposed to be doing. Systems protect us from that feeling. With good systems in place, we can manage our tasks and time, and not feel like we are struggling and barely surviving.

Since we feel more in control of the situation and our lives, that greater control filters down to our own willpower, and we also feel more in control of ourselves. We don't need to live reactively. We can live in a more orderly and organized way.

Target #3: Enhanced Ability to Assimilate New Challenges

Finally, life is not always predictable. Crises happen. Good and surprising things also happen. And we have to deal with them.

People tend to think that systems are rigid but, in fact, systems can be flexible and very helpful in handling new and stressful situations.

A good system allows us to deal with unexpected events and circumstances.

For example, Margaret works at a law firm downtown, and was scheduled to argue a case in court the same morning her son Matthew got the flu and her partner Dave was out of town. She can't go to court. Hopefully, her firm had redundancy systems in place so that another lawyer could step in and take Margaret's place.

But unexpected events are not always bad.

For example, Jill runs a graphic design firm and suddenly has good press and her orders are skyrocketing. That's an exceptional event that would test her systems, but it's not a negative event; her business is booming. Their systems must be able to handle a massive flow of incoming orders. You may have a contingency plan with independent designers waiting for you to call in to help complete the orders.

Your systems should be able to handle new challenges, both good and bad, as they arise.

CHAPTER 7
MAKING RIGHT DECISIONS

"We know there is a painful gap...between being aware of tremendous problems and challenges in the workplace and developing the internal power and moral authority to break out of those problems and become a significant force in solving them."

– Stephen Covey

Part of Self-Management Is Solving Problems

Self-control is a process.

This process begins with the expansion of our self-awareness.

The second stage is self-management. Although there are so many areas that we need to manage to achieve self-mastery, three main areas contribute the most toward personal mastery. These three areas of focus include:

a. Knowingly regulating emotions,

b. Manage time and energy wisely, and

c. Solve problems and make correct decisions.

If we develop these three essential soft skills, of possibly many other soft skills, our opportunity to manage and achieve self-mastery is within our reach.

Regulating emotions and managing time and energy, respectively.

Solve problems and make correct decisions.

Part of self-management is the development of our ability to cope with the problems we face and make the right decisions, which in turn allow us to release our potential and achieve our unique greatness.

Mastering Problem Solving to Realize Your Greatness

Until we develop the ability to solve problems and make correct decisions, we are far from achieving personal mastery. The problems we face daily stand in our way and prevent us from succeeding unless we creatively solve them and make the right decisions. If we hesitate to make difficult decisions or make bad decisions, we can get stuck in one place too long, or at least be unable to move forward and make progress. In this state, achieving self-mastery is unthinkable. Without developing the mindset, attitude and skills needed to solve problems and make right decisions, one cannot be in charge and free. There is a huge gap.

In his writing "The Eighth Habit: From Effectiveness to Greatness," Stephen Covey spoke of the existence of a gap. He wrote, "Between possessing great potential and living a life of greatness and contribution. Covey suggested that we fill the gap by developing the ability to get out of trouble if our desire is to realize our personal greatness.

Decision-Making Is a Part of Problem-Solving

There is a clear link between problem solving and decision making. Problem solving goes hand in hand with decision making. Robert Schuller stated. He further reasoned, "Unless problem solving leads to decision making, then what you are dealing with is not a problem.

Helen Reynolds and Mary Tramel expressed this in clear terms. They explained, "Decision-making is really a part of problem solving. There would be no decisions to make if there were no problems to solve. Problem solving consists of three operations: Problem analysis, decision making, and action."

When we lose this vision, we are unable to solve the problems that are in front of us all the time, just waiting for our decision. Henry Ford noted, "Most people spend more time and energy on problems than on trying to solve them. Jim Citrin identified what happens when we fail to make decisions to solve problems, "Uncertainty can lead to paralysis. And if you become indecisive, you're dead.

Paul was happy to give Dan a second chance.

Surprise! Dan received a call from Paul. He asked, "How are you, Dan?" Dan was surprised to get the call from the CEO and wondered why he had called. "Thanks for asking. I'm doing fine, sir!"

There was a brief silence. Paul proceeded, "How is the social skills development program treating you?" "I love it," Dan responded with excitement. Paul asked a follow-up question, "Has it been helpful to you? Dan assured Paul that he had liked the program very much up to this point and revealed, "As you may recall, I was hesitant at first. I've been wondering why I didn't go to it a long time ago.

They both smiled and laughed out loud.

Paul was so happy to know that Dan found the program very useful. He asked a specific question: "What was your last workshop about?" Dan quickly responded: "It was about solving problems and making right decisions. "Wow! Would you mind sharing with me a thing or two of what you learned in the workshop?" Paul asked politely.

Dan said, "Sure, why not," as he thought about what to share. Despite the fact that he had so many ideas, Dan decided to share with Paul the one thing he thought would resonate.

Dan cleared his throat. "I've learned so many things, but one thing I'd like to share with you is the idea I have that there is no problem big enough that we can't solve. I realized that it is possible to break big problems into small, manageable problems and solve them one at a time."

Paul agreed. "Knowing that we can solve any problem that comes our way takes away our stress, especially when we are faced with daunting problems. Thanks for sharing, Dan!"

No Big Problems That Cannot Be Handled

There is no problem we can't handle. Industrialist Henry Ford said, "Nothing is particularly difficult if you break it down into small jobs." As the pioneer who made cars affordable to the masses, he overcame insurmountable challenges by breaking them down. That's why he said, "There are no big problems; there are only many small problems. Similarly, Richard Sloma advised, "Never try to solve all the problems at once - get them lined up for you, one by one."

After chatting for a couple more minutes about other things in the project, they concluded their phone conversation. Once Paul got off the phone, he took a brief moment to reflect on the progress Dan had shown, and he was so happy that he was given a second chance.

Key Lessons

Embracing Problems

Dan began. "The most important lesson I learned was the importance of having the right mindset to succeed in problem solving and making right decisions. Rafael paid a compliment. "This is a great foundation. Dan continued, "Without this foundation, we will not take positive steps to work and enjoy the process as we solve problems and make decisions. We realized that many people see problems as:

- Bad things,

- Misfortunes, and

- Things to fear, to hate, to avoid at all costs.

Rafael remained silent for Dan to continue.

"I have had these opinions for a long time. These perspectives prevented me from consciously developing the soft skills needed to turn problems into opportunities. I have been defensive and reactive, in most cases. My concern has always been to get rid of problems as quickly as possible without taking enough time to understand them and eventually solve them properly.

Rafael reassured Dan. "Dealing with problems is not a bad thing all the time. To the extent that we set high goals for ourselves and try to move forward in life and our profession, we are forced to face problems and make difficult decisions. As we move forward to live up to our potential, problems come our way 'to prove' if we are up to and worthy of reaching our individual and collective goals.

Dan nodded and commented, "You're right. It's in our nature to set big goals. We must anticipate facing big problems as we pursue our goals. "They are two sides of the same coin! Rafael added.

To turn problems into assets, we need the right attitude toward problems. Theodore Rubin said, "The problem is not that there are problems. The problem is to expect the opposite and to think that having problems is a problem.

"Maybe it's better not to set big goals to avoid attracting big problems. Dan joked.

They both laughed.

Rafael quit. "Well, even though goals attract trouble, we shouldn't refrain from setting big goals just because they tend to attract massive problems. The alternative is not pretty. If we just fold our hands and stand by while life goes on, well, we don't have to worry about problems. They don't care about the people on that side of the fence.

Dan chose one side. With a wide smile and in a playful way, he said, "I prefer to be on the side of the fence where problems are frequent.

Problems Are Blessings in Disguise

Dan moved on. "The second lesson I learned was to accept problems as blessings in disguise. The more problems we have, the more opportunities we have to grow and improve individually and collectively.

Rafael liked Dan's perspective. He then shared his own experience. "I have witnessed in my journey that my significant growth came every time I overcame a problem. I firmly believe that every problem we face collectively is also destined to lead to another level of growth as a team. We have either arrived or lost if our life is free of problems and challenges.

The Future Is for Problem Solvers

The more problems we face, the more we develop our ability to solve them. This soft skill is in high demand now and in the future. The World Economic Forum, in its Report on the Future of Jobs, revealed that Complex Problem Solving is the main skill needed to succeed in 2020. In the report, this same skill is currently at the top. Therefore, to succeed now and in the future, we must continually develop and refine this soft skill.

CHAPTER 8
COMMUNICATION

Good communication is imperative in any environment where humans interact, but when it comes to the workplace, communication is even more critical because it is a crucial influence on business success. Success in business refers to having an organized team working to achieve organizational goals, meet production objectives, keep production costs low, have healthy internal relationships and relate well to customers. Securing market share is also part of business success, and is the result of all systems working well together, often because people communicate well.

Other benefits of good communication include:

- Makes employees more engaged: Communication connects people in the organization to a single purpose and goal. If the goal is clear, employees understand what they must do to achieve it.

- Makes the workforce more productive: Communication is a key factor in workforce productivity because it promotes understanding of each member's skills and talents and encourages creativity and innovation. Therefore, organizational planning is done taking into account the points of excellence of each employee. If the results are all excellent, then the company and its workforce will be productive.

- Avoid misunderstandings with customers: With excellent communication, customer needs and preferences will be clear, the customer will feel heard and understood, new information will be presented in a way that all parties can understand, and existing conflicts can be quickly resolved.

- Relieves conflict: Misunderstandings, feeling ignored and misunderstood often result in conflict. People also come into conflict when they do not understand how others communicate.

How to Resolve Conflicts

Below is a step-by-step tool to help you resolve conflicts that arise in the workplace, and in other forums involving interaction with people.

1. Do Not Burry the Conflict

When conflicts arise, don't assume they didn't happen, or bury them to avoid talking about them. Unresolved issues are time bombs that build up pressure, and the situation only gets worse over time. Therefore, conflicts should be addressed as soon as they occur so that there are no problems or hurt feelings while people are doing their jobs.

2. Speak with the Other Person

Approach the other party and let them know you are interested in talking about the problem. Invite them to choose a time and place to meet conveniently to discuss what happened. Make sure the place has minimal interruptions, if any, so that you have enough time to talk and solve your problems.

3. Listen

Listening is quite essential because it allows you to see the issue from the other party's perspective. Therefore, listen to what the other party is saying, and be prepared to react. Do not interrupt. Once you are done talking, summarize and restate what you said to seek confirmation, so that you are sure you understood everything that was said. When you need clarification, ask questions.

4. Take Note of the Points of Agreement and Disagreement

With the help of the other party, take note of the issues you agree or disagree with. At the end, ask the person to confirm his or her assessment. Make sure that both parties agree on the areas of conflict that need to be worked on.

5. Discuss Behavior Not Individuals

As you try to find out the causes of the conflict, it is easy to start attacking the personalities of others. Some people say, "I don't like it when you leave papers with sensitive information on your desk when you're away. Instead, they say, "When papers containing sensitive information are left on a desk without supervision, the company stands up to expose our clients' personal information, and we could end up with a lawsuit.

The first statement addresses the person's weaknesses, while the second attacks the fact itself.

6. Develop a List of Priority

Decide on the issues that are most important, and the purpose of working on them first before moving on to the less important ones. When you start discussing the topic, let your attention focus on the future of the company, and how you should work with each other to update the goals of the company.

7. Follow Through with the Plan

Stick to the list of conflict areas, addressing them one by one until you reach the end. Be sure to reach consensus on the solution of a particular issue before you move forward. Throughout, maintain a collaborative attitude so that you remain united, focused and committed to resolving your conflicts.

8. Forgive Quickly

When conflicts are resolved, it is natural to recognize that feelings were hurt, assumptions were made, and ignorant words were spoken. Recognize also that your perspective was wrong (if at all) and thank the other party for helping you see from a new perspective. Tell the person you are sorry and forgive them too. Superficial forgiveness is not enough because it causes resentments that get worse over time and undermine all the progress you have made.

How to Communicate Successfully

Below are some essential skills to help make workplace communication successful:

1. Encourage More One-to-One Conversations and Phone Conversations

Today, people prefer written communication because they are used to writing texts and publishing written content on various social media platforms. As a result, e-mails have become more popular in the workplace. However, if you are in a busy office and everyone decides to send you an email, you would have a fairly large load of emails to review and respond to each one of them would be an equally difficult task. The entire process would also take up a lot of your valuable time. However, if people switched to phone calls and individual conversations, communication would be faster and easier.

2. Encourage Open Discussions

Encourage people in your organization to speak up by letting them know that everything they say will be heard. Remind them whenever their opinions are important. When people are encouraged to speak, and their opinions are received with respect, they feel appreciated and valued, and they take pride in being part of the organization.

3. Let the Discussions Be Meaningful

If everything that is talked about in your meetings is unnecessary and useless, you will notice that attendance will start to decrease. People begin to lose interest in meetings and discussions because they perceive them as a waste of time. Too often, organizations hold meetings simply because the meeting is scheduled at the usual time. This is not correct. Meetings should be held only when necessary: at other times, communicate your ideas and additional information through phone calls or face-to-face conversations.

If you find that a meeting is still necessary, keep a strict time limit and stick to the agenda.

4. Get Visual Aids

Sometimes, words are not enough to express your point, and you will need a chart or other visual aid to help bring the point home. Use a photo, drawing, graphic, meme or short video to help you get your point across. Most people understand and respond better to visual information. They will also remember visual aids longer than if you just say a few simple words.

5. Be Careful When Wording Emails

It is difficult to interpret the speaker's tone when communication is done through a text. Through this means, your communication can go in any direction. Not surprisingly, the reader interprets in a context for which the writer had no intention. When this happens, people are unnecessarily offended just because they read the information in a particular way, even if it was not the intention. This happens especially in situations where the writer has left room for interpretation by writing in an ambiguous manner. However, if one takes care and is clear about what one is talking about, no one will misinterpret it.

If you must communicate through a written text, make sure you correct it to ensure that it delivers the tone you intended. Also, confirm that you use correct spelling, grammar and punctuation, as these can also be interpreted as rude and unprofessional.

6. Let Your Words Be Simple

The reality is that we are not all in the same situation when it comes to vocabulary. Therefore, to make sure everyone understands what you are saying, use simple words. Ambiguous words only lead to misunderstandings and may require you to explain yourself better again, ultimately wasting your precious time.

7. Act Out the Message

It is not until you see someone do something, or do it yourself, that the message behind it is completely absorbed. Words are easily forgotten, but actions, not so much. Acting out what you would want your team to emulate is a very effective method of communication because, first of all, you have shown them that what you want done is possible. Let people see you do what you would want them to do, and they will be challenged to do it. There will be no excuses.

8. Avoid Repetition

If you want to be taken seriously, don't sound like a broken record. Don't keep repeating instructions or trying to beat them with your words, in submission. Give your instructions only once and ask if they are clear to everyone. If some have not understood, repeat your instructions, and when this is done, step aside and let your people go to work. Demand good results and keep busy. That way you will earn their respect, when they do not see you hovering over them all the time, repeating instructions they have already heard.

CHAPTER 9
SOLVING PROBLEMS

Problem solving is generally considered from two perspectives. The first perspective is that there is only one solution to the problem at hand. Mathematical problems are a classic case of such problems. If you have an equation with an obscure one, you only have one solution. You cannot have multiple solutions to solve one equation. This type of perception is based on psychometric intelligence. The hindsight are problems that have constantly changing solutions. These are usually social-emotional problems. For example, your favorite shading is a problem because it changes almost constantly, and sometimes it can depend on your state of mind. Another model would be what to get you for your birthday. You may not recognize what you want, or you may want such a significant number of things that you find it difficult to decide.

This is a rational methodology. You must remember that all problems cannot be solved using this methodology. However, this will help you get started and help you work to solve your problem, whatever it is.

Define the Problem

Defining the problem is the most difficult part. We usually tend to stress about the problem before we try to identify what the problem really is. We perceive a problem, which may not really be the problem, and begin to worry about it. Instead, try to define the problem!

Defining the Problem with Assistance from Others

When trying to define the problem, you should ask yourself and others involved in the problem the following questions.

a. What are the causes of the problem? Here you may not identify the main sources in that capacity, but it is a start. You must remember that you are not blaming someone as the reason for the problem just at the beginning. The person may be the reason, but look at what led that person to be the reason for the problem.

b. Where is the problem really occurring?

c. How is the problem occurring?

d. At what specific times is the problem occurring?

e. With whom is the problem occurring?

f. Why is the problem occurring? Here you will need to write down the exact details regarding why the problem is occurring.

Finally, you will need to take a sheet of paper and summarize the answers above. You could start with "The following is not a direct result of".

Defining Complex Problems

In addition, this step requires you to follow steps a-f above. However, since the problem seems overwhelming to you, you will have to separate and simplify it. To define the unpredictable problem in general, repeat steps a - f for these smaller problems.

Verify That You Understand the Problem

Since you are working with others to identify the problem, it is easy to check whether your understanding of the problem is equivalent to that of your peers.

Prioritize Your Problems

In general, we are confusing the important issues with the urgent ones. The important issues are those that must be addressed first.

Sometimes it may be necessary to address multiple issues. You cannot work on all the problems at once, as you would not do justice to any of the issues involved.

Identify Your Role

It is important that you identify your role in the matter. How you perceive your role in the problem has a significant influence on how you perceive someone else's role in the problem. For example, if you are stressed, you may find that everyone else who is part of the problem is stressed. You may be just as quick to accuse someone else. If you feel sorry, you may be forgiving someone else's role in causing the problem. You may end up taking the blame entirely.

Identify Possible Causes to the Problem

There are many things you don't have the slightest idea about. Since you have very little information on the subject in question, you will need the help of your peers. You will need to understand the perspective of the people who are facing the problem just as you do. People may not be happy to provide the information you might be looking for anyway. They may be influenced by others, making it difficult for you to measure the cause of the problem. You may need to get the details separately. You also need to write down your perception of the reasons behind the problem. That way you can think about the different perspectives and then identify the real reason or reasons for the problem.

Try to Identify a Strategy and a Solution

Since you have defined the problem and also identified the causes of the problem, you will have to work on identifying the solutions. If it is a problem that you and a group of people are facing, you can use the brainstorming strategy to identify solutions that will help you solve the problem easily. This strategy cannot always be used. If it is a problem that you face on the personal front, you may not want to involve another person. At that point, you can use the strategy you are most comfortable with.

Select the Most Feasible Solution

You would have identified many solutions to your problems through the step above. Now you will have to select the best approach to solve your problem. You will need to consider the following when identifying the best solution to your problem.

a. Which solution will solve the problem in both the short and long term?

b. Are there risks associated with the solutions?

c. Is using the solution to solve the problem a realistic goal?

d. Is it financially viable?

e. Do we have the time to solve the problem through this method?

If it is a personal problem, it is not necessary to answer the fourth question for obvious reasons. You may find it strange to answer the second question as well. But you must realize that there are risks we may face in life when we try to solve a problem. There may be repercussions to any problem that may have been solved by a particular method.

Plan How You Can Implement Your Most Workable Solution

We will then help you plan how to solve a problem using the most feasible solution.

a. You will have to remember that a coin has two sides. In the same way, a solution used to solve a problem can have two sides. The solution could create a good effect or a bad effect. The consequences - good or bad - for the solution must be carefully considered.

b. What steps should be taken to use that solution?

c. Are there any changes in your systems that may need to be made? If this is a personal issue, you may need to identify if there is anything you need to change about yourself to overcome the problem.

d. You will need to check whether or not the solution steps are addressed. This is for your checkpoint. You will be able to estimate the time needed to solve the problem.

e. Do you need additional resources? If it is a personal problem, you may need to talk to a friend about it. You will need to identify that friend and see if he or she is available to support you. You cannot use resources that have gone through their lives. You can only use stable support, and you will get the required release.

f. You will need to plan your approach as a whole. You need to identify the time it takes to resolve your problem. Your schedule needs to fit all of your activities from the beginning to the end of the activity.

g. You will need to identify the person in charge of ensuring that your plan takes perfect shape.

h. Then you will need to create a separate plan to achieve your final goal. This is your plan of action and you will have to follow it word for word.

The most important thing to remember is that you must continue to follow this plan. You also need to be open to receiving feedback. If you identify that the plan has some aspect, provide feedback and make the necessary changes. You also need to be open to receiving feedback, either negative or positive. That way, you can come up with a foolproof plan!

CHAPTER 10
CAUSE AND EFFECT DIAGRAMS

Fishbone Diagrams

After identifying all the possible causes, you should stratify them, according to the different categories they belong to, so that you can organize your thoughts. You must also relate the causes to the problem. The fishbone diagram provides a clear way to represent the relationship between the root cause of the problem and all the possible factors that may be associated with it. A fishbone diagram is a visual tool that identifies the relationship between a problem and its possible causes. It allows one to categorize the possible causes of a problem and capture the ideas generated by oneself or other problem solvers, in relation to what is considered to be the root cause(s). The name fishbone comes from the design of the diagram, because it resembles the skeleton of a fish. The problem or process condition is represented on the right side, which is the "head" of the fish. Fishbone diagrams are usually drawn from right to left, where each large branch of the fish includes smaller branches containing more detailed causes. The main categories of causes are written in the boxes on the left side of the fishbones. These branches often come in the number 6, and are often called the 6Ms, because they represent the initials of the 6 most used categories: Machine; Method; Man; Measure; Mother Nature; Material. The defect is shown on the head of the fish, and the causes extend along the spine of the fish. The branches coming from the spine usually describe the main causes, with subbranches of those branches for the subsequent causes, with as many levels as necessary. The spine diagram can be used when a problem may be due to more than one major cause or may have multiple variables causing the problem: individually or in combination.

In combination with fishbone, the "5 whys" is a widely used technique. It consists of repeating the question "why", peeling off the layers of symptoms until a root cause is reached. Problem solvers usually apply the 5 whys to each of the smaller bones in order to get to the possible root cause. Each answer to the 5 whys results in a new why. This process of asking why often works best if the problems are of low complexity. Even though they are called the 5 whys, the 5 need not be the exact number of questions. It is important to keep the answers as straightforward as possible. There are some mistakes that should be avoided:

- Stop at the 5 whys when additional whys are required.

- Do not follow the answers.

- Do not create multiple paths for different answers.

- Not checking to see if the cause triggers the problem, in your location.

Example 1: Suppose you run a digital tablet manufacturing company that has received many customer returns related to its tablet sales. You address this problem using the five whys:

Question 1: Why are customers returning tablets?

Answer: 85% of tablets are returned because of scratches in the tablet frame.

Question 2: Why are there scratches on the tablet frame?

Answer: The tablets are inspected before shipment and any scratches would be found by the process operator. Therefore, they must be damaged during shipping.

Question 3: Why are they damaged during shipping?

Answer: Because when they are packed, the packing operators do not follow any operational procedures to avoid scratches.

Question 4: Why don't packaging operators follow any operating procedures to avoid scratches?

Answer: Because the packaging operators do not have the packaging procedure.

Question 5: Why don't packaging operators follow the packaging procedure?

Answer: Because it does not exist yet.

After that, a team is assembled to write a packing procedure, to make sure that the operators handle the tablet frames with gloves that do not scratch and that the frame is covered with a protective material cover. In addition, the tablets are inspected for scratches before they are packaged.

In this example, the 5 whys revealed many failures in the tablet shipping process, which was causing product returns and poor customer satisfaction.

The Work of Kaoru Ishikawa

Fishbone diagrams were introduced by Kaoru Ishikawa in 1968. Ishikawa introduced efforts in quality management processes at Kawasaki and these diagrams were used as part of those efforts. Apart from Kawasaki, there have been multiple reports of companies using fishbone diagrams in their manufacturing processes. It is believed that Mazda Motors used fishbone diagrams in the development of one of their cars. Since they were introduced by Kaoru Ishikawa, they are also called Ishikawa diagrams. Over the years, they have also been called cause and effect diagrams because of their use in cause and effect studies.

The basic concept of fishbone was first used in the 1920s, but only became popular in the 1960s thanks to the popular quality method called TQM. They were originally designed to help employees think outside the box and to help employees think of different possibilities that can lead to solutions that go beyond high-impact problems. The fishbone diagram quickly became popular in AACR as it was a method used for many years in root cause analysis. Although the fishbone diagram was introduced by Kaoru Ishikawa, the 5 whys were introduced in the Toyota company, by her management.

Why Reaching the Root Cause Is Essential?

Sakichi Toyoda, one of the founders of the Toyota Motor Corporation, and Taiichi Ohno, one of Toyota's production managers, are credited with being the first people to use the 5 pores in conjunction with the fishbone. This was made possible by the introduction of troubleshooting reports in the Toyota manufacturing plant.

Taiichi Ohno's goal was to make the RCA as simple as possible so that it could be used at any level of the organization. In addition to the 5 whys, the fishbone diagram is also frequently used in conjunction with brainstorming to direct problem solvers to list all possible causes of a problem. The main purpose of the fishbone diagram is to help problem solvers list the possible root causes of a problem, after going through its symptoms. A root cause is the combination of two factors: a "cause", which is the factor, and a "root", which is the deep, fundamental reason. Going through the various symptoms contributes to a deeper and more solid analysis of the root cause. The fishbone diagram has several uses, for example, it helps:

- Making sure a list of ideas is documented.
- List the results of the brainstorming.
- Organize thinking and mind mapping.
- Employees think outside the box.
- Involve people in problem solving
- Promote process and system thinking with visual aids
- Problem solving analysis with 5 whys or Pareto diagrams

Drawing a Fishbone Diagram

Fishbone diagrams are mainly applied during the analysis stage of problem solving. This is when you are looking for answers to your problem or problems. Once the source of the problem has been identified, it will be easier to act on it. Although a fishbone will rarely look the same for two different problems, there are some common steps that should be followed when making a fishbone diagram to ensure that a quality fishbone diagram will be created.

Making high quality fishbone diagrams will help you make a high quality analysis. Therefore, the better your fishbone diagram, the greater the chances that you will successfully get to the root of your problem. Spend as much time as necessary investigating all possible causes, because once you have the root cause, it will save you hours of trial and error efforts. To make a high quality fishbone diagram

1. Create the fish head, which will lead the problem to be studied. Be as specific and objective as possible.

2. Create the fish backbone, which is a direct line to the fish head.

3. Write the first branches of the fish's spine. Normally the main branches are 6 m (machines, man, materials, methods, measures, Mother Nature).

4. Each major branch should be divided into smaller branches. It begins placing first the causes already assumed.

5. Brainstorm on each branch to find the rest of the potential causes and place them within the smaller branches.

6. Ask the why of each cause.

7. Look at the fishbone diagram again:

8. Eliminate the causes that do not contribute to the problem.

9. Brainstorm for more ideas in categories that contain fewer ideas.

10. Identify and prioritize critical causes.

11. Confirm that the root causes are actually causing the problem by turning them on and off and observing whether or not the problem returns.

12. Develop an action plan to counteract the root causes.

There are several ways to make a poor quality fishbone diagram, which will result in ineffective results and, therefore, an ineffective root cause analysis. To make an effective fishbone diagram, you can follow some guidelines to avoid wasting your time and the time of other problem-solving personnel who may be working with you to create the fishbone diagram. Save time with:

1. Do not use the fishbone diagram as an alternative way to describe a problem or to find out if there is a problem at all. The problem must be described first, and only then should the fishbone diagram be applied, otherwise you may lose focus.

2. Check the causes on the diagram with data, to confirm that they are real causes. Unfortunately, experience alone or opinions are often insufficient. Be sure to back up your conclusions with facts, so that you know what causes are really affecting your problem.

3. Do not use the fishbone to list possible solutions, which should be reserved for the improvement plan brainstorming activity. The list of potential solutions, along with the verified causes, will delay your effort, because you will be confused.

4. Use the fishbone as a living tool while the problem is open. Fishbone should not be archived until all root causes have been addressed.

5. Treat one problem at a time, otherwise it may become too messy and confusing to use properly.

6. Do not place the business case on the fishbone diagram, instead it only contains the description of a problem and not the entire purpose of a project.

CHAPTER 11
IMPROVE YOUR ANALYTICAL THINKING SKILLS

Have you ever wished you had the ability to solve problems successfully and easily? If so, be much more rational, you may want to improve your thinking patterns.

Have you seen the new Sherlock TV show, this time played by the brilliant Benedict Cumberbatch? If you have, you probably envy his impressive ability to deduce and think, "Why is he doing this?" The truth is, you can do it too.

Okay, you may not be able to solve a complex murder case, but in order to promote problem solving and decision making, you could improve your logical thinking. In return, these skills will usually lead to your career and success in life.

Here are some tips and techniques that can motivate you to clear your mind.

Making Logical Conclusions

Although it may seem stupid to you, try to think of conditional statements and find small and perhaps insignificant cause and consequence facts. To begin with, let's say it's cold outside every time it snows. The expression would be, "If it snows, it's cold outside."

If the assumption (the first part of the sentence) is true in the conditional statements, then the inference (the second part) is also true. Try to do that with other things too (if I drop my cell phone, it's going to be ruined; if I don't eat, I'm going to starve, etc.) and see if that association or assumption premise still fits the other way around.

Play Card Games

Who said it must be difficult to sharpen your logical thinking? It's the other way around. Get your partners together once a week and play cards to stimulate your brain to think easily and clearly. Competitive card games are not only good for the soul and enjoyable, but they can also improve memory, concentration and analytical skills.

They are much better when technique is added to the mix. Children can play Crazy Eight or Go Fish, while adults can play Blackjack and Poker.

Make Math Fun

There is no doubt that math is one of the best exercises to improve your analytical skills. However, it can be an unattractive hobby for both children and adults. Fortunately, there are many fun ways to work on math for you. Through math games on different websites or using smart phone applications, both adults and children can find fun and mental challenges.

Playing Sudoku and other activities that involve handling numbers in fun and interesting ways will potentially improve the mind's ability to solve real problems quickly.

Solve Mysteries and Break Codes

Writing crime stories and novels allows readers to think critically. Through these films or television programs, a similar experience can be obtained. Try to solve a certain mystery before the main character of the story.

Don't be disappointed if it doesn't turn out the way you hoped it would. Just remember from the beginning of this article, the words of the famous hero: "When you eliminate the impossible, whatever remains, however improbable, must be the truth". So, eliminate the impossible and the improbable, and the solution will come to you. Another great activity of the brain is to decipher codes (created by your friends or found on the web).

Conduct a Debate

Have you ever been in dispute when you can't find the right arguments to explain why something is good or bad? We all have. Debates are good because they allow you to look for causes and consequences, turn them into strong arguments, and find the reasoning behind everything.

Because they need to think logically and make decisions on the fly, debates can sharpen your mind. So you can join a discussion group or have a conversation about economics, art, culture, literature, etc. with your family.

Be Strategic

Since logical thinking is about putting the pieces together, strategic thinking plays an important role in this process. Being a strategic thinker will not only overload the mind, but will also be a useful asset for work-related choices and even personal life success.

For this reason, some of the fundamental behaviors you can develop are planning (thinking about what is coming), critical thinking (questioning everything), analysis (looking for patterns), determination (concluding), and improvement (from your mistakes). Play strategy games (board games, card games, video games, etc.) and design a strategy for sports events to sharpen your strategic thinking.

Just as it is important to find your inner peace and focus on your faith, it is also important to keep your mind continuously occupied with challenging games and activities, so that you can develop your rational thinking, which is vital for a productive and therefore harmonious existence.

Evaluate Your Memory

Your brain is stimulated by training just like any other part of your body. Evaluating your memory is a fantastic way to give your brain a workout. See the number of minute details, schedule, or work you can take into account during the day.

Try to memorize small things every day. Prepare a food guide and dedicate it to memory as well. Memorize a short passage from a poem or novel. Wait an hour and see how much of what you have memorized you can remember.

Draw a Memory Map

A map of your home to work, a restaurant, the home of a close friend, or other place you visit regularly.

Notice the Details

Making a conscious attempt to identify things that are relatively useless can be a good tool to help you be much more rational. Do you see the new diminished journal in your good friend's hand? Should you make a list of your school and college actions? Look for punctuation errors in the texts? If the answer is no, it would be a fun time to start at this point. The more you process, the better your mind will be. You will end up being a more vital thinker over time.

Other Tricks Include

Based on logical thinking, reading. Practice in your reading to use inductive or deductive logic - Avoid common mistakes.

Inductive reasoning: You start with several instances (facts or observations) when you reason inductively and use them to draw a general conclusion. You think inductively if you perceive facts. Using the probability to generalize is called an inductive jump. Therefore, inductive statements are intended to produce probable and plausible hypotheses rather than to produce certainty. Your reader draws the conclusion he or she expects to obtain when your proof increases. You must ensure that the amount of evidence is adequate and not dependent on extraordinary or biased analysis. Make sure you have not omitted facts that invalidate the argument (called "neglected aspect") and have provided fair evidence that supports a predetermined conclusion (called "bias").

Deductive reasoning: You start with generalizations (premises) if you think deductively and extend to a particular instance to conclude that instance. Deductive reasoning also implies syllogism, a line of thought consisting of a major premise, a minor premise and a conclusion; for example, all people are foolish (major premise); Smith is a man (minor premise); therefore, Smith is foolish (conclusion). For example, to accept the argument, the reader must accept the concepts and principles he chooses as assumptions. Sometimes, there is no discussion about assumptions. It is important to analyze a syllogism with an undeclared major or minor assumption, or even an undeclared inference, because the excluded statement may constitute an incorrect generalization.

The Toulmin approach: The Toulmin approach is another way of looking at the mechanism of logical thinking. This model is less restricted than syllogism and allows for the important elements of probability, support or proof of the reader's objections ' premise and refutation. This approach considers that claims range from agreed facts or evidence (data) to an inference (claim) through a statement (order) that forms a fair relationship between the two. The order is often implicit in the arguments, and to be acceptable, as is the undeclared premise in the syllogism. The author can make a large assumption. Qualifiers like probably, possibly, certainly, and surely show the degree of certainty of the conclusion; refutative terms like unless the writer allows objections to be anticipated.

Falsehoods: There must be both plausible and real inference. A real argument is based on well-founded assumptions that are generally accepted. Learn to distinguish between fact and opinion (based on personal preferences) (based on verifiable data). A valid argument conforms to a reasonable pattern of thought.

Fallacies are failures in assumptions (truth) and logic (validity). They can result from misuse or misrepresentation of evidence, from reliance on faulty premises or omission of a necessary premise, or from distortion of the issues. Some of the main forms of fallacies are the following:

Non-Equity: a statement that does not follow logically from what has just been said; in other words, a conclusion that does not follow from the premises.

Hasty generalization: A generalization based on insufficient evidence or on exceptional or biased evidence.

Ad Hominem: Questioning the individual who asks a question rather than addressing the problem itself in an objective manner.

A Band Wagon: An argument that says, "Everybody does it and believes it, so you should do it. False track: Dodging the real problem by drawing attention to an irrelevant issue.

Claiming that there are only two options when there are more than two. False analogy: The belief that in some cases, if two events are the same, they must be unique. Mistake: An inference that in two different senses depends erroneously on the use of one word.

Slippery slope: The belief that it will be the first step in a downward spiral if an element is approved.

Over-simplification: A comment or point that leaves out relevant issues.

Question begging: A statement that reaffirms the point just made. Such a statement is conditional in the sense that a point mentioned in the assumption is taken as an inference.

CHAPTER 12
LEARNING HOW TO LEARN

Learning to learn is basically an ability to pursue learning and persist in the process. It is also a way of organizing a person's own learning, including proper management of information and time, both personally and in groups. It is a competence that includes awareness of a person's needs and learning processes, and even highlighting some of the available learning opportunities. It also involves a person's ability to overcome barriers so that he or she can learn perfectly.

This competency also means processing, acquiring and assimilating new skills and knowledge and also includes developing and seeking guidance. Learning to learn basically implies that learners build on previous life and learning experiences so that they can apply the skills and knowledge in various contexts: at work, at home, in training, and in education. Both confidence and motivation are very important when it comes to a person's competence.

The Essential Attitudes, Skills, and Knowledge Related to This Competence

In a situation where the purpose of learning moves towards certain career or job goals, a person must be fully aware of the qualifications, skills, and competencies that are needed. In all situations, learning to learn will always lead a person not only to know but also to understand their preferred learning strategies, as well as the weaknesses and strengths of their qualifications and competencies. In addition, you can also seek out training and education opportunities and available support and guidance.

Learning to learn skills would first require the inclusion of basic requirements that include ICT, numeracy and literacy skills that can assist in the process of promoting learning. At the same time that the above-mentioned skills are developed, an individual will be able to process, obtain, access, and assimilate the new skills and knowledge. This will also require effective and rapid management of the person's learning, work patterns and even career. Specifically, this will require perseverance in the learning process and concentration for longer periods of time. The individual also has the opportunity to critically reflect on the main objectives and purposes of learning.

Consideration should also be given to the need to devote time to learning with great self-discipline and in an autonomous manner. A positive attitude will include the confidence and motivation to follow and succeed in the learning process throughout an individual's life cycle. On the other hand, a problem-solving attitude will tend to support both an individual's learning process and the ability to manage various changes and obstacles. The desire to use prior learning as well as life experiences and the willingness to seek opportunities to learn and use knowledge acquired in various life contexts are basic characteristics of a positive attitude.

Learning How to Learn, a Vital Skill for a Lifelong Student

Even those who consider themselves life-long learners sometimes struggle with optimizing their learning to get the best results. Learning to learn is one of the vital skills that should be mastered by anyone who wants to be a competent and avid student in a given area of study.

The Illusion of Competency and Procrastination

Some of the challenges you may have to face as an apprentice may include the illusion of competence, procrastination, and even dropout midway through the course of education. However, there are some surefire ways that can be used to overcome all of these, and you will be forced to put them into practice by deliberate means. When it comes to learning to learn, Barbara talks about learning in short bursts of time but in a consistent manner. She says this is one of the most effective ways to learn. Sitting for almost four hours without moving does not do your back any good. It is also very unproductive for your learning process.

Focused and Diffuse Modes

It is also very important to be in a focused learning mode, before going into a fuzzy mode, either by choosing to take a nap or doing certain exercises. This is one of the safest ways to help the brain make the necessary neural connections and build lasting knowledge into its memory system.

Don't hesitate to test your knowledge, in the hope that reading it once more or watching a movie on the subject will activate it. It is important that you feel comfortable in your state of discomfort. This is done by testing your knowledge by carrying out certain challenges that will ensure that you do not forget what you have said.

It is also very important to keep increasing the complexity of the challenges you might be experiencing when trying different problems. This is one of the best ways to flex your long-term memory muscles. It is known as intercalation. At first, it may seem very uncomfortable but it is one of the best practices to try.

Challenging yourself on an ongoing basis will help you get rid of the illusion of competition that may arise after you have faced a number of challenges. There is nothing that can really deprive learning of the power of deliberate practice. Keeping an open mind as a learner is also very imperative, lest you run the risk of falling into a situation known as Einstellung mentality.

Adults tend to develop their ways of doing things and their perceptions, although it is a process that can impede the learning process if an open mind is not maintained. Although our long-term memory serves us well, there are times when it can set in motion and even prevent us from learning. Our brains should always be open to reconditioning and continuing to challenge what we already know.

Procrastination is basically the action of postponing or delaying something that is very conscious of the urgent needs that need to be done.

Chunking

Chunking is basically an idea of breaking down what a person has learned into small concepts. The main goal here is to learn each of the concepts in a way that makes them seem like a familiar puzzle piece. To be able to master a given concept, one must know it and understand how it will fit into the larger picture.

According to Dr. Barbara Oakley of the University of California, San Diego, the first step in learning one thing is to study and prepare the whole process. This includes scanning a piece of writing or a course syllabus to get a general idea of the big picture. The second step is to look at the example, before doing it yourself. The last step would be to do it over and over again.

Illusion of Competence

You should also be aware that there is something called the illusion of competition. There are many ways to make us feel as if we have mastered a given concept. For example, one of the most common illusions of learning competence is to look at a solution and think that that solution can be easily reached. Other methodologies that normally lead to this type of illusion of learning are also underlining or highlighting. On the other hand, short notes that tend to summarize the main concepts are much more effective.

Bite-Sized Testing

In order to avoid the illusion of competition, it is important to test yourself every time you find a new material. A simple example of this mini-test is known as "recall". It is not so important that you pass these particular tests without making any mistakes. Remembering the mistakes, and correcting them later, are very crucial steps when it comes to solidifying your learning process.

Recall

A few years ago, Dr. Jeff Karpick researched the subject of recovery practice. The main goal of this research was to offer scientific support to take just a couple of minutes to remember or summarize the piece you are trying to learn. It goes beyond taking a particular thing from just a short term memory to what can be described as long term learning. It is also very important to note that even remembering the material in various physical environments can help you understand the material regardless of any physical cues the brain may have. This is something practical that you can even try after reading this. You can take a moment and try to point out some of the points you remember.

Over-Learning

The main point in favor of this particular point is to avoid spending too much time in one session going through the same material over and over again. Here, the law of diminishing returns will definitely apply. It would be better to spread it out over many sessions and several learning modes.

Interleaving

Once you have gained a basic understanding of what you are trying to learn, you can apply the interlayer to help you master the main concepts you have learned. By practicing jumping from one problem to another that requires various techniques, you will be able to solidify your understanding of the concepts by learning how to choose how to apply them in different situations. It is also very important to know when to apply a certain concept, as well as how to apply it.

Process over Product

Whenever a person is faced with a delay, they should always think about the process over the product. There are people who would normally postpone when they feel overwhelmed by a certain thought of getting somewhere.

The Metaphors and Analogies

Analogies and metaphors are often considered very important study techniques. The best teachers use metaphors and analogies in their speeches. And, being able to talk about what you have learned is one of the main skills that creates a distinction between a good developer and only a great one.

Therefore, making a deliberate effort to teach what you have been able to learn to someone else becomes very important, and in doing so, you will have no choice but to explain the concepts with the narrative analogies and metaphors.

There are a number of opportunities in the daily practice of software development to teach and get lessons from other people. You may be able to match a given program, comment on it, or even get applications. You can also sign up to give a code talk on a given topic.

CHAPTER 13
MIND MAPS

The more you use your brain, the smarter it becomes and the more you can think rationally and make decisions. Logical thinking is rational thinking, which consists of two parts: rational affirmation and rational criticism. That is, having the ability to find and solve problems and the tool to help rational thinking. Mind maps are the best tools for rational thinking.

1. Turn the research topic into a question and you have a definition problem. Then use it as a tip to start your research.

2. Start quick thinking by using horizontal thinking to list all possible answers and perform "problem analysis". (parallel thinking) Think of all the ideas you acquired on a mind map as thick branches.

3. Use slow thinking, use vertical thinking to analyze the factors behind individual responses, categorize them, go deeper in "problem analysis" and collect data when necessary. (thinking logically)

4. How to think slowly. List the strategies for each individual cause and how to prioritize them. (second level of vertical thinking)

5. Use analytical tools to analyze the situation over a wide range.

6. Then list the solutions one by one according to the answers.

7. Start with a list of all the questions. Or use a two-value analysis to list all the "pros and cons" or "cons" that you do not want. You can also divide them into subtopics and make them less thin.

Mind Map to Plan Future

Mind mapping is a useful tool that can help us fill the gaps in our knowledge and experience, as long as our objectives are clear. Even when things are difficult to understand, mind maps can help us turn them into something easy to understand.

However, with some differences, such a powerful thinking tool can be transformed into a pure image. It would be an honor if you could learn the true essence of mind maps from the examples presented here. I also hope you can experience the greatness of mind maps and have confidence in your abilities when you achieve results. You can plan your future with a clear understanding of your goals and your strengths.

Goal Setting Using Mind Maps

Goals are useful only if they help people to act and inspire them to go somewhere from their current position in life. For most people, the path to follow is often unclear, with no way to see where they are going and no way to see all the possibilities of the future. For good things to happen in the future, the seeds must be sown now. The chances of achieving the goals can be increased through planning. You have to plan for the next ten years from the end of the day and you have to plan for the short, medium and long term to make sure that time goes by. Your goals will be met over time.

Below are the types of goals you can plan for using different mind maps. Use colorful sketches and paste them in your room so you can see them every day when you wake up.

- Goals for Tomorrow: What to Achieve Tomorrow

- Monthly goal: what to accomplish the next month.

- Short-term goal: this coming year to three years. Divide your medium-term goals into several milestones, plus the optimistic and realistic goals you want to achieve.

- Medium-term goal: three to five years. It can be the next step in your career, or it can be the specific type of training or course you are looking for.

- Long-term goal: five to ten years. The desired life profile is the lifestyle you want to have, including work, family, etc.

- Life goals: within the next 20 years. You are waiting for the big picture of your life and what you want to achieve at the end of your life.

Steps to Draw Mind Map for Setting a Goal

1. Start with a goal and think about how you want your life to be 20 years from now. If your life goals are too abstract, at least start thinking about them in terms of long-term goals.

The bigger the goal, the more likely it is to affect your life. But we only have the ability to master the small goals, the long-term goals in a number of small, cumulative goals to achieve small goals; there is a chance to really care about the long-term goals. Remember to think about what interests you and what makes you happy. This state of mind is the psychology of "flow", a feeling that one's mental energy is totally invested in a certain activity, as it is accompanied by a great sense of excitement and accomplishment.

Experience and think about the activities that make you flow. But at the same time, keep an open mind, give yourself more opportunities in different areas, try to do it and maybe you will discover a new you in the process. One thing to watch out for is taking things one step at a time. Don't expect sudden, drastic changes. Change gradually and you will have a chance to achieve your goal. Create different branches on the mind map and map them to your goal with your arrows along with alternative options.

2. Set medium-term goals and include things that give you a sense of accomplishment.

   Some people have a life goal, but the motivation to implement it is not strong, it may be that this life goal is not what your heart really wants. Passion, you can rely on a teacher or some activity to give you a brief burst of energy, but these people cannot motivate you in the long run, so many people continue to attend motivational camps, look around for a stronger motivational teacher to motivate you to become a career student in motivational courses. The more you know the value of what you do, the more motivated you will be to do it well.

3. Set short-term goals and include deadlines.

   Short-term goals can be used to increase your productivity or meet a deadline. Make a mind map with basic sorting ideas surrounding the tasks to be accomplished or a deadline with a bright color, which can keep you on your toes. Use illustrations to highlight the immediate task to be done and touch it up when it is completed.

Mind Maps for Story Marketing

In recent years, it has become very popular in the United States to market your ideas by telling stories. This is called story marketing. It's not just for people who sell things, as long as you want to plant your ideas in someone else's head; you need to learn this trick. Because a story is a kind of sugar-coated package, through which the hard to accept point of view is packaged so that when you hear the story, you accept my point of view.

1. To gather material from the story without any purpose. In fact, as you observe, pay more attention to things around you, more attention to slow thinking, your mind will naturally remember many stories. You can bring a cell phone or a tape recorder at any time to record. Take the ordinary activity as the main branch, begin to carry out the observation.

2. Find a common point between today's story and previous ones and use that common point to start developing independent mind maps.

3. Analyze the main characteristics of each story. Use the additional branches to list the characteristics of the story and write down as many ideas as possible so that your brain can form associations while looking at the mind map.

4. Practice telling the story. Use the mind map to recall the narrative order of the story and practice it in front of the mirror before presenting it to your target. By using the mind map, you can augment the story's marketing techniques so that you can reach the minds of your audience.

The Study Program for Adults Using a Mind Map

Learning is the most effective way to invest in yourself. It is a tragedy in education. No one thinks of reading as a way to be more resilient in the future, to be more capable of solving problems, to be smarter and to help people live better. No wonder there are so many intellectuals with no qualifications and no skills.

Do a self-analysis using mind maps about why your own thinking ability is not enough and why you should develop your skills. The first step in improving your thinking ability is to get rid of resistance to it. Regardless of the current learning process, focusing on future outcomes will give you the resistance you need. You can also write down your reason for the resistance, which will help your brain see more clearly why you are really resistant to thinking.

The key to successful self-learning is in two steps: setting specific and clear learning goals and knowing what can be done now.

1. Specific and clear learning goals.

   Learning is a process of absorbing information, knowing what you are missing, you must try to absorb that kind of information, to really improve your ability. Do not copy others, learn from others what is very good, this kind of learning mentality will only make you become as ordinary as the public, it will not let you have more than the public professional. Take the time to set your goals to be more accurate in your reading selection, so you don't waste time reading a bunch of readings you can't use.

2. Choose the learning flow according to the type of content.

3. Find out what you want to read this year according to your life stage, then go to the store and fill out the list first.

4. Make a reading plan.

5. Insert the planned date for the application.

6. Mark the finished article and mark it with a new date.

7. Find your favorite reference.

   There are thousands and hundreds of self-study references on the same topic. The content is basically the same, but the difference lies in the way of arrangement and arrangement. Taking the time to find a reading first is much more effective and saves time than reading several readings later. After all, more readings, with which everyone is unfamiliar, equals more study and no one feeds back the same. Having several readings piled up in front of you at the same time will only increase your nervousness and make you afraid every day that you won't be able to finish them.

8. Study the exam questions for each subject and find out the proportion of the questions.

   Over five years of exam questions, the benchmark is relatively low. If you have some free time, do some research. Find out the last five years of exam questions, one by one with reference to the written ones, find out the proportion of the three main questions.

9. Calculate the amount of time you spend studying each month.

10. Set monthly progress goals for each reading.

Set monthly progress goals and deadlines for each reading so you can maximize the psychological impact - the right amount of stress can boost productivity.

11. Develop a monthly study schedule.

12. With the reading, make a monthly study time plan.

CHAPTER 14
USING MIND MAPS TO DEVELOP APPROACHES

Mind mapping is a technique for analyzing issues and developing approaches in a non-linear way. Mind mapping uses markers in the flip chart paper, whiteboard markers, or computer software to make mind maps. Completed mind maps include sentences, link arrows, lines, and sometimes drawings. The types of mind maps involve problem solving, projecting, and understanding.

Problem-Fixing Maps

A mind map is a useful tool that is used during staff brainstorming sessions, once the goal is to create ideas quickly, without instant logical feedback. Displaying the mind map throughout the semester allows team members to observe the ideas created, which awakens more thoughts. This procedure creates a favorable momentum for problem solving.

A challenging brainstorming session begins with the leader recording the topic as a phrase or small image in the middle of what is to be developed on the brain map. As staff members become involved with the opinions, the recorder brings in colored radios that radiate from the heart theme. Each of the rays represents another part of the topic and can be labeled with a word or a graphic. As the session progresses, staff members' observations lead to the inclusion of smaller lines coming out of the radios and arrows that demonstrate the connections between objects on the different radios.

Project Maps

Planning an event, planning the launch of an item, creating the strategy to close a mass sale, and other actions can create project mind maps. Updated from time to time to reflect changes in the status of the work, they live only until the completion of the work. The life span of work mind maps is usually only a couple of days or months.

Knowledge Maps

Knowledge mind maps include information recorded once and retained for future use, occasionally replacing existing files. Some are adjusted and updated over time, while others are not updated. Mind maps that describe business procedures, which occasionally include checklists, are cases of understanding mind maps. Used multiple times over a very long interval, understanding mind maps is important for maintaining the company's background, the never-recorded knowledge that is only present in the minds of workers. Knowledge mind maps can be especially valuable for new workers when discovering procedures to carry out recurring actions. The useful life of knowledge mind maps can be years.

How Mind Maps Can Assist Your Creative Thinking

A mind map is a visual form of equipment to capture, store and organize ideas. By accumulating subtopics in a disorderly manner, mind maps make it possible for teams to handle problem solving in a natural way.

Instead of taking hard-to-read notes or disparate meetings, mind maps bring teams together and facilitate collaboration on a wide variety of work.

5 Types of Mind Maps

There are five types of head maps. Direct thought, notion and arbitrary word maps are ideal for free brainstorming among almost any group. Flowcharts and dialogue mind maps are used by the agile team for retrospective spark, preparation, along with other work tasks.

1. Simple Mind Mapping

A mind map is a visual diagram in the form of a bush or tree, where the important groups radiate from a central node, and the lower categories will be the sub-branches of the larger ones.

A mind map is a free default application in Miro. It is possible to focus on real thoughts and use only a few hotkeys to build the map. In addition, with Miro, you can put images, videos and other visual elements next to the brain map to animate and expand your thoughts.

Measurements to make your map:

- Start in the middle of a blank canvas, giving your mind the freedom to distribute and communicate ideas freely and naturally.

- Use colors everywhere; this gives more vitality and life to the brain map.

- Use an online keyword as it gives your brain map more flexibility and power.

- Use images in everything. A picture is worth a million words and allows you to use your creativity.

2. Concept Map

A concept map is a graph used to illustrate the connections between theories in a brainstorming session. An idea is a frame of thought defined by an explicit "focus question". Mapped theories represent a hierarchical structure that allows for better understanding of the topic and building stronger arguments.

A concept map differs in brain mapping from design. It usually follows a hierarchical arrangement and reveals more complicated interrelationships between theories (a theory can be related to more than just the parent node).

To start mapping theories, you simply need to focus on the ideas. Here is an easy guide to the procedure:

Insert a form or sticker with the general topic you want to know more about. Make sure it is the answer to a specific question.

- Brainstorm the list of topics on the topic. Use the sticky note style to follow the thread of your thought and keep the concepts as succinct as possible.

- Start mapping the topics around the idea and then connecting them with lines. The most significant ideas should be closer to the center and the less significant ones closer to the border. Insert the text to describe the connections more clearly.

3. Random Words

Random phrases are a brainstorming technique that motivates your creativity to create unique insights and fresh perspectives on the thought or problem you are facing. By evaluating your environment, you develop new ideas that can help you solve the problem.

By forcing you to use a random word to find a solution, you will almost certainly go beyond the limits and attack the problem in another way.

This is the way to use this method of brainstorming:

- Identify the problem or challenge you are facing.
- Using a mind mapping tool, make the starting node with a random note. This term has to be totally arbitrary and irrelevant to your problem or challenge.
- Applying the shortcuts, write down as many ideas as possible that are connected to the arbitrary word.
- Using an observation tool, examine the links between your arbitrary institutions along with their difficulty or challenge. Write down the thoughts that come to mind.

4. Flowchart

A flowchart is an incremental algorithm, workflow or procedure displayed with outlines of different varieties and arranged with arrows.

Flowcharts help to imagine a particular procedure to help, understand and detect defects and bottlenecks. There are several types of flowcharts, and although some of them need specific types of shapes (like ovals or diamonds), a very simple site map or business procedure will use text boxes.

The best way to make a flow chart:

- Kick your thinking process into gear by incorporating the initial product.
- Use checkpoints around the first thing to start drawing in a connection within your mind mapping applications. You will notice the menu where it is possible to decide on the thing that is coming, producing your flow of thought as easily as possible.
- Customize the look and feel of this flowchart, using item menus for both arrows and objects.

5. Dialog Map

Dialogue mapping is a facilitation technique. The mapping promotes shared understanding of a complex problem, in which technical and social complexities have been established.

When a group of intelligent individuals come together to solve a complicated or challenging problem, the frequent question is: how do they see the whole picture and know what the real problem is? Teams around the world can see the big picture in real time and preserve shared knowledge, remote accessibility and knowledge retention. The built-in brain mapping tool can help dig deeper and brainstorm faster.

Dialogue mapping contrasts very well with agile practices and could be a very effective tool to provide focus, clarity and advice to agile actions. It can even be used for retrospective meetings, making it easier to understand the next improvement that the agile group will produce, make sure it is scrum, fdd, lean, rup or any development group.

The best way to make a dialogue map:

- Produce the initial node using all the mind mapping tools. Start with a query or a problem. It can be something as simple as "agenda" or as complicated as "what do we do to be better product programmers?

- Start adding thoughts using shortcuts.

- Insert "pro" and "con" arguments to each idea. Highlight the positives and negatives with various colors using the brain map toolbar.

- To solidify mutual understanding, complete with a list of what has been identified.

Head Maps: Paper vs. Virtual

Mind maps are rapidly replacing lists, summaries and other types of linear business for an assortment of applications. Almost everyone, such as professionals and students, can benefit from their use in college, work, or perhaps in mundane applications such as grocery stores and to-do lists.

Traditionally, they have been made with paper and pencil.

The benefit of this method is that this type of mind mapping can be done anywhere, anytime, and you have access to it. In addition, even individuals who are uncomfortable with technology can use this method.

The learning procedure is occasionally aided by handwriting elements, and you can add as much color and as many examples as you want to your own map.

Unfortunately, handwriting is not necessarily the optimal solution.

They could get torn, dirty, lost, and they only take up space. They take longer to make than the virtual one. The virtual ones can be produced with mind mapping applications, of which there are a variety, and they have some benefits over the hand-drawn ones.

They require less time to make them, changes can be made easily and at low cost, they do not need physical space to buy, and they look more professional.

The only disadvantage of the virtual ones would be that, of course, they need a computer to make them, and people occasionally find themselves making a map at home when they want to talk to other people at work, instead of using it there, or even trying to make a mental map at work but using their computer applications.

These problems, however, can be solved using a great mind mapping program.

This allows you to create an individual on any PC; it is an excellent benefit if you are doing work-related work both at home and at work.

Being able to save the maps you create allows you to start working on a project at work and then finish it at home or vice versa. It also allows you to make a mind map at home or on your laptop during a trip or a long bus ride, and then take it to work to share with your co-workers.

While conventional, pencil and paper maps alike, as well as virtual ones, such as improving your business and productivity, many men and women are discovering that digital maps are easier to store, organize and share. You can even make adjustments to some virtual mind maps without the map falling apart, unlike the newspaper.

CHAPTER 15
UNLEASHING YOUR CREATIVITY

Brainstorming and Idea Generation

The first act of creating new ideas seems like the natural place to start. It is a part of the creative process that is often overrated, as editing and selecting ideas can be just as important. However, this is where the creative process usually begins, so this is where we will start.

The brainstorming act is the process of rapidly creating ideas. Brainstorming is widely used, but often without following the rules to optimize the process. The concept of brainstorming was first named by Alex Faickney Osborn and presented in his paper "How To Think Up". Below are the rules he formulated for effective brainstorming:

Go for the quantity - the more ideas, the better. By developing an abundance of ideas, you are more likely to discover something great.

Don't be critical unless you have to be. By reflecting and criticizing at that moment, you will stifle new and unusual ideas.

Push for new and unusual ideas. Following from the top, try to push creativity towards what is unusual and different.

Combine the ideas with each other. Bringing ideas together often allows for the creation of something new.

Of course, generating ideas is the natural application of brainstorming. This can be recorded on lined paper in the form of a linear list, or in a more scattered and non-linear way.

We will return to the above rules and apply them in subtly different ways to facilitate a more developed approach to creativity in general.

The Principles of Brainstorming Applied to Other Areas

Applying the principles of brainstorming to other areas of creativity will have the same turbo-charging effect as generating ideas. Perhaps the closest cousins of brainstorming are jamming (with music creation) and free writing (with writing).

The principles of pushing for quantity, eliminating judgment, pushing for the unusual, and combining ideas will boost creativity, regardless of the medium.

When you write freely, you write at the speed of consciousness and completely remove the filter, following the mind where it wants to go. A similar process takes place when musicians play together.

Experiment by applying these principles to your own creative field - write down these 4 key principles and apply them regularly.

An important caveat to creating in this way is to make sure you are recording what you create. This will allow you to get back to work and be critical in editing your work. Just as brainstorming should take place on paper, free writing and jams should also be recorded. If you don't record what you create, you can't go back and look for the parts that you think are great, the parts that can become the valuable pieces of your album/business.

Returning the Filter – Focus and Selection

Once you have performed your act of free creation, you will have to return to your work and find what is great and must be preserved. As with everything creative, there are no hard rules for doing this. However, below are some principles that can help in the process of deciding what to cut:

Follow your intuition... what feels best?

Choose the three best ideas.

Leave a little space between creation and editing: a few days, a night's sleep, or at least a walk.

Clarify your creative goals. What is your creative identity? What problem are you trying to solve? Who are your influences / who are you trying to imitate?

After editing and cutting out what you don't want, there is a process of "cleaning up" and establishing the final polished piece. This is an essential part of the creative process (especially if you are taking your art "to market"), although often the least enjoyable. Pay or befriend someone else to help you through this phase, as being 100% accurate in editing and cleaning up your own work is not easy, and often not even possible.

Produce Prolifically

The essential rules of brainstorming can be expanded to form "macro" principles that can be applied to your creativity in a broader sense. By being prolific in general (an extension of "Go for the quantity - the more ideas, the better"), you can enjoy benefits similar to those enjoyed by being prolific in brainstorming.

Going for the exceptional amount in a broader sense (e.g., many novels, albums, paintings, or whatever your art creates) will provide you with the following benefits:

You will have the full experience of the process, so you can refine each part, for example, writing an introduction, half and end of your novel.

It will help reduce fears and self-criticism as you cross the finish line again and again.

More opportunities to experiment, fail and learn how to improve your work.

More opportunities to create something exciting and to reach your target audience in the right way. For example, if you send 10 short stories to a publisher, they are more likely to pick you up than if you send only 2.

Apply the rules of brainstorming holistically and on a macro level to help optimize your overall creativity. Whenever possible, push for new and unusual ideas, combine what works, and hold back criticism to a necessary extent.

Keep and Revisit Your Work

Over time, a body of work will inevitably accumulate. If you are prolific in producing work, as I recommend, this will happen before you know it. It is important that you then keep your work, order your work and review it regularly. The following are some of the benefits of doing this

Although your creative career is new and fragile, if you do not maintain and review your work, you will be less aware of the improvements you are making. This will decrease your drive to keep going, so regularly look at your work to remind yourself how far you have come and to maintain motivation.

Wider trends and patterns will become evident that may not be clear when looking at individual pieces or across a small range of your work, for example, you may notice that you stick to similar themes in your paintings. You can then better plan and integrate these recurring aspects (or cut them out) to make your work better and more desirable.

By reviewing a wide range of your work, it will become clearer what mistakes you are repeating. Again, look for patterns and take notes in your work to help create your awareness of recurring errors and things you don't like.

It will reveal ways to synthesize your work and/or create something new, for example, combining your best guitar riffs from a series of works to create an exceptional piece could create the most spectacular song you need to advance your industry.

Sentimentality strikes us all. When you're gray and old, nostalgia is going to show up at some point - reminding yourself of the poetry/songs/commercials you made on your creative journey will feel good.

Externalize Creativity

"Ideas are worthless until you get them out of your head to see what they can do."

– Tanner Christensen

Every "creative" can benefit from the development of the external tools he uses in the creative process. Using a worksheet will allow you to contain these tools and have them ready and in one place.

A primary use of this worksheet is as a dumping ground/collection of ideas. Also, consider including work from your creative influences, especially anything that you like and could integrate into your work in the future. Whether it's a collage of your favorite magazine ads or a portfolio of your favorite poems - build a collection.

It will also be useful to have a space to externalize the creative process itself; this will help free up the mental RAM and act as a bicycle for your creativity, allowing it to go faster than if you try to do everything in your head.

This set of creative tools can take a variety of forms. It can be a series of writings, or plastic pockets arranged in a folder - whatever works for you. The more organization you can bring to this worksheet, the easier it will be to use. Using a digital worksheet is also a great idea - making your creative work easy to store, digitally editable and highly portable. However, many find that working with a simple paper and pen is an easier, more practical and creative way to manipulate their work. If you find this to be the case, consider writing or taking photos of your work and putting them on a digital worksheet regularly so you can have the best of both worlds. Evernote and OneNote are both excellent programs for this.

The following are possible categories/folders you could include - they are a great start.

A list/assembly of the creative people/minds you like. Idolize your heroes, learn more about them and write down their lessons. Include some biography, if possible - maybe their creative habits, what inspires them, etc.

The work you love. As I said before, you have to build that collection of the things you love. It's important to write down what you like about them as well to better identify trends and common themes that you might want to integrate into your own work.

Work that you admire for its creativity. In addition to the work you like, think about finding work that you can appreciate for its creativity. It may not be the art you want on your walls, but either way, you know it has quality and/or originality that can help inspire you.

Idea creation and brainstorming: a shameless and messy space to write down everything you can think of.

Synthesis of ideas. Here you can gather ideas and connect and create the possible ideas that will be formed into letters or themes.

Records of old work, along with separate notes or notes you made when you revisited them.

As your work grows, you can develop a folder for each of the above, and then maybe a couple of chronologically ordered folders. No matter what kind of creative you are, use creative worksheets/folders to outsource your work and record everything.

Use Diagrams to Further Facilitate Your Creativity

There are several diagrams that will help you create, organize, edit, analyze and synthesize your creative work.

Venn diagrams, for example, will be useful for synthesizing ideas and getting inspiration from different places. Finding where your work intersects will reveal the commonalities that can spawn the best, most compelling, and most original ideas.

Mind maps are also exceptionally useful. They are especially useful for:

By creating ideas, thanks to the associative branches, connections to new ideas can be created quickly and naturally.

Analysis of ideas and deconstruction of an idea. Do it by putting what you want to deconstruct in the center and then working outward.

CHAPTER 16
BUDGETING AND FINANCIAL LITERACY

What Is Financial Literacy?

Financial literacy refers to the skills and techniques that anyone can acquire to gain control of their finances. It is not that some people are naturally good with money, but that they have had to take the time to learn specific skills that are often not taught in the traditional way. These skills need to be reinforced just as you would reinforce any other skill you have mastered throughout your life. Although financial education is not something natural, it is something that can be learned regardless of age or income. People with financial literacy have a clear understanding of these three key financial factors:

1. Budgeting

Knowing how to create and follow a budget is one of the most crucial skills for financial education. As mentioned, creating a budget is not just about seeing where your money goes, but creating a plan that allows you to cover your monthly expenses and plan for the future. With a clear budget, you can have more peace of mind and feel confident in your money management skills.

Creating a budget allows you to see exactly what you can afford to spend each month by designating specific financial goals for each area you want to contribute. When you are financially literate, you understand that delaying the instant gratification for buying what you want now will be much more beneficial to you in meeting your true money goals. Creating a budget is something that is not intimidating but is an effective way for individuals to see and become more aware of what they really want. They use this budget to finance their current lifestyle, while also working to finance the future life they have only dreamed of before. Sticking to a budget is what allows them to turn their dream into reality.

2. Emergency Funds

An emergency fund is one that covers all monthly expenses. This total should equal about three months of expenses. But three months of covered bills is not enough if you are out of work, facing a serious illness or injury, or suffering another sudden blow to your ability to earn a substantial income. Today, it's safer to have an emergency fund that can cover at least six months of your total expenses.

As you increase your financial knowledge, you will see how quickly and easily you can begin to build an emergency fund and grow it to cover your monthly expenses for up to six months. This emergency fund gives people the peace of mind of knowing that their income is low or that they are concerned about the safety of their job.

An emergency fund is essential to cover any major financial setback we don't see coming. By preparing for them, you will be less stressed and overwhelmed when these sudden, unexpected turns occur. People with financial literacy not only have an emergency fund, but it is considered a crucial component to their overall financial goals. This emergency fund is what allows them to relax and be less stressed about funding all their other desires. Having a clear sense that they can make bigger plans because they have a good cushion to support them if something goes wrong is the reason why those with financial literacy achieve greater success.

3. Debt

Half of our monthly income is spent on debt repayment. Credit card bills, student loans, mortgages, car payments and other debt are what make it seem like gaining control over your financial situation is impossible. One of the top priorities for those with financial literacy is to pay off their debts as quickly as possible.

They learn which debt must be paid off first and which can be paid off slowly over time. They understand that while they have a significant amount of debt, they cannot fully finance the future life they desire. Financial literacy takes into account that time and money are wasted in paying off debt and this significantly impairs our ability to save or invest in our future.

Perhaps you accumulated a greater amount of debt in your 20s than in your 30s, you are still paying off. This is often the case, as most individuals are never taught that using credit cards to pay for the things they want now, without having the money, is a direct path to years of financial stress. Once we understand that these debts significantly impact our ability to save, then our money will work for us the way we want it to. Taking steps to get rid of debt will allow you to make much more progress on your financial goals.

Becoming More Financially Literate

Financial literacy is a skill that can be reinforced and will allow you to better manage your money. It is what will allow you to save for the future and avoid unnecessary financial stress. Financial education is what will allow you to fully understand how to create a budget that works to achieve your financial goals. It is what will allow you to learn to save more and spend less. Through financial literacy, you will learn how to borrow money and have a payment plan in place when you need to make big money purchases like a new house, car or college tuition. It's what will help you invest your money in the best way, so you get more return.

If you really want to feel in control of your money, you will make it a habit to be more financially literate. You will be eager to understand how you can make your hard-earned money work for you in multiple ways. You will have more confidence in your ability to achieve the goals you have set for yourself and to see your money from a new perspective.

Having more financial knowledge will help you understand exactly what financial struggles have been holding you back. When you have a better understanding of how debt is holding you back, impulse purchases are holding you back, or unaccounted for expenses are causing you more stress, you will learn to handle the money you have with more awareness and purpose.

Financial literacy really highlights the importance of making your money work for you. You won't be discouraged by how little you have to save right now, especially if that small amount is after you've made a significant dent in your debt. This is what allows you to understand that saving a little now is more important than not saving at all.

Make it a habit to learn about financial literacy. Most people lack a basic understanding of how to create and maintain a budget, but even those who have a clear understanding of how to budget themselves lack other components of financial education. They don't understand how to create a plan to really pay off their debt quickly, don't allocate their money in the best places to account for "unexpected" expenses, and postpone saving until everything else has been covered. In addition, there are a number of things you can learn to increase your financial knowledge, which will allow you to better understand how to manage your money.

Knowing the difference between debit and credit cards, paying taxes, different insurance policies, or how to build a retirement fund are all components of financial education that many lack.

Take responsibility for your savings and expenses. If you know you have big goals for your future, but instead of saving, you're spending on going out to dinner or expanding your closet, you lack the financial knowledge and responsibility that will get you where you want to go. Take responsibility for where you are in your financial planning and your future.

You will learn how you can easily increase your financial knowledge, however, this should not be the starting point. Getting as much information as possible about personal finance is the key to preparing for future financial success.

CHAPTER 17
MAKING BETTER DECISIONS

In this chapter, you will learn about the different decision-making styles people have. It would be unwise to assume that their decisions only have a personal impact. There are certain decisions you make that will affect the lives of others, so it is important to understand your decision-making style. If you are a leader in any way or intend to lead people in the future, you need to read this chapter.

There are four general styles of personal decision-making. These are: Managerial, Analytical, Conceptual and Behavioral. You should know that no one fits completely into any one category. It is likely that you have traits that cut across two styles.

On the other hand, there are also group decision styles. These relate to the way you tend to lead a group of people when you make a decision. They also fall into four categories. These are: autocratic, democratic, collective and consensus styles. Each of these affects a group differently and can be effective in unique situations. If you are in business, you need to understand these styles.

So which of these decision-making styles best describes you?

Personal Decision-Making Styles

Directive Style

If your decision-making style is managerial, it means that you value structure above all else. You are aggressive and expect instant results when you give an order. When you encounter a problematic situation, you take charge, make quick decisions, and expect everyone else to do what they are told without asking questions.

As a managerial decision maker, you have learned to rely entirely on your own experience, knowledge, judgment, and information. You are very strict with the rules and have excellent verbal skills that allow you to give clear instructions.

However, there are some limitations to this style of decision making. You tend to act very quickly without waiting for all the facts. This means that you are likely to make rash decisions without evaluating other alternatives. It is also possible that your decisions provide short-term benefits but not long-term solutions.

Analytic Style

If this is your style of decision making, then you are a born problem solver. You love to examine all kinds of problems, challenges and puzzles and solve them. You are innovative and enjoy dealing with large amounts of data every time you are asked to make a decision. Clearly, analysis-paralysis means nothing to you. No matter how challenging the problem, you are adaptable enough to handle it all.

On the other hand, however, you are also a slow decision maker. The fact that you tend to wait for all the data and facts to come in before making a decision means that your decision-making process can take a long time. To some extent, some people may describe you as a control freak.

Conceptual Style

As a conceptual decision maker, you see problems from an artistic perspective. You tend to be very creative when solving problems. In fact, you try as much as possible to find solutions that are fresh and new. Unlike a managerial decision maker, you believe that any solution must be long-term. You try to think about how your current decisions will impact the future. As a result, you are a risk taker and extremely achievement-oriented.

Behavioural Style

You are a natural peacemaker who believes that every decision should bring people together and avoid conflict. You are very diplomatic and are known for persuading people to see your point of view. Since you are a people person, you prefer to work in groups so that everyone agrees on the best action to take. This gives you the opportunity to help people reconcile their differences and agree on an acceptable solution.

Group Decision-Making Styles

Autocratic Style

It is a style of decision making in which you, as a group leader, have full control over every decision. You don't even bother asking your group members for their opinions or ideas on how to solve the problem. You simply decide what to do based on your own perception and internal information. As a result, you are completely responsible for the positive and negative outcomes of your decision.

The autocratic decision-making style is very effective when the group needs to make a quick decision, for example, during an emergency. However, this style also brings many challenges within the group.

Group members may not be enthusiastic about implementing a decision that was made without their input. For example, if the decision negatively affects employees, morale will drop and they will resent the manager. Therefore, productivity within the company will be affected and the manager can no longer be seen as a credible leader.

Democratic Style

This particular style allows you to make quick decisions involving the whole group. As a leader, you give up your control and ownership of the decision making and allow the group members to vote. The decision that gets a majority of the votes will be adopted and implemented by all.

The problem with this style is that, unlike the autocratic style, there is no sense of individual responsibility. No member can be held responsible for any decision the group makes, and if something goes wrong, a member can refuse to accept responsibility because they voted against the decision in the first place.

Collective Style

This is where, as a group leader, you get everyone's input on the situation and involve members in every step of the process. However, the final decision rests with you alone. Encourage the members of your group to share their ideas and any information they may have about the situation. As they do, you gain a greater understanding and a wider range of perspectives on how the problem can be resolved. At the end of the day, you analyze the information you have received and make your decision.

In the collective style of group decision-making, you have to accept full responsibility for the outcome of your decision. The advantage of this style is that everyone has the opportunity to get involved and participate in the process. For you to be successful as a leader, you must develop excellent communication skills and become a good listener. This is the best way to get a clear picture of the situation so you can make the best decision possible. On the other hand, the fact that you have to wait for the group to give its opinion makes the decision making process very slow.

Consensus Style

This is quite similar to the democratic style, but what makes them different is that in the consensus decision-making style, the decision must be unanimous. As a leader, you have no control over the final decision and you do not have to accept individual responsibility for the outcome. Everyone must agree, otherwise the decision cannot be considered consensual.

The greatest benefit of this style is that it creates a strong sense of commitment within the group. Everyone feels that their opinion matters and plays a role in the success of the group. By involving every member of the group, you will increase the likelihood of success. The consensus style of decision making is generally used when you have a small group of people who will work together over an extended period of time. A good example of this is a business partnership.

The only drawback is that the decision-making process will be slow. It is also difficult to teach a group of people to work together in this way and still maintain harmony.

How Seasoned Executives Make Decisions

When you are at the lower levels of a company, your main responsibility is to make sure that the products go out the door and that any problems are solved immediately when they arise. In other words, taking action is everything. When you climb the ladder, your job is not to take action. Now you have to decide which products or services are worth creating and the best method for developing them. In other words, if you intend to become an effective manager as you move up the corporate ladder, you must learn to change the way you use information and analyze options.

There is one caveat, however, that you should heed. If an ambitious lower-level manager tries to adopt the decision-making style of a higher-level executive too quickly, he or she will be exposed to failure. Likewise, if a newly promoted senior manager gets stuck in the decision-making style of a lower-level executive, he or she will ruin their career. The key here is to ensure a smooth and gradual transition pattern.

But how does this transition happen?

Research shows that a successful lower-level supervisor uses a decision-making style that is the complete opposite of that of a successful CEO. As a manager moves up the ranks, there seems to be a gradual progression toward a more participatory approach with greater diversity of opinion. However, the supervisor who spends most of his or her time in the workshop must be more direct and more command oriented. They do not have time to listen to everyone's input because quick action is required.

This narrative makes sense because when a manager is at the top of the hierarchy, he loses touch with what is happening on the floor. Therefore, their decision-making style should be geared to getting as much information from multiple sources as possible. For a senior executive to be successful, they must encourage people to give them information so that they can critically analyze all the data and select the best strategy. In fact, the most successful business executives become more flexible, open and analytical in their decision-making style as they move up the corporate ladder.

But at what point does this change occur?

There seems to be a "zone of convergence" at the beginning of the management hierarchy, right between the manager and director stage. At this level, an executive will discover that the style of decision making that was effective in the past no longer works. Therefore, most managers simply try to strike a balance by adopting new styles while retaining much of the old thinking.

But this is where things get interesting. Most successful managers are able to leave behind their old decision-making styles and adjust to the new styles. This rapid evolution is what drives them forward in their careers. However, unsuccessful managers seem to be stuck in this convergence zone for too long. They realize that their decision-making style is not working, but for some reason, they don't know how to handle the situation. So they try to use a variety of styles at the same time. They try to be direct today and participatory tomorrow. They are action-oriented, but they also try to be open to other options. Instead of allowing their decision-making style to evolve and progress up the ladder, they stick to the old ways of doing things. Unfortunately, this is where the least successful 20 percent of managers fall and stagnate for the rest of their careers.

CHAPTER 18
SUCCESS WORKS WITH STRUCTURE

Success usually works with structure. You must create a system that brings the flow of success into your life. Systems are vital because when they are created, they last longer and give more significant benefits than random, hit-and-run scores. It means that there must be measures in place for one to succeed in life or for an organization to excel. Left to chance and probability, a person cannot succeed because the odds of failure exist in life and one finds that without hard work, what is easy to achieve in life is failure. You are more likely to fail if you do not work at success. One must work at success and this trial is very important if we are to succeed in life.

Keeping in mind what I have just said, I say here that those who seek to walk the path of success and live in the strength of greatness must first find out what those who have succeeded have done. Surely there is a way and a method to success, and it is discovered through hard work and walked and lived through constant work and applied wisdom. Of course, I must also mention here that in living successfully, there is also the principle of momentum. It is true that as one becomes familiar with the ways of living successfully and sets up structures that ensure success and keeps away from the follies that destroy simple men, that person will live in the fortress of success and greatness. Life, it must be said, works with principles. God has designed the world to work that way. And if you know the principles of how to run a business or how to support and train your children, you are more likely to be successful in your business than the man who shoots at "general management. Believe me, I've been on the shooting range many times: it's almost impossible to hit a target if you don't aim and follow the principles of marksmanship.

Just as there are principles of being a shooter, being a sniper, there are principles of hitting life's targets. On the shooting range, those who are most successful are those who study what is required and apply the principles consistently. We used to say a joke many times when we were on the shooting range that a bullet can smell blood and be directed to hit a human being as long as there is a person in that direction. It was a joke and we would talk about it with laughter. I just wanted to tell people to be careful and not to shoot in the direction the staff was, because people could get killed. Aiming while on the shooting range, and in life is a requirement for success.

It should be understood that the easiest way to succeed in life is to put in place structures that ensure success. This includes a good education. When you have a certain level of education, you will have a certain amount of benefits and opportunities that accumulate in your life because of the education you have. This is the structure. It would be difficult for one to randomly obtain, on a daily basis, the benefits that accrue to one who has a graduate degree. Life doesn't work that way. Through chance, a person would risk something good, but if that thing is really a chance, it would take a long time for the benefit to land in their lap. But if there is a structure in place to ensure a certain benefit, you are going to have that benefit routinely, at measured intervals. If you can have a well measured and calculated success for your life, you are better off. It means that you will also have the opportunity to seek out successful new ventures.

It's not just about formal education; it's about structure in other areas of our lives. We must establish ourselves to succeed through the life we live, the movies we watch, the radio we listen to, the readings, the friends and the associations we make. The skills that one has, like photography, horticulture, landscaping, music, sports, and all these are the structures that we put in place so that success is not a random affair for us, but a designed way of life. Organization. Keep the right friends: keep the mentors in your life. Have close friends who hold you accountable.

And we must keep in mind that the structure also has to do with the internal affairs of our lives. It is about our emotions, our beliefs and our philosophies. This is true because ideas have consequences. Emotional imbalance is a danger and can cause failure in a person's life. And only the wrong beliefs. If your ideas about how the world works are wrong, you will be making wrong choices. This may be true for a person who believes that he or she can meet a person for two weeks and marry them. This is a philosophy. Some people have done it before, and it has worked for them. What is true now is that the chances of making a mistake in that situation are very high. So, this is a belief system that you have, and it becomes a structure because it shapes your life. What we believe and think is how we will appear and become the parade ground of life.

A man will not stand without bones, and a fish will not swim without the structure of bones. Any success we achieve will come from the structure, and any success that is sustained will be sustained by the structure, a system that is created to maintain that success. It is like the steel structure of a building, it keeps the building straight and strong for many years. A success that is presented to us without having the essential structures, without building pillars and foundations to support it and keep it strong, will not be sustained. That's why such investments as real estate, farmland, investments in livestock such as cattle, sheep and other high value animals are creating a structure. This is because with a structure for success in place, even when we sometimes fail and go bankrupt, we are able to rise up because we have the means in our lives to rise up again. This also applies to nations. Investments like bridges, railroads, roads, processing plants, seaports and airports, communication assets, good and reliable partners, a well-educated population with good national values, all this is a structure in place to keep success together, and to stand up with, in a situation where we do not perform well.

In his writing, a political treatise, The Prince, the Italian politician and diplomat, Niccolò Machiavelli writes and guides how a prince will win a kingdom. He also, importantly, gives advice on how a prince can maintain his kingdom and how not to lose his own once he is a prince. When you review all these details that are brought to light for the prince's guidance, you will see that he talks about creating a structure. For example, it talks about how a prince should always make sure he is well armed and that it is in his best interest to constantly prepare for war. The prince who neglects the enterprise of war, Machiavelli argues, will lose his kingdom very easily.

CHAPTER 19
ACHIEVING PEAK PERFORMANCE

There are so many opportunities in the world today. The same opportunities come with your technology, and then, distractions follow. How is it possible for someone to reach their peak? Is there a way for someone to improve their performance and achieve happiness?

Having a sense of purpose is very vital for busy people. With such a mindset, one can achieve personal satisfaction. And so, people strive to prepare themselves to perform better. According to survey studies, two main things can result in peak performance: finding one's balance in a volatile environment and being mentally healthy.

To achieve peak performance in any endeavor in life is to do your best to get the best results. Thinking about it, it might seem impossible to get the maximum results in everything we set out to do. However, one only has to look at the great achievers who reached such heights with maximum performance. Yes, maximum performance can also be achieved.

In fact, some people do not achieve maximum performance. Therefore, one way to achieve great results is to learn from the mistakes of those who fail. Everyone; strong and weak people have 24 hours. But while some use this same resource to grow, others fail with it. Why? Most people lack focus, while others are not passionate enough. Many others throw their hands up in the air at the sight of a challenge. However, before thinking about others with these characters, it is better to look at yourself first. Which of these characters do you have and how can you overcome them to achieve maximum performance?

Proven Ways to Attain Peak Performance

Everyone wants to reach great heights. Success has many friends, but what is success for you? This question is important because different people have different perceptions of success. The reason is that we all have different reasons to strive for a goal. You may want to run a business, be a good father to your child, build the best technology in the world, be the fastest man on earth, or want a quiet spiritual life. The truth is that anyone who tries to achieve the best results in any of these activities has a motive that drives them.

There is an impulse, a desire that pushes you, and you are aware of it, but knowing does not make the journey any easier. Knowledge makes it more difficult, but you must realize that you are not alone in the journey. The path to achieving maximum performance and becoming the best at what you do is difficult, but if you can follow the directions that follow, it will not be as impossible as you thought. Now, let's take a look at the proven ways you can achieve maximum performance.

Health: Take Care of Yourself

You need to make time to take care of yourself. You can go to the gym often or to the spa for a good massage. You can also play soccer or anything that increases your natural energy. For each individual, taking care of yourself is unique. Be sure to put aside the effort to do it every time and do what's right for you.

Your Mood: Be Careful of Bad Moods

Neuro-Linguistic Programming (NLP) shows how enthusiastic reactions are physically anchored in your body. For example, if you are having a terrible day, and need to change your temper before going out to work or looking for a job, here is a primary method to do so: look up at the ceiling, raise your arms noticeably around it, and wave your hands at the ceiling. Chances are your mood will be better than before when you do this.

This behavior shows how optimistic physical gestures can improve our attitude. In addition, these hopeful gestures can be repeated to improve your mood. So, whenever you need to improve your temperament, look up at the ceiling, raising your arms while your hands greet the ceiling. A movement in the disposition and a smile should not be so bad as to add to it.

Energy: Make Use of Passionate Moments

Everyone meets pinnacles and valleys in their vitality. The mystery is deciding the hours of the day when you feel most revitalized or the hours when your energy sinks. During the moments of excitement, perform the most significant task of your day, and when you don't feel motivated, you can make the tasks easier.

Also, when you reach the calm of the night, when you don't feel energetic, don't go after caffeine or sugar. Instead, take a 26-minute break.

This will increase your performance by 30%. High-tech organizations like Google and Apple have "break cases" where their staff can slack off for 26 minutes. Even if you're not resting at all, you'll get a similar benefit if you lie down and stay calm - without examining the advanced devices, or any interference at all.

Music: Stimulate Your Brain

Some tunes make you feel amazing, and others get on your nerves. The peak performance test demonstrates an apparent design output from the mind. For you to experience peak performance, the two sides of your mind have to be in sync.

Let me explain this to you. Some tunes make you feel amazing because they harmonize the brain waves of your two analytical hemispheres. You can feel this impact when you have a smile all over the place, and you need to move to the rhythm of the music.

On the other hand, any physical improvement that makes your vibration grumpy or that you don't feel good regularly, results because the stimulus shook the brain waves of your two brain halves of the globe out of sync.

Concentration: Work on What Works

Comply with the 80-20 law. Your main goal is to do the most important work at the beginning of the day and leave the less important work behind. You need to put most of your effort into areas that can result in significant accomplishments in your job or profession.

The Pareto Principle is simple but very meaningful to achieve your maximum. It is named after Italian financial specialist Vilfredo Pareto. In 1906, he discovered that 80% of the land in Italy is for 20% of the population: this is the basis of the rule.

The most significant thing about Pareto's finding was that this appropriation of the 80/20 occurs incredibly often. For example, 20% of his clients represent 80% of his business. Also, 20% of your time produces 80% of your results. Etc.

The Pareto Principle, or "80/20 Rule", as it is commonly called today, is an extraordinary rule to develop your work. For example, let's say you can understand that 20% of your time produces 80% of the results of your work, you can invest more energy in those exercises and less time in others. In the same way, by recognizing the qualities of the 20% of your most important clients (who occupy 80% of your work), you can discover more clients like them and significantly develop your deals and benefits.

Vision: Look Beyond Momentary Problems

From employees to competitors, from innovative experts to specialists, and the most outstanding ones always imagine themselves achieving their goals and being successful. The brain cannot differentiate between what is genuine and what is not real; it responds to their feelings. Practicing visualization expands your performance capabilities. Around the time of the night take five minutes and visualize yourself playing well tomorrow. See yourself prevailing in meetings, working at your highest potential, and achieving a goal of leapfrogging.

Be Alone: Enjoy Your Company

Spending time alone can be quite refreshing; it helps build your physical, mental, passionate and deep self. This time revives you, developing your ability to perform better. You should allow yourself to rest from the pressure of being confidently close to others. Being surrounded by individuals regularly wears down your ability to manage your state of enthusiasm, causing exhaustion as you try to regulate your behavior while with them.

Being distant from others gives you a time for self-reflection as you try to get your mind in the moment. Being with yourself gives you a feeling of harmony and inner peace. Time alone allows you to consider what is going well in your life, what you need to improve, and the things you need to change. The rewards of being with yourself are incredible. The knowledge you gain, which can be a challenge to gain with friends, will improve your performance on all levels.

Improve: Work on Expansion

After having achieved the task of the week, it is an ideal opportunity to expand their qualities, which is the later stage to achieve maximum performance.

If you want to write a 90,000 word literary work and during the last two weeks you have only written 1,000 words every day, in that moment you have accumulated the propensity and quality of writing. Since this is your quality, you can decide to grow from there. Within a week, you can set a goal of producing 1,500 words every day. The goal you set for yourself of writing your literature in 90 days can happen in 75 or even 65 days.

If what you're doing doesn't work, you shouldn't work too hard at it. The qualities you are expanding on should be the ones that lead to your long-term goals, not the immediate ones.

It is simply a challenge to try to fix every imperfection you have. You can achieve anything you set your mind to in your brain, but that doesn't mean you have to end up being amazing at everything. Instead, you need to end up being amazing at a couple of things.

Stress: Be Emotionally Balanced

Managing your stress level, which is the ability to avoid panic under pressure, is equally critical to achieving maximum success. Being emotionally balanced when facing stressful events is important if you want to achieve maximum performance. Managing your feelings helps you better manage stress, which in turn makes it easier for you to focus on your work while performing it smoothly. The result of this is peak performance.

You can reach your peak performance by making large, constant movements. Peak performers are the opposite of people who experience the harmful effects of burnout. High performers maintain balance and strength over long periods of time, just as they remain optimistic under difficult conditions. All this can be achieved by being passionate, maintaining an energetic attitude and being disciplined. By learning the methods and ways that lead you to achieve your best, you continue to advance your career and stay on top of your game.

CHAPTER 20
COGNITIVE FLEXIBILITY

Cognitive flexibility encompasses multiple skills, all related to our ability to quickly adapt our thinking to reflect the changes or complexities of our environment. It allows us to find out and clearly understand even ill-defined problems and generate several possible solutions to a given problem. In a constantly changing world, it is essential to take steps to improve cognitive flexibility, and one of the best tools to immediately improve this executive skill is a growth mentality.

Whether you choose to adopt a growth mentality, or a fixed mentality can have a dramatic impact on your life. A growth mindset encourages persistence in the face of challenges, while a fixed mindset can encourage you to give up. Think about how many opportunities will open up for you if instead of saying, "No, I'm not good at that," you say instead, "I could learn to do that! What a great new experience this will be.

People who invest in their own cognitive flexibility not only create more opportunities, but also strengthen their ability to solve problems and change tactics midway, which is essential to successfully navigating our complex and rapidly changing world. As with other executive functioning skills - or any skill, for that matter - practice is the key to strengthening cognitive flexibility. The shortest path to becoming a better problem solver is to solve more problems, which can often be done simply by facing the challenges that arise in life. The more you go out into the real world, encounter real problems, try to solve them, fail and try again, the more you will strengthen your cognitive flexibility. You can also hone these skills with the brain exercises and tricks we are about to explore.

Flexible Problem-Solving

I once worked with a woman, Marie, who lived in fear of the drastic changes and reorganization that was taking place in her workplace. As Marie explained to me, she had a lifelong strategy of dealing with uncertainty by preparing for the worst. She believed that if good things were going to happen, she would have to work hard at it, and she also believed that she had to work just as hard to make sure that bad things didn't happen. He didn't trust the idea that something good would come into his life and that difficult situations would be resolved in his favor.

I suggested that he try to change his perspective and asked him if there was anyone in his company who wasn't afraid of the changes that were taking place. He thought of his co-worker Stan. He was surprised that Stan believed everything would work out and didn't put any energy into stressing himself. He had an easy faith and confidence in the goodness of the world. Whenever she and Stan talked about the reorganization, he was optimistic and confident that they would be okay no matter what.

Marie imagined that she was Stan, adopting his attitude to describe the situation from her point of view. Her fear began to dissipate just by pretending to be him. When she saw the world through his eyes, she realized the price she had to pay for always imagining the worst-case scenario. He also realized that the future can never be known for sure, but that, in itself, could be exciting. She discovered that when she felt hopeful, she felt good in the moment, which impacted everyone around her.

With this new attitude, Marie realized that even if her job was eliminated, she would get a severance package that would give her time to find a job she could enjoy even more. In short, the positive feelings she came to experience created the ability to see a wider range of positive outcomes. Marie adopted a growth mentality, and so can you, starting with the first brain cut here.

Role Play – What Would Oprah Do?

When a problem or struggle seems overwhelming to you, remember a role model or someone who has an inspiring story. Oprah Winfrey is a good example. She overcame a childhood of poverty to become one of the most successful inspirational media figures. She is a great choice for this brain hack, but you can choose anyone you love or admire and know personally or just from reading and movies.

Use your imagination to explore what it would be like to be this inspiring person and how they would handle the situation you are facing. This opens up new potentials. You can easily get into this brain hack by pretending that you are an actor and that this person is the role you are playing. Imagine that you are acting, thinking and feeling as this person would. Ask yourself: "What is the most different from being this person?" and "What does it feel like to be this person?

Then think about the problem you are trying to solve, and ask yourself, "How would this person solve this problem? As you embody this role, think about the first action step this person would take to begin to realize this solution. That is your next step of action.

Tips: Pop Your Bubble

Their life experience is often limited by their gender, race, social and economic class, education and family history. Most of us live in personal bubbles that we assume to be the "true" reality. These bubbles convince us of falsehoods, such as the idea that we cannot or should not change because others will look down on us. But there is a whole world of possibilities outside of our personal bubbles. When you practice seeing what's outside your bubble, opportunities for problem solving will come up.

Stop Approval-Seeking

Psychologists use the term "seeking approval" to describe decision making based on what other people think. It can be as small as choosing your clothes to fit into a group rather than expressing your own style. It can be as big as taking an awesome job instead of a low-paying job that is more in line with your talents and interests. If you value the approval of others over your own, you will not be able to discover what you like, where you want to live, what kind of career you would thrive in, etc.

Unfortunately, many of us are controlled by our fears of what others will think of us. It may be that the solution to a problem requires you to take actions that others would argue with, disapprove of, or discourage. Start noticing your fears about how things look to others. When you notice them, you have the option to go beyond them. Then, loosen up the new views by changing from "What do others want me to do" and "What will others think of what I do" to "What do I really want to do? This opens up a whole new perspective.

Exercise

Find Your Inner Compass

Remember a choice you have to make soon or in the future. If you don't face a choice, make one that is likely to happen. Write it down in your journal or worksheet. Then list all the possible choices.

Then, write down the answers to these questions:

- What would my closest partner or friend recommend that I choose?
- What would my parents recommend that I choose?
- What would my friends recommend that I choose?
- What would other important people in my life recommend?
- What would I like to choose?

Finding your inner compass doesn't mean you have to challenge what others think you should do. They might have good ideas that you agree with. However, if you still feel stuck in your decision making, consider consulting a coach, therapist, or expert in the field related to your decision.

Tips: Career Selection

Give yourself permission to try new jobs if you are not thriving in your current workplace. In a post called "How to Pick a Career (That Actually Fits You)", in the blog, Tim Urban compares the concept of having a lifetime career to entering a tunnel you don't get out of until you're 40. Who wants to stay in a tunnel, especially if it's dark and gloomy? There's no need to feel like you have to stay. Maybe you can ask for a promotion, ask for a transfer, or launch a job search while you're at the job you have now.

Seeing Yourself from Different Perspectives

Being able to see yourself and your life from multiple perspectives not only helps you think creatively but also helps you regulate your emotions. I have already talked about seeing a problem from someone else's point of view, but now I suggest you see it from your own, from different versions of yourself. What do I mean? Well, let's say I wrote an article about the 10 best ways to get a client who never thinks he's good enough to cry into therapy. Number one on my list would be to ask, "What would your 16-year-old self say about the life you've created for yourself?"

When I ask this to my clients who are struggling in their lives, they almost always realize how much they have overcome and that, by the standards of their 16-year-old self, they have achieved enough to be truly happy. "You're doing great," their younger self would say. Unfortunately, adults develop a tunnel vision, and with each new improvement in life, they lose this perspective.

However, some people may do this exercise and feel they have let down that 16-year-old self. If that's you, remember that you have a reading in your hands to teach you the skills you may have been missing. If you feel that way, reassure the 16-year-old that you are back on track and working towards your dreams.

CHAPTER 21
METHODOLOGICAL BELIEF

Methodological belief is a critical thinking skill that involves a special kind of role-playing. Using this skill, you adopt the other person's point of view and support it vigorously for a limited period of time - usually 5 minutes or less. During this period of time, you think of as many reasons as you can to support this position. You put yourself in the other person's shoes.

The purpose of this skill is to provide you with an understanding of an opposing point of view. Once you have used this skill, you will have a better understanding of the opposite point of view. You will be able to understand to a much greater degree why the opposite party thinks as they do. You will be familiar with their frame of reference and will be able to resolve disputes and conflicts more easily by understanding what is important to the opposition and why.

Methodological belief requires some practice. The easiest way to begin using this skill is to deliberately choose a point of view from the opposition. Once you have chosen it, write down on a piece of paper all the reasons you can think of to support this position.

Let's start with the next topic: the war in Iraq. Should we stay there or withdraw? Whatever you believe, take the opposite view and support it. Here are some examples.

Stay in Iraq:

Finish the job, train the Iraqis to defend their land.

The soldiers will die in vain if we withdraw now.

Retreating now will admit defeat.

We must continue to fight terrorism.

Withdraw:

We have achieved our goal. We overthrew the Hussein government.

We have occupied the country enough.

Iraq and other countries need to get involved.

Enough of our troops have died there.

The same technique can easily be applied to a business environment. Consider a classic management issue: use the authoritarian approach to management or use a collaborative approach.

Authoritarian:

Maintain strict control.

Get results.

Proven results have been around for a long time.

Workers know what to do and when and how to do it.

Collaborative:

Provide workers with more autonomy.

Increases creativity.

Promotes good morale and a positive environment.

Encourages people to work to their potential.

Now it's your turn - consider the opposite viewpoint and choose the one you would not normally support. Use the Methodological Belief for five minutes and support that opposite position. Write down on a piece of paper as many reasons as you can identify to support the opposition.

The Methodological Belief is a skill that needs to be practiced, like any other skill. Sometimes, after a person has used this skill, he or she changes their view and supports the view of the opposition. More often, however, he or she will not necessarily change their viewpoint but will have a much clearer understanding of the opposing viewpoint. You may come to understand why someone thinks this way and what their frame of reference is. This information can help you resolve conflicts and reach agreements. In fact, it can help in negotiation.

Why Compromise Is a Lose-Lose Proposition

The idea of using the Methodological Belief is not to gain influence and try to manipulate the opposition or even compromise. In a compromise, both parties lose something. They both give something to stir up a conflict. The Methodological Belief gives you a greater understanding of the other person's framework. The question to be asked is: how can we resolve this conflict and satisfy both parties? There is no guarantee that the Methodological Belief will accomplish this. But, you will have a better understanding of what the opposition wants and why that is so important to them.

Synergy

When both parties really want to resolve a conflict, it is sometimes possible to find a solution that is greater than the sum of the individual parties to the negotiation. Negotiation is a complete reading in itself and far beyond the scope of this paper. However, I emphasize that methodological belief can lead to creative solutions. I would like to suggest a simple action that can be done in a negotiation. - Make both parties sit on the same side of the table. Instead of opposing each other, they sit on the same side and work together toward a resolution. It doesn't always work, but neither does negotiation. Some conflicts can only be resolved with time, a lot of time.

One of the difficulties of the Methodological Belief is that "trying to believe someone we don't agree with makes us feel vulnerable" (Elbow, 1986, p266). An individual usually feels uncomfortable when looking at or discovering something that is different from his or her perspective (Sargent 1984)). Distress" is defined by Selye as anything that is uncomfortable (Selye, 1974). When it comes to using the Methodological Belief, initially, you can feel uncomfortable, especially if you have strong feelings about the particular issue.

In my critical thinking classes, I often introduce a fairly low level, non-controversial topic initially. One exercise that I often use is the topic of civil disobedience. I have my students read an excerpt from Thoreau's Civil Disobedience and use the Methodological Belief to address the question of whether it is okay to break the law. Then I move on to more controversial issues such as the death penalty or abortion. Such issues present a real challenge because they are so emotionally charged for most people.

Another difficulty with the Methodological Belief is self-centered thinking, which is the tendency to see everything in relation to oneself (Paul, 1990, 548). Ironically, the Methodological Belief is the antithesis of self-centered thinking, because it promotes awareness and a willingness to see all points of view - regardless of one's personal feelings or interests (Paul, 1990, p198).

Despite the challenges presented by the Methodological Belief, it is an extremely valuable skill. It allows you not only to see the other side but also to temporarily adopt the opposite point of view. Instead of "putting yourself in the other person's shoes," you are "getting inside their head. In fact, Elbow states, "give me the view in your head. You are having an experience that I am not having. Help me to have it" (Elbow, 1986)

To be able to use this skill successfully, you need to be able to take the opposite view and realize that you are only doing it for a limited period of time (5 minutes). What you are really trying to do is find as many reasons as possible to support this position. Imagine that you are a lawyer and you have to defend a position that you personally oppose. But, as a professional, you are obliged, even compelled, to defend this position. Therefore, you need to know as many reasons as possible to support this viewpoint. You don't have to agree with it, but your goal is to understand it better. Why would anyone think that way? What would be their frame of reference? What is important to them and why? The answers to some of these questions are what you will learn using the Methodological Belief. You should "look for evidence and favorable reason to support the belief in question. (Elbow, 1988, p276).

The Methodological Belief, or the "belief game" as it is sometimes called, has some rules. The basic one is the 5-minute time limit. Another rule or more than one suggestion is to look for something that is interesting or useful about the point of view. As I have described above, it is best to practice this skill initially with a non-controversial topic. If you are a manager or supervisor, keep in mind that what you consider non-controversial might be an important issue for others. It is best to check with others first before trying to use it.

For Managers

A good manager knows how to motivate employees and get the best effort and work out of employees. Too often, when a manager has a "problem worker," a person who is not adequately fulfilling his or her responsibilities, the manager, after talking to the problem worker, will begin to build a case for termination. While such a step may be necessary, it may be more beneficial for the manager to use some methodological belief to understand the problem worker, especially if there is a conflict or opposing viewpoint. I am NOT talking about an employee who is disrespectful, defiant and/or appears to be deliberately difficult or breaking company policy. By using the Methodological Belief, it may be possible to understand the problematic worker's point of view. It is very easy to simply fire an employer. However, think about the time involved in recruiting, hiring and training a new employee. The Methodological Belief provides you with a way to understand an opposing viewpoint - to understand what is important to that employee and why. This skill provides managers with a specific way to accomplish this - to gain a better understanding of individual views that are in opposition to their own. This can be a very valuable skill.

Summary

- Methodological belief is a powerful critical thinking skill that allows you to understand an opposing viewpoint.

- For a limited period of time (5 minutes), you adopt the opposing viewpoint and support it vigorously.

- The technique requires practice and presents a real challenge because, initially, it can make you feel vulnerable or uncomfortable.

- If you have very strong feelings about the subject and/or are polarized, this skill can be difficult to use.

- If done correctly, you will better understand the opposition's point of view. This could lead to improved chances of resolving a conflict or negotiating a settlement.

CHAPTER 22
KEEN OBSERVATION SKILLS

Observation is fundamental to any analytical process, and is actually what is done in the first place. In fact, human beings continue to observe things and events around them, sometimes only accidentally and at other times as a deliberate move in their critical observation.

The Art of Observation within Varying Fields

Passive Observation

Any idea what passive observation means? Well, it's what you do casually almost every minute you're awake. It means what you register with your common senses continuously, without even planning it. You see, by varying the colors that objects carry around you, the shapes too, you register different smells and sometimes odors, you feel different textures with your hands or other parts of your body, and you even notice that moving objects change speed, and the environment changes temperature.

All of these observations can be made casually, or they can be the result of an exercise that you have deliberately planned to carry out: spontaneous observation, or observation as part of critical thinking, in which you may wish to gather information in order to carry out some critical analysis.

Psychological Observation

Observations of a psychological nature are often made during experiments or on a normal day in the course of natural behavior. In psychology, observations are of a visual nature, and sometimes of a vocal nature. So, essentially, video and other devices that record sound are used as tools to assist in the observation and analysis of those observations.

Meteorological Observation

In the field of meteorology, specialized tools are used to make observations on meteorological elements. Here, we are talking about observing temperature changes, issues related to atmospheric pressure, the degree of precipitation and humidity and also the intensity and speed of wind.

The observations are actually very crucial in this field, as a basis for an extensive and deep analysis.

Medical Observation

The medical field, like the meteorological one, depends to a great extent on the observations made. In this field, observations are made in order to make a diagnosis and decide on the appropriate treatment. Here tools are used to take note of the patient's heart rate, blood pressure, body temperature and so on. Once this wide range of data is collected through observation, it is used to determine the course of medical action with respect to the patient being observed.

Experience

Experience is the strongest pillar of critical thinking skills, and this is because it is your personal life experiences that often influence the direction of your critical thinking process. These experiences include things you discovered when you were very young, and things you experienced only this morning.

Let's take the example of a child painting a chair at home from his palate of colors. As he does this, he learns some universal truths, like what a painted surface looks like. If his mother admonishes him for painting his chair, he learns that people can get upset when he interferes with their objects without permission.

How about when you're cooking in the kitchen and washing the dishes? Aren't there some principles you learn during these processes that help in critical thinking? You learn how ceramics respond to heat as opposed to glass items, which helps you in the future when analyzing situations in critical thinking. Nor can you underestimate the lessons you learn from your adolescent experiences. Inevitably, they influence your critical thinking skills.

Indeed, even your own personality can be influenced in some way by your experiences. For example, if a ridiculous pose by your child during a photo shoot makes people laugh, the child may get into the habit of doing that trick when he or she wants to get attention. All of your experience can be useful in helping your child's critical thinking, but what seems to play the most important role in shaping and refining his critical thinking skills is his interpersonal experience. Why do you think this is so? Well, you learn from others what you should anticipate when you behave in a certain way, and also how you should react when others behave in a certain way. These experiences influence the way you behave, and although it takes more than experience to develop strong critical thinking skills, these experiences are the most convenient ways to learn new critical thinking skills.

Reflection

When something is seriously considered, or what can be called serious thinking, it can be called reflection. Reflection is really necessary for critical thinking. You cannot take things and events as you see them, without considering them or thinking about them properly. For example, you may have observed something happen and lived the experience, but to form a reliable opinion, you have to consider the circumstances in which the event occurred, the people who were involved, the probability that what happened might have changed, and other factors.

In this case, your reflection would help your mind process your experiences and sift through the relevant parts of those experiences that are irrelevant to your decision making. You must be able to reflect on things so that you can reason about events and so that you can correctly communicate those events to others. The reality is that reflection influences the way you perceive yourself, as well as the way you perceive the world in general. You should also keep in mind that other people involved in these experiences may have a different point of view that is equally valid.

Reasoning

Reasoning is how you think and how you understand the issues in order to draw conclusions or make judgments. Reasoning is based on logic, and also on the available evidence.

Even when you are learning in school, you appreciate things better when you can reason, because you can review the facts and supporting evidence and come to a logical conclusion about why things happen a certain way, or why things in the past happened the way they did. Reasoning is what helps you decide what is most important in your life and what needs to be left out. It supports your critical thinking process, leading you to gather your different thoughts as well as any information you have, in preparation for taking whatever steps you feel are necessary. In short, reasoning helps you to have a better understanding of the subject at hand.

Now, are you always reasoning the same way? Of course not! How you reason will probably depend on the facts you have, the circumstances in which things happened and so on. Therefore, you will see the reasoning classified differently as in:

Moral Reasoning

Here, it is his moral standard that comes into play, and he uses it to reach a conclusion on the matter in question.

Inductive Reasoning

Here, some particular information is taken, and from that information, some general conclusions are drawn.

Deductive Reasoning

In this category of reasoning, it is general information that is used to draw conclusions of a specific nature. Whatever form of reasoning you apply, the point is that you are trying to reach conclusions regarding a certain issue.

Would you like to have examples of when reasoning is used?

Here:

On a Daily Basis

Surely we do not use logic on a daily basis to solve problems that arise in the course of our work and in other areas of our lives. In fact, you do. Even the people we come into contact with call us to reason. If you think about it, some of those people's ideas are hateful, and some people often have questionable morals. In those circumstances, only your reasoning skills can help you make the most appropriate decisions, such as how to relate to each of those people, and also which of their ideas to adopt and which to ignore.

In the Course of Business

Have you noticed that many employers are impressed by employees who can reason? That's a factor they look for when conducting job interviews. They want employees who can draw conclusions from given facts and scenarios. This is important so that employees can make decisions aimed at taking advantage of business opportunities, and even decisions aimed at protecting the company's brand. Decision makers need less supervision.

In the Field of Sports

When it's time for practice or actual game time, a sports team takes time to think through how they will approach the game and tackle it, and they do so by taking into account the competition or supposed skills of their opponents. In short, the team must reason out the best moves to make, and in what form or order, to ultimately beat the opposing team.

Communicating

Communication can be considered as the exchange of thoughts and information between the parties. Isn't this what you do almost continuously? Although you may have taken it for granted, you can appreciate that serious issues tend to go smoothly as long as you have thought critically about what to say before actually saying it. In fact, there is a saying among the wise that it is important to think before you speak.

If you want to be a great communicator:

- Take deep thought seriously.

- Take into consideration other people's perspectives.

Only after doing this are you sure that you are giving an answer that is justified at the time and in the circumstances that prevail.

Take Away Lessons

What needs to be removed here is that it is important to be fair in the assessment of situations, and it is also important to be rational in decision making. This is useful in your career, in business, in your social life and practically everywhere. Finally, all critical thinking skills are very important to your success and to the way others see you. If, for example, as a manager, you suspect that one of your employees is stealing things from what you have observed, and also from your personal experience of how people tend to behave when they are taking things away from the company, you don't just reflect on what you suspect and reason out what the implications are of retaining or not retaining the employee. You are also able to communicate your thoughts to that employee.

Otherwise, if you miss a step, such as communicating, and only sign the employee's letter of termination, how would you know if another employee is purposely sabotaging this particular employee? Without effective communication, how would the other managers and employees be sure you fired this employee for fair reasons?

Your skills combine observation, facts, input from all sources, and your experience and ability to handle each situation based on your own power of critical thinking.

CHAPTER 23
THE THEORY OF MULTIPLE INTELLIGENCE

Howard Gardner believed that the conventional concept of intelligence was too restrictive and limited and that IQ measurements overlooked the other "intelligence" an individual might have. He discussed the prevailing belief that one can only learn through reading and writing or through a lecture in class and that one's understanding can only be measured through a test or essay questions.

According to Gardner, he had the opportunity to study human nature, particularly how human beings think during his years at Harvard College under the influence of individuals such as cognitive psychologist Jerome Bruner, psychoanalyst Erik Erikson, and sociologist David Riesman. The theory of multiple intelligences was conceived and developed after working with two very different groups - one is a group of normal, gifted children and the other is a group of brain-damaged adults.

In the course of his observation and research, he discovered that people have various learning methods and thought processes. Therefore, it is somewhat restrictive to adopt only the traditional theory of intelligence, which focuses merely on a single general intelligence.

Gardner's theory opened the door to more research studies as well as advances in the field of education. It has become so popular that educators believe it validates their daily experience with their students. The theory provided educators with a conceptual framework for school curriculum development, teaching practices, and student assessment. Educators have been able to improve their teaching methods to better accommodate a wider range of student needs.

Howard Gardner's theory has been criticized by both educators and psychologists. They claim that the word "intelligence" is too broad to be defined by only eight (at the time of its initial introduction) types of "intelligence," and believe that this stated intelligence only represents personality traits, talents, or abilities. In addition, Gardner's theory also lacks supporting empirical research.

Despite the criticisms, Gardner's theory is gaining popularity with other educators. Even teachers are beginning to integrate the theory into their teaching philosophies and practices. As a result, students begin to understand more about their strengths, abilities, and talents.

The Two Types of Intelligence by Cattell-Horn

According to the American psychologists, John Horn and Raymond Cattell, there are two types of intelligence: fluid intelligence and crystallized intelligence. The theory presents that a person's general intelligence is a product of both inherent and acquired abilities.

Fluid Intelligence

Psychologists described fluid intelligence as the general ability to process abstract ideas, solve problems, identify patterns, discern relationships, and give reasons. These factors are generally influenced by one's inherent abilities and are not learned through education, training, or experience.

Fluid intelligence is used to respond to riddles, create strategies, solve problems, and solve puzzles or mysteries. It can be said that an individual identified as "street smart" has a high fluid intelligence. Another example is a person with high navigation skills.

One way to determine this type of intelligence is its adaptability and flexibility, particularly during various situations or circumstances in which it could be applied. However, fluid intelligence tends to deteriorate during late adulthood, as certain cognitive skills related to fluid intelligence decline as people reach this stage.

Crystallized Intelligence

On the other hand, crystallized intelligence is the opposite pole to fluid intelligence. This type of intelligence can be acquired through learning, experience and education.

While fluid intelligence remains fundamentally throughout an individual's life, crystallized intelligence can progress and develop further. For example, knowledge of a person's vocabulary can be increased by learning more words and being exposed to several people with whom one can speak. Another example is gaining culinary skills through constant learning and practice, as well as exposure to various cultures.

Interrelationship and Distinction

Between fluid and crystallized intelligence, what is more important? Both types are equally essential for an individual to function in his or her daily life. For example, when taking a math test, one needs to rely on both fluid and crystallized intelligence - fluid intelligence to be able to work out a strategy to solve problems; and crystallized intelligence to employ the exact formulas that are needed.

Cattell believed that both fluid intelligence and crystallized intelligence are facets that make up general intelligence. Therefore, both types of intelligence are interrelated and different at the same time. Crystallized intelligence is established through the inversion of fluid intelligence when an individual goes through a learning process. By using fluid intelligence, acquired information is transferred to long-term memory and ultimately becomes part of crystallized intelligence.

That said, crystallized intelligence and fluid intelligence are closely interrelated. Crystallized intelligence is formed when fluid intelligence is used in the course of acquiring information and learning about it. By using fluid intelligence to reason and think about problems, information can then be transferred to long-term memory so that it can become part of crystallized intelligence.

Changes in Crystallized Intelligence and Fluid Intelligence

Both crystallized and fluid intelligence can change over the course of a person's life, with some mental abilities maturing at various points.

Many believe that fluid intelligence peaks fairly early in life, but recent studies suggest that some characteristics of fluid intelligence can mature into 40 years of age. On the other hand, crystallized intelligence can only peak at 60 or 70 years of age.

Here are some details to remember about crystallized and fluid intelligence:

- Many features of fluid intelligence reach their apex in adolescence and begin to deteriorate around the age of 30 or 40.

- Both fluid and crystallized intelligence progress through childhood and adolescence.

- Crystallized intelligence continues to develop throughout adulthood.

Developing Crystallized Intelligence and Fluid Intelligence

As crystallized intelligence is apparently something that can be improved through learning and that means that the more knowledge a person has accumulated, the more crystallized intelligence will be obtained. Therefore, in order to improve this type of intelligence, education must be expanded, either formally (for example, by expanding university studies) or informally (for example, by reading a lot and acquiring different experiences).

Until recently it was believed that fluid intelligence was no longer modifiable. The latest research suggests that brain training can help enhance certain characteristics of fluid intelligence even in older adults.

Studies of intelligence conveyed that people do not have much control over their intelligence. In addition, it was primarily determined by genetics and that training programs intended to help increase IQ levels only achieve a small amount of success. However, a recent study by Columbia University suggests that fluid intelligence can be improved by using brain training that focuses on working memory, a form of short-term memory that concentrates on what an individual is currently thinking.

Working memory is essential, as it involves the ability to mentally manipulate stored information for a limited period of time. For example, a person trained in a specific working memory task might perform better in that particular task. Moreover, the researchers also found that training increased unrelated cognitive skills, such as the ability to solve new problems, which were completely independent of the knowledge gained and the ability to reason. Basically, a person can improve his or her ability to employ the abstraction of ideas as easily as he or she employs knowledge-based reasoning.

Sternberg's Triarchic Theory of Intelligence

Another psychologist who advocates multiple intelligence is Robert J. Sternberg, who formulated the Triarchic Theory of Intelligence. He proposed that there are three types of Intelligence: practical, analytical and distinct. This theory comprises three sub-theories which are related to a specific type of intelligence.

- Contextual (Practical Intelligence) - or the ability of an individual to relate successfully to his or her environment or to get along in varied contexts.

- Experiential (Creative Intelligence) - the ability of the individual to deal with new situations or issues or to propose new ideas.

- Componential (Analytical Intelligence) - the individual's ability to solve problems or the ability to analyze situations and provide solutions through available information and resources.

It was not until 1985 that Sternberg proposed his theory in opposition to the idea of general intelligence (g), which is the common basis for measuring intelligence. General intelligence is what psychologists call "Academic Intelligence".

Sternberg presented his argument on the basis that practical intelligence or the person's ability to react and adapt to his environment, as well as creativity, is significant in measuring the level of an individual's general intelligence. Furthermore, he argues that intelligence is not something fixed, but is composed of many skills that can be further developed. His arguments led to the creation of the Triarchic Theory of Intelligence. Sternberg divided his theory into three sub-theories.

Contextual Sub-Theory

Under this sub-theory, intelligence is believed to be intimately interconnected with the individual's environment and therefore based on the way the individual functions in his or her daily life. This includes their ability to adapt to their environment, to select the most appropriate condition or environment, and to shape that environment to fit their needs and desires.

Experimental Sub-Theory

Contextual sub-theory is based on the belief that there is a continuum of experiences, from the novel to automation, to which its intelligence can be applied.

Component Sub-theory

The component sub-theory specifies the potential set of underlying mental processes that affect behavior and how behavior develops.

There are at least five component areas that are significant for creativity according to studies of creative people.

- Expertise - Creativity is a product of hard work (Ericsson, 1998; Weisberg, 2006). Knowing more about the topic they are working on through careful studies, creative people have developed expertise

- Risk taking - Creative people are always willing to take risks in their approaches to new ideas.

- Imaginative thinking - Creative people see things visually, giving them different points of view from different angles of different ideas.

- Intrinsic interest - Creative people love to work on projects regardless of their compensation to give way to their passion. Research has shown that those who are paid for their creativity are often less creative than those who are not (Hennessey & Amabile, 2010).

- Working in a creative environment - In fact, most creatives were helped, supported and challenged by others working on similar projects (Simonton, 1992).

CHAPTER 24
TECHNIQUES USED BY SUCCESSFUL PEOPLE

Making intelligent decisions and having quick thinking techniques is the goal of every human being. We are always going through difficult times when we need our thinking skills to make difficult decisions, and without great thinking techniques, we are doomed to fail in this life. It can be extremely difficult for people to make the right decisions in life because sometimes we are guided by instincts of fear and anger. It is important for each person to learn to make decisions that are not influenced by our emotions. Our current emotions are not the best to support us when we are faced with difficult decisions because they do not reflect what the future holds for us. What should be done is that one should be able to get out of all the things that interfere with one's judgment and achieve balance by looking at the big picture.

One person who is good at making the right and smart decisions in life is a famous investor who is also a billionaire named Warren Buffet. When you make a decision, you need to consider the long-term effects your choices will bring.

Warren Buffet

This is a man considered to be one of the greatest investors that has ever existed. According to Warren Buffet, it is very important that every human being be able to step out of the present for a moment to make wise decisions that will endure over the long term. To achieve this, Buffet encourages people to have a very high level of thinking. In doing so, one is able to carefully evaluate the effects of all actions beyond anything one may see at the time of making one's decision. This is how most people who have succeeded in life make their decisions. Buffet recommends the implementation of a strategy that she believes will help anyone she meets. This strategy is called the 10/10/10 method.

The 10/10/10 Method

If you are the type of person who has grown up making short term decisions, advancing to a high level of thinking can be a challenge. This is where this method comes in to help people like you move forward effortlessly. This method suggests a very simple but effective rule of always asking yourself three essential questions before making a decision as it will help you get rid of any doubts you may have within yourself. The three questions are:

- How will you feel within 10 minutes of making your decision
- How you will feel within 10 months of making the decision
- How you will feel 10 years from now after making the decision

The three questions are very crucial for every human being since they help to evaluate the decision he is about to make in terms of short, medium and long term. This is because sometimes what seems very important in 10 minutes can be very useless or not so important in 10 months. However, something that was not important in 10 months may be extremely important in 10 years. When you think along these lines, decisions tend to be at a very high level. Your decisions will be very effective because you have considered all the factors of short-term effects on future effects.

Implementing this strategy is not very easy and may take some time for you to adapt. However, you should try to practice every time you are faced with a difficult decision or simply any decision because it will improve over time. This method helps people realize that everyday decisions are very important because they eventually determine the quality of life in the long run. Every decision you make every day has to be the right decision because that is what will help you improve your life. Every gradual step you take is essential; that's why you can't ignore the small choices you make. The 10/10/10 method will help you analyze the complete order of the different actions. This method is what Warren Buffet attributes to his success in making the high-level thinking decision, and it can work for you too.

Bill Gates

This is a man well known for being a co-founder of Microsoft and the second richest man in the world in 2019. With a net worth of $98 billion, this man definitely has strategies we can borrow to help us make smart decisions. Bill Gates is known for being a person who thinks differently than others. He is also said to be a man who has the unique ability to find flaws, spot opportunities, and even connect puzzles. This is a man who is able to adjust to different life scenarios in any given situation and therefore has been able to learn from various perspectives.

10 Ways to Help You Think like Bill Gates

You can't be Bill Gates, but you can definitely ask him for some wisdom, and these are some of the great strategies he uses.

1. Priorities - Time is a very important resource, but it is also very limited. When you know this, then you begin to question what is worthwhile and what is not. According to Bill Gates, knowing what to prioritize will save you a lot of time instead of going around in circles on something that is not worthwhile.

2. Anyone who requires a smart answer should ask a smart question - Smart questions help you explore a wide range of options that you would have missed if you hadn't been smart about simple questions. This is a skill that has worked for the Microsoft brand through the implementation of precision questions. Seven categories fall into this skill:

- What to go and what not to go, this is where you ask if what you're about to ask is worth asking, or you can just let it go.

- Clarification: in this, you get to know what you are supposed to do to make sure you get the right message.

- Assumptions - this is where you learn about all the assumptions so you can clarify them

- Critical questions. All the necessary questions are clarified here, such as discovering the truths.

- Causes - you will find the causes of all that is needed

- Effects - what will be the consequences?

- Action - what is the right action to take?

3. Make data-based decisions - in this strategy, be informed first before making any decisions. To do this, you also need to thoroughly evaluate all the sources from which your data come. Where most people fail is when they first make emotional decisions, then try to get data that supports their choices. What a smart person does is to put aside emotions and enter into critical thinking.

4. Let go of your ego - what you do in this strategy is distance yourself from the problems as well as the solution. By doing so, you can strategically examine both the problem and the solutions from all angles and know the details you need to know. Remember, you are not trying to prove that you are right, but what you are doing is finding out if the solution is really right. Therefore, you are able to separate your emotions by not taking it personally.

5. Frame the problem - this is simply framing your problems as you would a photograph to get a better view of it. When you frame your problems, you are able to determine what is worth focusing on in terms of what should be inside and what should be outside. You will only know your problems well when you frame them, and you will learn how you can address them from that. Some of the questions that should be framed include

- Who are the clients?

- What are the priorities and needs of your customers? What are your competitors doing? How is the market? What can you do to respond?

- How is technology affecting your business? What should be your priority for the company?

6. Get perspective on problems - this means examining all angles of your problems. You must be flexible enough to be able to change the way you see things from one side to the other. This means that you have to conduct thorough research in which you get to know what others think about your problem. There is a lot you need to learn about your problem, and you have to be open-minded so that you can see all the angles of your problems. Here you can take advantage of smart people who do not have experience in the field so that you can know how to solve the problem accurately.

7. Problem modeling - when you make an abstract model of your problem, then you are able to scrutinize your problem in small details. This is a good strategy because when you start with the complicated factors, it will wear off. Bill Gates has used the whiteboard to help you with this method. Using a whiteboard, you can quickly sketch out your thoughts and focus on them at that angle. The board is very useful because it allows you to draw a problem and a solution on the board itself. Some models may be wrong, but they are still useful as they will help you learn things you would never have without the model.

8. System and ecosystem - sometimes, like Bill Gates, you have to have an engineer's mind. This is where you see the problem as the system. So, you have to ask yourself questions like what are the parts, how does it really work, how do the two work together, and the inputs and outputs. From the system, then you move on to the systems of systems or the Ecosystem.

9. Looking at the problem over time - You must try to play with your problems and solutions, no matter how challenging they seem to you. You have to consider possible future trends and their impacts, consider sustainability. Some things may seem great for a short time, but when you consider the time factor in them, they may not be worth it. When you consider time, you protect yourself against future challenges and learn how to protect yourself.

10. Think strategically - strategies are what determine your outcome and the actions you will need to take. There are some tips you can use to put them into practice:

- Consider the core of your business - what are your goals, what is the mission and vision, and what are the values you want to be guided by.

- Internal analysis - what are your strengths and weaknesses, what resources you have. And what are your capabilities.

- External analysis - consider the analysis of the competition, find out the opportunities and threats and also the market conditions.

- Organizational design - considers structure, controls and incentives and finally people and their cultures.

- Implementation - what roles and responsibilities should be carried out and by whom? What are the action plans and accountability measures?

- Functional strategies - this considers the marketing and sales process, how operations will be developed and the human resource.

- Strategic choices - here we consider the business strategy as well as the corporate strategy.

CHAPTER 25
LOGICAL THINKING

The simplest explanation of critical thinking is that your thoughts are more the truth. If you take nothing else away from this book, the importance of facts and logic cannot be emphasized enough. The most crucial thing you can do to develop yourself as a critical thinker is to support what you think, say, and do with facts, and to subject it to logical scrutiny.

As already stated, critical thinking is the ability to analyze the facts in order to reach a logical conclusion. A fact is a statement that can be supported by external evidence or observable experience. Facts are true, and they are true. Elementary, you say? The definition may be simple but its application has been the subject of philosophers and scientists for centuries. We will talk more about the facts later, but for now let's say that it is something we know to be true, whether it is because we observe a certain action, scientists tested a physical principle in a laboratory, historians have used rigorous methods to determine its existence, and so on. Facts are the building blocks of critical thinking.

Logic is the mortar that binds the facts together. Logic is simply the set of rules and relationships that govern claims about truth and falsehood of statements. In plain language, logic allows us to determine when we can say that two different statements lead to a new statement. The classic example in first year philosophy classes is "All men are mortal. Socrates is a man. Therefore, Socrates is a mortal man. It sounds basic both because all of us have already internalized some level of logical thinking, and because this common sense statement disguises a law of abstract logic. In this argument, the premises, or starting points established as true for the sake of discussion, allow us to make a new statement. We also know that we cannot say "All mortals are men" because our experience shows that there are mortals who are not men.

In this case, logic does not allow us to make the statement "All mortals are men. It does not follow from the premises, and it creates an invalid relationship according to other rules of logic. Logic prevents us from making contradictory statements, from saying things that simply do not make literal sense.

A defendant's alibi is a simple example of logic preventing invalid conclusions. If we know that the defendant was in a different place during the actual crime, we dismiss the case because we also know that a person cannot be in two places at the same time. This is also why we tend to be suspicious of politicians who make contradictory statements - you may want to do something when you are in office or you may not want to do it. Saying two different things is not only confusing when it comes to predicting a candidate's policies, it is also logically invalid.

Logic allows us to assemble the facts into new perceptions, rather than letting the facts simply exist as so many pieces of a broken puzzle. Instead, facts make logic have real consequences, rather than simply remaining abstract figures on paper. Facts and logic are the basis of critical thinking, so get into the habit of identifying the facts and logic behind the statements and attitudes around you, including your own. You may find considerable gaps in this area, allowing you to question things and present new ideas, or you may reinforce those statements with facts and logic. The point is that in critical thinking, supporting our statements is as important as making them in the first place, and there are specific ways we should support those statements.

Intellectual Rigor

Just as there are certain rules that determine whether a food is safe or whether a ball has been thrown out of bounds, critical thinking asserts that there are rules regarding how we justify our thoughts and statements.

United States Senator Daniel Moynihan once said that "Everyone is entitled to his own opinion, but not to his own deeds. This is a classic statement of critical thinking. We will talk more about the facts later, but for now let's say that a fact is a statement that has "truth value," that is, it can be true or false. An opinion is a subjective matter. We may have a strong feeling about it, but it is not true or false in any sense beyond the mind or heart of the opinion holder. When we affirm something as a fact, we are inherently making a statement about its truth value and why we are claiming it is true or false. Confusing facts and opinions is a symptom of confused thinking, and critical thinking tries to eliminate that confusion.

How we arrive at the particular truth value of a certain claim must conform to standards of clear thinking, evidence, and rationality. Let's say someone made the statement "All redheaded people are stupid. You could take that statement at face value, but that would not be an example of critical thinking on your part. You could try to interview every redhead in the world, but even if you could do that, you'd probably soon find yourself with a smart redhead who would refute the speaker's statement. So how could that person justify that statement? You could say that you have met many gingers and found them stupid. Again, many redheads are not the same as all redheads. Besides, how did this person establish his stupidity? Do they have an intelligence test? Was that test designed by people with valid intelligence measures? It is likely that no such test existed. Like all statements of prejudice against a group, this statement will eventually have to resort to a subjective value judgment that has no real value-for example, an opinion that is used to support a false statement.

The intellectual rigor of critical thinking can often seem harsh or insulting. After all, every time these standards are asserted, there will be different levels of people meeting or not meeting them. "How could you vote for that person" is a well-known question that can expose a lack of critical thinking on the part of the voter and even a sense of self-conceit on the part of the questioner. Voters do not always vote rationally, according to the facts, or even according to their own long-term interest. They often rely on first impressions, catchy slogans and rhetoric, or the opinions of those around them. Critical thinking may not always put the best person in the office, but it will be the best method for making that determination. Awareness of wrong thinking is painful, but it is necessary if we are to ensure that critical thinking informs important choices.

Intellectual rigor may seem the most discouraging aspect of critical thinking, but it is also the most rewarding. It requires effort, concentration, time, and probably some reading and study when we are especially pressured for an explanation. However, we are also challenging those around us, and ourselves, to reach a higher level.

Seeking Straight Answers

Another big part of critical thinking is the ability to explain why something is being done with a careful and reasoned explanation (instead of simply saying "Because I felt like it" or "Someone told me to do it"). Although this may sound rather lofty, at the same time your explanation must be clear and orderly. It must reflect a clear line of thought, going back to the premises of the facts and sticking to the facts as well as to the subject at hand. Irrelevant information, ideas that don't flow or tangents off topic are another sign of poor discussion.

Have you ever met someone who has answered a question without actually answering it? Did he or she go off-topic or switch immediately to a completely new topic? Critical thinking ensures that you stay on point. Directing the person back to the question not only demonstrates a sharp mind, but simply gives you an answer to your question.

Did the person respond to your question with a lot of jargon, for example, with technical terms only known to experts, with vague terms or clichés, or without a clear beginning or end to his or her answer? In other words, did they provide deliberately careless or confusing answers? Ask them to make their response clearer by sticking to simple terms. Critical thinking is not (always) a matter of complex language, fancy terms, or long answers. Clarity of thought and communication is a hallmark of critical thinking.

Thinking about Your Thoughts

Many organizations have powerful mission statements, which outline the purpose and philosophy of the organization, so that both management and staff can always remember why they are working there in the first place. On the ground, projects often get derailed because project objectives are no longer the focus of attention. Sometimes, simply asking why certain things are being done again can help people focus on the objectives again.

The "Why" question can often lead to the "How", generating broad questions that can lead to specific understanding. "How did I come to believe in the things I now believe? may sound like an unnecessarily abstract - and possibly intimidating - question, but it can also lead to a better understanding of ourselves and our values. Instead of answering, "That's just what I believe," you begin to have concrete, articulated explanations for your beliefs.

Above all, critical thinking is about method - about how we arrive at a judgment. That is why a scientific experiment operates according to accepted practices based on scientific data: so that the experimenter can say that his or her results are based on an established method, not on mere conjecture or a sloppy design that might have yielded the results. That's also why we have standards when it comes to things like construction or food safety. The method that leads to the result must be sound in itself, or we cannot rely on that result.

In your own life, simply asking "What was my chain of thought that led to this decision or judgment" is a crucial act of critical thinking. You may discover that you did not have all the necessary information when you made a decision - or that some of your attitudes are rather the result of particular education and listening to the same ideas.

Instead of being something passive that we do between actions, thought becomes an active guide to those actions, something that we are aware of and can therefore scrutinize in order to improve it.

CHAPTER 26
A LOGIC ANALYZER

Philosophy and science often express two very different types of attitudes in the human mind. The scientific mind seeks truth, that is, ideas that are valid, that are in agreement with the fact. At a high level, it builds a theory that connects and explains scattered and dark points in its isolation. But this cannot satisfy the philosopher. The very essence of knowledge and truth is problematic for him; he needs to get to the deeper meaning of what the scientist is doing.

The results of philosophical reflection do not include proposals or justify proposals. When real progress is made in the history of philosophy, it is not so much the results that are at stake, but the attitude towards the issues: on what was perceived as a concern, or on what was accepted as a false question and omitted as such. When, therefore, in his famous critique of the principle of causality, Hume showed that we only experience the sequence of events and never an internal connection that unifies them, his reflection did not acquire a lasting interest in a metaphysical proposition -an axiom around which other schemes are divided in a crystal of truth- but in clarifying the meaning of the causal proposals: In this sense, philosophy can be called the logical analysis of our thoughts. Hume analyzed the concept of cause.

Many non-technicians who hear the word logical analyzer struggle to understand what the system is or the advantages of using it.

A logic analyzer is electronic equipment that can display signals on a digital circuit to help you understand. This tests the voltage of "logic" electrical signals that might otherwise be calculated too quickly.

Although logic analyzers appear similar to oscilloscopes, there are a number of differences that allow each piece of equipment to be used for a variety of tasks and measurement requirements.

Once data is captured, the analyzer can convert it to a variety of formats to facilitate analysis and further experimentation. It can also transfer the data to different software and hardware computers.

The Varieties There are three main variants on the open market due to the large number of applications and specifications of a logic analyzer.

All of them are classified in separate categories.

Mainframe analysts find a monitor, controls, device, and spatial chassis to mount the necessary hardware. They can be configured by the user according to their specific requirements and needs.

Stand-alone units are those that are ready for use with the various manufacturing programs.

The third option is PC based analyzers with computer hardware connected via YSB or Ethernet. The computer software receives and stores the data for analysis and measurement.

A fourth alternative (hybrid) are analyzers known as mixed-signal oscilloscopes that combine the functions of both machines to make them easier to use.

Selecting the Basic Application Logic Analyzer, The drawbacks of traditional oscillators and logic analyzers are the lack of display and memory that can help the user to test and evaluate.

Since many tools are used by professionals who may not only want to capture and archive their information, but also analyze it for troubleshooting and scientific research purposes, it is not surprising that some handheld devices have proven to be ineffective.

However, an analyzer that required a "traditional" monitor and "tower computer" to use the hardware or software would have made its use nearly impossible, particularly when dealing with rough terrain or space-to-space shifts.

Advances in the field of laptop and handheld computer technology have contributed to the technological progress used to manufacture and develop logic analyzers that can be adapted to new and modern laptop computers, offering the best of both worlds in a compact and simple situation, but helping software to analyze, troubleshoot, and make decisions in a field.

One such logic analyzer is the Proto-PIC USB logic analyzer, which allows users to fully benefit from the powerful and useful machine with the portability and features needed to get the most out of it.

Considering that computers and all electronics usually run on electricity, you must remember that every operation is based on a signal: on or off (which means one or zero electrical circuits) for any task. If you need to test a logic circuit inside a gym, you need a specific test device called a logic analyzer.

This tool checks all types of circuits on the logic board and tells you if the channel is safe or not, if there are no breaks in the harness or wiring of the board being tested, i.e. that all circuits are complete. The analyzer has samples placed along the logic path. These sound meters are designed not to interfere with the signal, simply to observe, if you will, as a person on the sides, to see that the appropriate signal is given. You can think of it as a neutral government, calling for a game between your feet (yes or no, on or off).

After mounting the logic analyzer, the device waits for a "cause" or "specific" action (if so, then that...) Data is captured and converted to a designated format once the desired signal is detected. This style can range from creating assembly code (remember the first language for computer programming?) to drawing programs. Data can be stored and distributed in various ways.

If the technician is properly trained, he can take this information and debug the device or activate the captured data to perform specific actions. The technician can detect and locate any trouble spots that are found. He then re-tests to see if the entire problem area has been found and repaired. It almost becomes a game in the game or in the development itself in a way.

For any company that produces electrical equipment, for serious work or games and that depends on flawless logic circuits for its final product, logic analysis equipment is an absolute necessity. There are many different testing grounds on which logic analysis must be performed to ensure a quality product. So, get your Game Boy out of hand and look for the facts in the ring.

Sentiment and Opinion Mining Analysis

The phrases "opinion mining" and "sentiment analysis" are usually equally important. The process of opinion mining or sentiment analysis in today's world has become essential. The free flow of information and participatory collaboration is what the modern world believes. Participatory contact has led to an increase in traffic flow in terms of SMS and the status load on social networking sites. Essential information about the behavior of ordinary people can be obtained by watching all these SMS conversations and status uploads.

The implementation of sentiment analysis in everyday life in recent years, the people they serve have been significant for large organizations dealing with large numbers of people. These may include clients, consumers, customers or the general public. As such, organizations should always consider what the public thinks.

It is not an easy task to gather information from the public because the population represents a heterogeneous set. Everyone tends to think differently. The need for emotional research comes here. With the help of sentiment analysis tools, forecasts are almost accurate.

The areas that require the most useful analysis are large corporations, advertisers, political parties (particularly before elections to predict the role of political parties), commerce, and financial institutions. During the study, analysts can often be confused by the presence of certain words, phrases, or sentimental details. It is strongly recommended that a sentimental dictionary be used in cases such as this.

A sentimental dictionary is a broad collection consisting of alphabets, vowels, nouns, and other discourses, along with different meanings and related phrases. WordNet, General Inquirer and SentiWordNet are among the most common sentimental dictionaries. The deposits of these feeling dictionaries are always expanded by many active members and frequent feedback. The benefits of applying this particular analysis approach include logical analysis of logic gates and circuit algorithms. It helps to carry out a complete analysis of a specific subject and also at high speed.

The analysis tools provide both positive and negative feedback; almost one hundred percent was accurate.

Analysis tools are useful to provide even the general public with emotions.

Resources are the perfect way to provide knowledge about changing trends in public behavior.

When taken together, all these advantages make emotion analysis the ideal tool for making forecasts by analyzing rivals, evaluating a specific product and providing valuable input to different organizations, media and political parties.

Getting Decision Making Right

No transaction can be made until a decision is made: to take an idea, to buy something, to agree on a deal, to choose one thing over another or to take an action in any way. With the most efficient solution, the most accurate data, or the best idea or social justice, no new things happen, and no change occurs until there is consensus and action. We can be right, logical, practical and moral, and acceptance can escape us no matter how "right" or "fair" the new decision is.

After all, any decision is a change management issue. Whether it is a personal decision or the result of corporate, scientific or professional decisions, a decision reflects the introduction or elimination of the status quo of something that would be accomplished through new or different knowledge. Decision-making, therefore, is not just about facts, input or output, risks, complexity or acquired knowledge, but also about the process of acceptance, buy-in and the system's ability to adjust.

Most decisions are based on fair decisions or use data or reducing biases, but the arbitrary structural part of decision making is often ignored: decision making is incomplete, before or after an acceptance direction appropriate to the status quo, regardless of the validity of the conclusions.

Too often, we believe that "useful data" is the basis of "fair" practice. But if we all wanted that, there would be far fewer losses. How can we possibly end up wrong even when we have reason on our side? By shifting the focus from rational decisions, risk, data, probabilities, and chances - the best outcome - to allowing our subjective inclinations to broaden the search, adoption, and possible parameters, decision making can be more productive.

For decades, we have practiced decision making with a clear emphasis on a "fair" outcome based on facts. The most applied organizational concepts seem to be weighted averages and data or accuracy. We still seem to equate good choices, risks, and tasks in decision making with "useful data. People "make" casino decisions, "gathering probabilistic incentives, and determining the best route between them. After years of trial and error, however, they focused on helping people make sound, rational decisions as a limited success. He was to be judged "not by his performance - whether right or wrong - but by the process he allows. The problem lies in the subjective and personal purpose of decision making.

Our mostly inconsistent values have narrowed the scope of results by limiting our search criteria, restricting our interests and objectives, and diminishing acceptance even before we meet weighted parameters, data, or' objective truth". In other words, our method restricts the entire range of options. We are not even curious about anything beyond what we know in our hearts or what is real in our intuition. Our unconscious is sabotaging our choices. We need to shift the focus away from evidence and objectively correct answers and instead manage our structural and subjective bias.

CHAPTER 27
FACTORS THAT IMPACT YOUR THINKING

To become a more conscious and attentive thinker, you will have to understand the factors that could affect the inner workings of your brain. We will take a look at some of the more prominent things that could be impacting your thinking in a positive or negative way. You will be surprised at the number of factors influencing your thoughts.

The Infamous Nature vs. Nurture Argument

Some people wonder if this question will ever be answered because it is quite similar to the chicken versus the egg at first sight. First of all, thoughts originate in biology, and I am sure you now understand why. The brain is a biological organ that is very susceptible to change, but it comes before the environment. We are born with a brain full of neurons that fire in multiple directions. Therefore, genetics can never be underestimated. Let me present you with both arguments so that you can find clarity.

We like to assign percentages to environmental and biological factors in psychology as a general rule. These percentages vary, and I will give you a breakdown of them. Intelligence is usually assigned a genetic portion of 70%, and the remaining 30% can be credited to the environment as an example. Many psychologists believe that the environment and biology work hand in hand to develop our minds to be what they are today. The fact that the environment plays a role is undeniable, but your brain and the genetic code it contains are already there. The environment, which can consist of anything external, influences your brain, and the neural network forms and adapts to this stimulus.

Don't get me wrong either. Yes, biology is the underlying factor, but our environment regulates the biophysical aspect of our brain. You have learned how our neurons, or nerve cells, circulate every two months and how their receptors are attracted to the new orientation of the outside world. Let's look at a child whose brain is newly impressionable. The parenting style a child chooses represents the child's outcome. I don't disagree with this. A child who grows up in a neglected home is prone to insecurities in his adult life. That reinforces the parenting argument.

However, think about an inanimate object for a moment. A stone is a non-biological object, and when you mistreat it, the nonexistent genetics cannot change. This stone cannot become an insecure being because it is not a living being. Now let's take an animal, for example, specifically a mammal that has the genetic strands closest to us. An abused monkey will behave in an inappropriate way because its biology in the brain is being formed to create negative thoughts.

The conclusion is that the environment cannot have an impact on us without our gray matter changing and adapting to our surroundings.

External Influence

Let's take a closer look at how the environment impacts on human brains to expand their knowledge. San Francisco State University conducted a study on people to further solidify the existence of control from external sources (San Francisco State University, 2015). They achieved the result they suspected and more when they learned that our consciousness can be influenced without our being aware of it. This only proves that the processes in our brain are so fast that we often misinterpret them.

However, 52 participants were exposed to black and white images linked to familiar words that varied in length. Some of these images were of a fox, a bicycle, and a heart. Participants were asked not to verbalize the words in their minds or the length of these words. Their automatic responses were to do what they were asked not to do. A total of 73% of them verbalized the words internally, and the others counted the number of letters in each one. This experiment triggered two different thoughts that were unintentional and confirmed that we do not think consciously.

Our subconscious is in control and reacts quickly to an external source, whether we are instructed or not. These people were asked not to do what they did, but the thought planted itself in their minds when they heard the directions.

Psychology professor Ezekiel Morsella explains that we should not see this as a total loss. It can be advantageous in some scenarios when the mind automatically blocks out unwanted thoughts. This study has helped him to understand uncontrollable and repetitive thoughts. We have learned that the brain is highly adaptable with practice, and is part of our evolution.

What can alter our thoughts and embed automatic thoughts? There are numerous outside contributors, and I will review some of them with you. The moment we are faced with any situation, large or small, our minds see a divided path.

Your past experiences play an important role because they determine how you see the world, yourself and others. They have shaped your neurons into a form or pattern over time. You understand that this is not something that happens overnight. The confirmation bias is born in the wings of memories of the past. How you experienced something determines how you expect to perceive it in the present and in the future. Another persuasive factor in brain patterns is the difference of opinion you have compared to another person. The next contributor is the way you see yourself. How relevant do you perceive yourself? Now for the end, I would like to discuss: The level of commitment you have to the circumstance at hand will determine your thoughts and decisions as well.

The Ghost of Our Past

All of the contributors to your thinking process and your ability to solve problems are at the root. This is how nutrition comes to light once again in shaping our biology. Every person who crosses your path and every experience you succeed or fail with is spinning the wheels of your machine. I will discuss heuristics to explain how our decisions and the thoughts that drive them are rooted in our past. Heuristics is another concept to explain how we come to a quick decision - similar to quick thinking. But it relates to the path we choose when our thoughts run free. It is, in fact, the method we choose to reach our decision. Heuristics is a huge factor in decision making, and we need to make acceptable business decisions.

If we look at the influences of the past, we can understand that a decision made yesterday will influence our decision for tomorrow. This applies to both good and bad decisions. I will use John from our previous discussion as an example here. John had difficulty in his business yesterday because he saw the bad comments on the Internet after offering the customer a month's worth of cheeseburgers to make up for the hair on his burger. This experience automatically releases small bits of memory in John's brain, and will now determine how John will react to his customers today and in the future.

The customer added a line to his comments that hit John hard. It could lead to both positive and negative results in future decisions. The customer suggested that the owner or manager should remove the burger immediately and replace it with another burger as a first act of correction. This was not John's first thought. He went directly to the negotiations while leaving the contaminated burger on the table. John feels like a failure now because he did not react appropriately. His idea of appropriateness is in the customer's commentary. Business owners strongly believe that the customer is always right, and this can impact John's future decisions. We do our best to avoid the mistakes of the past with the information our brain collects.

Confirmation bias is another derivative of our past. Let's go back to John's original response at the restaurant yesterday. John grew up in a home where he was not shown any value or worth and is a very insecure individual. His father constantly told him that he could never be anything. John approaches the table with an automatic mouse height, and the customer sees his vulnerability immediately. The client threatens him with detailed feedback and gives John no room to negotiate. He finds himself begging the customer for a solution, looking weaker with every word he utters. John cannot see a solution that will save his restaurant from the inevitable disaster, and the customer is imbued with arrogance. Let me tell you a secret before we go any further. Yes, it is the customer who allows his business to prosper, but it requires a balance between kindness and respectful assertiveness.

Another scenario is the commitment that John holds on to. He might have a friend who had a similar incident at his restaurant, and it wasn't a month before they closed their doors forever. This is John's life and livelihood. He sees all of his investment in this business and may even carry an unhealthy attachment to it. His fear can escalate horribly because he automatically assumes that the end is near. What will he do if he loses his business? How can he afford his home and take care of his children? There is nothing wrong with engaging in a thought process, but there is a fine line between the irrational and the logical. John's thoughts and decisions are driven by the depth of what is "in the hole of commitment."

Factors such as age and gender may also play a role. He has grown up with the belief that older people are more knowledgeable. John is a 40-year-old man, and the client who is complaining is a teenager. This may cause John to disregard his client's opinion. On the other hand, let's make

John a sexist scholar. The client is a young woman, and he has these deeply engraved biased notions about women who have no valid opinions. Keep in mind that these are all examples of clients I have dealt with in my practice, and the distorted notions are not mine. The same could apply to someone who presents himself as uncultured and unsophisticated. The person's appearance could influence John's sensitive judgment.

CONCLUSION

This is perhaps the ultimate goal of analytical thinking: truth. Truth is a slippery and difficult concept to define to everyone's satisfaction. To complicate matters, because of cultural differences, it is possible that one person's perception of truth may differ from another's. However, we tend to believe that despite these obstacles, there is an objective world out there and that we can have some knowledge of it.

Knowing that there is a truth of the matter and discovering what that truth is is not the same thing. Determining the truth can be difficult or even impossible. Finding a factual truth may involve obtaining evidence that is hidden - such as secret government files; evidence that may not even exist today - such as evidence of life on other planets, or evidence that is virtually impossible to obtain at all - such as what courses of action will lead to the most happiness.

What about normative disagreements, that is, disagreements about what we should do or how we should behave? It may be that if the parties to an argument disagree on a fundamental normative claim, such as which moral theory is preferable, then there can be no resolution of the disagreements that result. This does not mean that it is useless to try. The resulting arguments and discussions will help us to better understand those intuitions and inclinations that make us human and to better understand the limits of our rationality.

The point of this is to demonstrate that it is possible to find what appear to be rational justifications for one's beliefs, no matter what they are. The important distinction is that they are used to support a belief to which one is committed, regardless of whether it is true or not. Of course, people are not all the same and we all react differently in different circumstances. So some people will change their beliefs, even deeply held ones, as a result of rational argument. However, this is unusual. Most people will not.

1. Debates

Remember, with analytical thinking, we are concerned with getting to the truth or making a good decision. Often, to determine this, we can engage in discussions with others. Public debates, whether in parliament, on television, in debating societies or in the courts, are a feature of liberal democracy. Unfortunately, often in such debates, the search for truth is set aside and becomes a matter of winning. Good debaters will use some of the analytical thinking techniques I have covered here. They may also deliberately use fallacies and cognitive biases to persuade. They may use ad hominem attacks; they may use false statistics or mere statements instead of evidence-based claims; they may take advantage of ambiguities of meaning or be misleading about what they mean. In addition, the debates are immediate. Thinking about a difficult problem can take time, and if a factual statement is important, it may need to be verified. You never hear one side of a debate say, "You know what? That's an interesting point. I'm going to go and think about it.

Debates are also stressful. Stress doesn't usually lead to good quality thinking. If instead of engaging in a debate, you are in a negotiation, it is often the case that the winner is not the one who has presented the best arguments, but the one who can stay awake the longest. Good decisions are not made in conditions of extreme exhaustion, but often it is precisely at that moment that they are made.

2. Ensuring Our Beliefs Are True

It is not only corrupt politicians, power-mad rulers, corrupt officials, or debaters who win at all costs who are guilty of bad thinking. It is all of us. And most of the time. Our brains are lazy. They require a lot of fuel to keep them going, so as I have said on other occasions, we often make a decision or come to a conclusion that feels intuitively right and follow it. We are not as interested in the truth as we would like to think. And now, that you have finished reading this book, you should have the skills to make sure that you arrive at the truth with much more regularity and accuracy than before. No doubt you will continue to make mistakes, but at least you will be prepared to admit them and take corrective action.

The purpose of this reading is to give you the skills necessary to help you arrive at the truth or the best course of action or the most probable explanation. This may mean taking a different approach to your thinking. It will mean accepting that you may be wrong. It may mean giving up certain preconceived ideas or beliefs. It can mean taking positions that are at odds with your friends, your family, your teachers, your bosses or your leaders. It can mean being isolated. It can mean being brave. It can mean being persecuted for your beliefs.

Being committed to the truth means following the logic of an argument wherever it leads, even if it is to a place you would rather not go, rather than trying to force an argument to fit your preconceptions.

These are just a few suggestions of how you can make better choices. Ultimately, it is up to you to make a committed decision to be a ruthless seeker of truth. Such a course is not for everyone, but if it is for you, then I hope this has been of some help. Good luck!

Made in United States
North Haven, CT
05 October 2021